# THE
# Astonishing
# General

# THE
# Astonishing
# General

## THE LIFE AND LEGACY OF
# Sir Isaac Brock

### WESLEY B. TURNER

**DUNDURN**
TORONTO

Editor: Cheryl Hawley
Design: Jesse Hooper
Printer: Transcontinental

**Library and Archives Canada Cataloguing in Publication**

Turner, Wesley B., 1933-
  The astonishing general : the life and legacy of Sir Isaac Brock / by Wesley B. Turner.

Includes bibliographical references and index.
Issued also in electronic formats.
ISBN 978-1-55488-777-4

  1. Brock, Isaac, Sir, 1769-1812. 2. Generals--Canada--Biography. 3. Canada--History--War of 1812. 4. Canada--History--1791-1841. I. Title.

FC443.B76T87 2011          971.03'2092          C2011-901143-3

1   2   3   4   5        15   14   13   12   11

We acknowledge the support of the **Canada Council for the Arts** and the **Ontario Arts Council** for our publishing program. We also acknowledge the financial support of the **Government of Canada** through the **Canada Book Fund** and **Livres Canada Books**, and the **Government of Ontario** through the **Ontario Book Publishing Tax Credit** and the **Ontario Media Development Corporation**.

Printed and bound in Canada.
www.dundurn.com

| Dundurn Press | Gazelle Book Services Limited | Dundurn Press |
| :---: | :---: | :---: |
| 3 Church Street, Suite 500 | White Cross Mills | 2250 Military Road |
| Toronto, Ontario, Canada | High Town, Lancaster, England | Tonawanda, NY |
| M5E 1M2 | LA1 4XS | U.S.A. 14150 |

*For my grandchildren*

# Contents

# Preface

Isaac Brock is the subject of this book. It tells of his life, his career, and his legacy and of the context within which he lived. Readers interested in the War of 1812 or the British army and navy or American forces, diplomacy, and politics, or in the history of native peoples, will have to look at other works, some of which are listed in the bibliography.

The literature on the War of 1812 is large and growing and so it is a fair question to ask: why another book about Major-General Sir Isaac Brock? In the most recent study of Brock, M.B. Fryer offers her answer to this query, "Perhaps I have something different to say."[1] The same question could be asked of this book and my answer is similar. With the approaching bicentenary of the War of 1812, there is growing interest in all aspects of that war, its participants and victims, and its legacies. One of the most enduring legacies on both the United States and Canadian sides was the creation of heroes and heroines. The earliest of those heroic individuals was Major-General Isaac Brock who, in some ways, was the most unlikely of heroes. For one thing, he was admired by his American foes almost as much as by his own people. Even more striking is how a British general whose military role in that two-and-a-half-year war lasted less than five months became the best known hero, and one revered far and wide. I find this outcome to be astonishing and approach the subject from that point of view. This concentration on Brock should not diminish anyone's admiration of other heroic figures — Tecumseh, John Norton, Oliver H. Perry, Winfield Scott, and Laura Secord, to mention a few. Compared to them, however, the way Brock acted and what he achieved in so short a time were so unexpected that I believe the most appropriate term for them is astonishing. Let me outline, in brief, my thesis.

Isaac Brock was born into an upper class family on the island of Guernsey. He purchased his ranks in the army, except his captaincy, up to his Lieutenant-Colonelcy when he gained command of a regiment, the 49th Foot. He had only one experience of participating in combat before going to the distant British colony of Canada where he spent ten years in command posts that involved principally administrative duties. It was in the last year of his life that he achieved immortality as a fighting soldier and leader of Upper Canada. Ironically, a majority of the people whom he died defending against an American invasion had been born in the United States. He also surprised in other ways. In spite of his high-class origins and military status he proved to be a commanding officer who understood the feeling and needs of the common soldier. He enforced traditional British army discipline but when necessary allowed sufficient variance that showed his humanitarian concern for his troops. He led the militia (who were essentially civilians) and co-operated easily with native leaders and their followers. He showed remarkable insight into the enemy's intentions and attitudes and by swift, decisive action he gained a complete victory over his opponent's stronger forces.

No person on the British or Canadian side from the War of 1812 became memorialized as immediately and as much as Isaac Brock. His combat record during the war appears unimpressive. As a Major-General, he participated in two battles. He won one almost bloodlessly against a demoralized commander. He died early in a second battle yet he is remembered not as a failed leader but as its victor, thereby displacing Roger Sheaffe, the general who led the forces to victory over the American invaders. Other individuals subsequently received recognition for their contributions to Canada's defence — Tecumseh, John Norton, Laura Secord, Lieutenant-Colonel de Salaberry, and Sir Gordon Drummond, to name a few. What is astonishing about the glorification of Brock is that it began among the Upper Canadian population immediately upon his death, remained strong during the rest of the war years, and has continued ever since. Even Americans at the time recognized his outstanding quality as a military leader. The elevation of Brock to the status of a great Canadian hero was, in part, a product of the times,[2] but more it was due to how he acted — as I attempt to show in the following pages.

Brock was a man of his age, the late eighteenth and early nineteenth centuries. Those times in Europe, North America, and elsewhere were tumultuous. When he was born, 1769, Britain was triumphant as a result of victories in the Seven Years' War, which had resulted in large territorial additions to her empire. Ten years later the British Empire was fighting a losing war against American colonists who had proclaimed their independence. Isaac's brother, Ferdinand, was killed in that war during the Spanish siege of Baton Rouge on the Mississippi River. Another brother, John, was serving in the 8th Regiment of Foot on the Canadian border.

A second decade later, revolution had broken out in France and the monarch was being held as a prisoner in Paris. Within a few years, Europe "would be plunged into one of the largest and longest wars of its history ..."[3] and Brock was an ensign in the 8th Foot. Whoever decided that his future would lie in military service, he dedicated himself to it. The rest of his life would be determined by the vagaries of war. The context of his early years and his career during his years in Canada need to be described in order to explain his actions and legacies.

## Notes on Terminology

Among historians there is debate about the appropriate terminology for First Nations people, the official governmental term now used in Canada. I agree with Carl Benn's approach and apply it in the following text.[4] That means I refer to tribes or nations as they were called in the 1812 period and by names commonly used then (e.g., Seneca); also, I use the names of leaders, often called chiefs, commonly used then (e.g., John Brant). Benn explains that the Six Nations Reserve was normally called the Grand River Tract in 1812. I follow his usage of using "native" and "aboriginal" without capitalization, and "Indian" only when the term was used by historical figures or in official agencies. Many terms used in 1812, as well as earlier and later, are now considered politically incorrect or demeaning to the people in question, but their use in a historical context provides accuracy and authenticity and in no sense is intended to offend anyone or any group.

It may be helpful from the outset to have a clear idea of what is meant by the terms "Canada" and "the Canadas." British North America is a collective term for the seven British colonies in North America: Newfoundland, Nova Scotia, New Brunswick, Prince Edward Island, Cape Breton, Lower Canada, and Upper Canada. Some contemporaries referred to Canada meaning Lower and Upper Canada, but the term "the Canadas" is more accurate. Lower referred to the lower stretch of the St. Lawrence River, while Upper denoted the upper part and beyond. In effect, Lower Canada was the equivalent of modern day southern Quebec and Upper Canada the equivalent of southern Ontario. The term Canada refers to the confederation (called a Dominion) that was created in 1867 with four provinces to which all the others later adhered. Canadian means the citizens of that nation. In the early nineteenth century, Canadian usually referred to French-speaking residents but could also mean the English-speaking people who were often called English or Upper Canadians. However, for convenience I sometimes refer to Canada (for the Canadas) and to Canadians meaning the residents of either one or both Canadas.

Donald Hickey explains the most usual contemporary designation of warships. For American vessels he uses US followed by the type (e.g., Frigate, Sloop, etc.). For British vessels he uses HM followed by the type. In 1812 the British warships on the Great Lakes were operated by the Provincial Marine, a branch of the army, and so he designates them PM followed by the type. The change to Royal Navy control came in May 1813 when Sir James Yeo arrived to take command and, thus, HM would replace PM.[5]

I follow the practice of many military histories of this period by using figures to designate British infantry regiments or battalions and words for American ones. Thus, the British 49th Regiment and the American Thirteenth Infantry Regiment.

*Accoutrements* (as in "arms and accoutrements"): A soldier's pack straps, cartridge box or pouch and straps (belt), haversack, canteen, slings, bayonet belt, and bayonet scabbard.

*Adjutant General*: His job was to relieve his commanding officer of detailed work. He was the general's chief administrator, although in the War of 1812 he might be called upon to assume combat responsibilities. Prevost's adjutant general was Colonel Edward Baynes. See Hitsman, *Incredible War of 1812*, 32; Sutherland, *His Majesty's Gentlemen*, 60.

*Battalion* (see Company): Was the basic British infantry unit and would be commanded by a lieutenant-colonel. Often, "battalion" and "regiment" were used interchangeably. Three battalions made up a brigade, which would be commanded by a brigadier-general. During the Napoleonic period, the British Army had 104 "regiments of the line," each having one battalion and some as many as six.

*Bateau* (*batteau*): Flat-bottomed boat designed for shallow waters or river rapids. It was powered by oars with sometimes a simple sail.

*Canister* (U.S.) or *Case Shot* (British): This was a tin filled with small lead bullets for use against infantry. Usually used at a range of 200–500 yards. It differs from chain shot, which was naval ammunition used against enemy rigging.

*Carronade*: A gun with a short barrel, which differentiated it from a long gun. The carronade required a smaller gun crew and smaller charges than a long gun but had a shorter range (about 500 yards). A ship could mount more carronades than long guns of the same calibre because they were lighter.

*Company* (see Battalion): A company was supposed to have up to one hundred men and each battalion was supposed to have ten companies. Eight were known as centre, or battalion, companies. The other two were flank, or elite, companies, the grenadiers on the right and the light company on the left. A captain commanded a company and he would be assisted by subalterns (i.e., lieutenants and ensigns).

*Gun* (long gun): Fired on a flat trajectory and longer range than carronade, mortar, or howitzer. Calibre denominated by weight of its roundshot (e.g., a 6-pounder fired a 6-pound roundshot). The 6-pounder was the most common artillery piece used by both armies.

*Parole*: A promise given by a captured soldier that he would not fight again until he had been formally exchanged with a man captured by the other side. The parolee would be allowed to return home but he would usually sign a certificate of parole and his name would be entered on a list. See Gray, *Soldiers of the King*, 39–41.

INTRODUCTION

# The World of Isaac Brock

Major-General Sir Isaac Brock, K.B., is a well-known name to many Canadians, but less is known about the world in which he lived, served his king, and died defending Canadians. It was a world very different from what we know today, yet, with many unfortunate similarities. When he was born in 1769 (Napoleon and Wellington were also born that year), the world was dominated by the great powers of Europe — Britain, France, Austria-Hungary, Prussia, and Russia. Britain had recently gained overseas territories by conquest from France but was soon to lose some of its most developed colonies and see the creation of a new nation in North America. Nevertheless, Britain's industrial and financial strengths were growing, its empire continued to expand and it was becoming mistress of the seas.

France recovered from its losses of the Seven Years' War (1756–63) to help the American rebels win their independence, but its monarchy was inept and out of touch with its people. The result was revolution that produced a bloodbath in France, unstable revolutionary governments, war with neighbouring countries, and, eventually, dictatorship. During those years, Napoleon Bonaparte rose from the rank of a second lieutenant in the artillery to that of a general commanding the army in Italy and, later, in Egypt. He returned from there to help in a seizure of power to become first consul and, finally, in 1804, emperor of the French. The other great powers — Austria and Russia — fearful of revolution fought the French but their generals were no match for Napoleon.

Britain was most concerned that no single power should dominate Europe and that any country controlling Antwerp and the mouth of the Scheldt posed a serious threat to British maritime communications and security.[1] Thus, the British sought allies against Napoleon and undertook campaigns (1799, 1809) to gain control of Antwerp and the mouth of the Scheldt. Brock would have experience in the first of these assaults.

Nelson's naval victory over the French and Spanish at Trafalgar on October 21, 1805, produced British dominance at sea, but on land Napoleon's control increased. On the 20th, he defeated the Austrian general Mack at Ulm and in December smashed an Austro-Russian force at Austerlitz. At Jena and Auerstadt (October 1806), he destroyed the Prussian Army and occupied Berlin; Frederick William agreed to a peace treaty on Napoleon's terms. The next year, at Tilsit, Napoleon forced the Czar of Russia to make peace and recognize his conquests in Europe.[2]

The Royal Navy imposed a tight blockade of the ports of western Europe in order to starve Napoleon of food and military supplies. His response was to intensify his attack on Britain's economy, a warfare that extended back at least to 1796.[3] In the Berlin and Milan Decrees (1806–07) he closed the ports of western Europe to British ships as well as neutral ones if they had previously been to a British port. This was the beginning of what was called the Continental System. Fortunately for the British economy, France, its allies, and European neutral countries could not do without some products obtainable only from Britain. Consequently, these countries found ways to circumvent the Continental System.[4] In response to Napoleon's decrees, Britain issued orders-in-council (1807) that sought to prevent or strictly regulate all trade with the ports of France or her allies. Neutral vessels were required to report to a British port before they could proceed to a continental one. In pursuit of their ends, both powers stopped and seized the ships of neutrals, many of which were American. This Anglo-French contest sowed the seeds of great future troubles because to the

Americans Britain's actions violated the freedom of the seas, while the British regarded these measures as essential in a war for national survival. Neither nation was prepared to back down in this dispute.

The Royal Navy, which grew to a strength of about 145,000 men and some 700 ships by 1812, faced enormous demands for manpower.[5] The chief method — although not the only one — that the navy used to obtain seamen was impressment. A press-gang of reliable seamen was sent ashore in a British port and they went about seizing men from streets and taverns and even homes. Crews of outward-bound ships were exempt but not those of returning merchant vessels, and those men might be snatched before their ships even docked. Other categories of people were exempt, including foreigners, but it was often difficult for Americans to prove their citizenship and the burden of proof fell upon the victim of the press-gang. Once taken, the men were locked up aboard a small ship and asked if they wanted to volunteer. If they said yes, they received a cash bounty; if no, they were still pressed into the service but without a bounty. It was a brutal process, widespread around the coasts of England and Scotland and often resisted by force.

One of the greatest irritants in Anglo-American relations arose from the Royal Navy's practice of boarding neutral ships in order to impress British subjects and deserters from the navy. Many American ships were stopped on the high seas and sometimes American-born seamen were taken. It was not always easy to determine who was a genuine American citizen because certificates of citizenship were freely issued and even forged ones could be bought. Furthermore, the British government held the view that a British subject could not renounce his nationality without permission. The American view was different and it is not surprising that the United States government strongly resented the often high-handed behaviour of Royal Navy captains. Between 1793 and 1812, an estimated 8,000 to 10,000 American seamen were pressed into the British Navy, with the largest number, some 6,000, taken between 1803 and 1812.[6] Impressment actions, at times, produced conflict between British and American ships — which will be looked at later.

In June 1808, when Napoleon put his brother Joseph on the throne of Spain, the French emperor seemed to be at the height of his power; but the Spaniards rose up in revolt and their new monarch fled. In August, Arthur Wellesley landed in Portugal with British troops and took possession of Lisbon. This was the beginning of the Peninsular War which tied down thousands of French troops there, but likewise committed Britain to major land warfare for an unpredictable future. Therefore, from 1808, Britain could spare little in troops or supplies for defence in North America. A large reinforcement (the 7th, 8th, 23rd, and 13th regiments of foot with equipment) had been sent under Sir George Prevost to Bermuda, Halifax, and Quebec early in 1808, but not much else could be done until 1814 when Wellington's veterans became available for this distant war.

Ironically, Wellington's Peninsular Army depended on American grain for its food supply and this need would affect Britain's naval strategy toward the United States when war came. The British issued licences so that American ships carrying "Flour and other dry Provisions" to Portuguese or Spanish ports would not be seized by the British Navy or privateers. There is a reference to the British in one month in 1812 issuing 722 licences for such shipments to Lisbon and Cadiz.[7] The effect of licences issued by British officials as well as by Vice-Admiral Herbert Sawyer and Sir John B. Warren was to retain New England's goodwill. American ships also carried American newspapers, which were valuable sources of information. The cost was high because all transactions had to be paid in specie. So while troops fell up to six months in arrears of pay and Portuguese muleteers and middlemen as much as a year, American merchants returned loaded with British gold and silver "that would gorge New England's banks by the war's end and help pay for subsequent industrial development."

After the War of Independence, one of the most serious issues facing the United States government was relations with aboriginal peoples. Americans were rapidly moving westward and their government's policy toward native peoples was based upon assumptions that within United States boundaries aboriginals were a conquered people who could expect their land rights to be extinguished to accommodate American expansion. In the 1780s, through several treaties and military actions, it became clear that the United States government intended to push settlement well beyond the Ohio Valley.[8] The Northwest Ordinance of 1787 reasserted American sovereignty over the region and provided for new states between the Ohio and Mississippi rivers. The ordinance declared that native "lands and property shall never be taken from them without their consent;" but it went on to state, "they shall never be invaded or disturbed, unless in just and lawful wars, authorized by Congress."[9] To many American officials, as well as land-hungry pioneers, this ordinance made no difference to their actions and demands on Indian tribes. The result was almost continuous frontier warfare in the 1790s.[10]

In August 1794, at Fallen Timbers in Ohio, an American Army led by Major-General Anthony Wayne inflicted a crushing defeat on a confederacy of tribes. Their hopes of British help were dashed when the commander of Fort Miami held back his troops and closed the fort's gates to native refugees. That refusal would be long remembered.

The native leaders were also aware of the outbreak of war in Europe, which meant that their old ally, Britain, would have to concentrate on its own defence at the expense of aid to them. Both Britain and the United States desired to settle a number of disputes, one being the continued British occupation of "frontier posts" within the boundaries of the United States.[11] In November 1794 the two countries made a Treaty of Amity, Commerce and Navigation (named Jay's Treaty after the American secretary of state) and the British agreed to evacuate the western posts by June 1, 1796. The posts they withdrew from included such major forts as Detroit, Niagara, and Mackinac (also known as Fort Michilimackinac). Western New York and all the territory north and west of the Ohio River was now firmly on the United States side of the boundary. Aboriginal nations had little choice but to accept Wayne's offer to negotiate and the outcome was the Treaty of Greenville (August 3, 1795) by which the natives surrendered the greater portion of the Ohio Valley.

New states soon appeared: Kentucky in 1792, Tennessee in 1796, and Ohio in 1803, the same year that saw the purchase of Louisiana.

President Jefferson, in a special message to Congress in January 1803, made it clear that his government's policy would continue to encourage native peoples to abandon their traditional way of life in favour of agriculture, "domestic arts," and industry (i.e., become like Americans). In a private letter in February, he made it clear that any tribe that resisted would be defeated and driven out of its territory.[12] The Greenville boundary rapidly became redundant as settlers poured across it and native lands continued to be purchased, particularly by the Treaty of Fort Wayne of 1809, which led to the acquisition of much of eastern and southern Indiana. The author of the treaty was William Henry Harrison, governor of the Indiana Territory since 1800, who repeatedly used divide-and-conquer tactics to acquire lands along the Wabash River for American settlers.[13]

Desperate resistance to American expansion continued in the Ohio Valley, but tribes were driven westward and along the Wabash River they reached the furthest limits of their traditional territory. If they retreated westward, they would intrude into lands of other aboriginal peoples, some of whom were traditional enemies. The dispossessed tribes "were perplexed and disorganized. All they needed was a sign, a Messiah."[14] He appeared in the person of a Shawnee prophet, who took the name Tenskwatawa and preached a doctrine of return to a traditional life and rejection of white ways. His teachings found wide appeal to tribes in a large area of Ohio, Indiana, and the upper lakes, and many people flocked to his settlement of Prophetstown at the mouth of the Tippecanoe River in Indiana. Toward the end of first decade of the nineteenth century, these western tribes formed a new defensive alliance around Tenskwatawa and his brother, Tecumseh, but most Iroquois refused to join. Eventually, American troops would march against this new confederacy at Tippecanoe.

British-native relations rested upon mutual benefits focused primarily on trade, but wars in North America with France and the American War of Independence created needs for military cooperation. The British government created the Indian Department, the fundamental purpose of which was to maintain the allegiance of

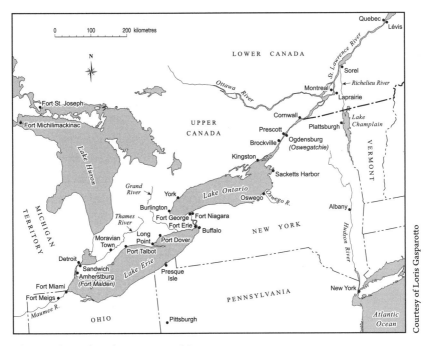

*The Canadas and northeastern United States.*

Courtesy of Loris Gasparotto

native peoples, and from 1774 "British Indian policy ... [was] ... geared primarily to ensuring the preservation and defence of Canada through the military use and assistance of His Majesty's Indian allies."[15]

As a result of withdrawal from the western posts, the British began to construct new forts within their own territory: Fort George near the Lake Ontario mouth of the Niagara River, Fort Amherstburg on the Detroit River, and Fort St. Joseph on the island of the same name at the mouth of the St. Mary's River in Lake Huron. Each post would have a superintendent, storekeeper, and other officers of the Indian Department, whose tasks included distributing gifts to aboriginal allies, maintaining bonds of friendship, and keeping detailed reports on native attitudes and actions. Expenses of the department were paid from army funds, which sometimes produced "nasty conflicts over military and jurisdictional authority and areas of responsibility in the management and administration of Indian affairs."[16]

The British territory most threatened was British North America and its principal colony of the Canadas. Quebec or Canada came under British rule in 1760 (confirmed by the Peace of Paris in 1763) and was developing its unique characteristics. The influx of thousands of Loyalists after the American War of Independence had forced the British government to create a new constitution for Canada and to divide it into Lower and Upper Canada. The Constitutional, or Canada, Act of 1791 provided for a governor of the Canadas with a lieutenant governor in each section to preside over the elected legislative assemblies and appointed legislative and executive councils. From the outset, in Lower Canada French-Canadian members dominated the assembly but they did not have influence with the governor equal to that of the aggressive English minority that predominated in the appointed councils. There was a steady increase of antagonism between the two language groups, occasionally dramatized by the clash of their wills in the Legislature. The governors sent out from England managed to work fairly well with both groups until the term of Sir James Craig that began in October 1807. We shall pick up the story in a later chapter.

Settlement had moved slowly up the St. Lawrence River past Montreal, and farms and villages were confined mainly to the shorelines of lakes (Ontario and Erie) and rivers (St. Lawrence, Niagara). In effect, there was little competition for land between natives and settlers, whose population was small and increasing only slowly. The contrast with the rapid advance of American settlement south of the lakes and the resulting displacement of large numbers of native peoples was obvious to all. Furthermore, in the Canadas the fur trade was still vital to the colony's economy and that required close co-operation between Europeans and natives, which often led to intermarriage. Canadians, therefore, tended not to regard natives as threats to their settlements, but, instead, when war threatened, they could be seen as potential allies.

Let us return to Europe to discover the origins of our hero.

Near the western end of the English Channel and closer to France than to England are tiny specks of land known as the Channel Islands.

They are the remnants of English holdings in Brittany, Normandy, and other parts of the mainland. Guernsey, officially the Bailiwick of Guernsey, lies forty-eight kilometres west of the coast of Normandy. Like the other Channel Islands, it is a dependency of the British

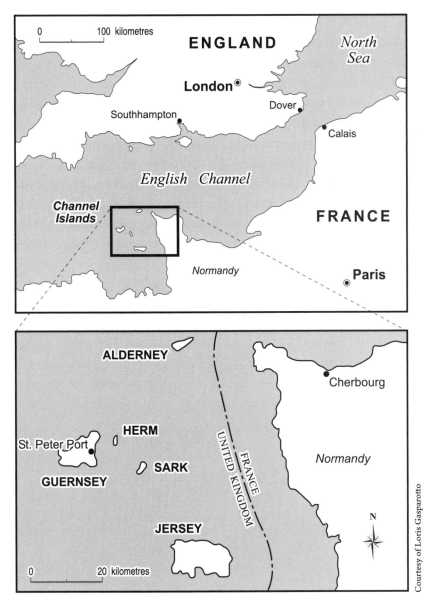

*Channel Islands, credit to G.R.D. Fryer.*

23

crown, but has its own lieutenant governor and chief minister who presides over a cabinet (Policy Council), which is elected by the Legislature (States of Deliberation). Its Royal Court is presided over by the bailiff and twelve jurats. In this small, semi-independent island world, the Brock family traces its ancestry back to Sir Hugh Brock, who was driven out of Brittany in the fourteenth century. The family lived in the island capital of St. Peter-Port and by the eighteenth century was playing a prominent role in island society and government. William Brock, who died in 1776, is considered the common ancestor of the present Guernsey family of the name of Brock. One of his sons, John (b. 1729) was the father of Isaac.[17]

The Brock family could be classified as "gentry" and its members intermarried with each other while the men, according to Donald Graves, "eagerly sought commissions in the British army or Royal Navy."[18] Families like the Brocks, Le Merchant, and Saumarez of Guernsey and similar ones on the other Channel Islands provided officers for British forces in the eighteenth and nineteenth centuries. Isaac would be born into that tradition.

## CHAPTER ONE

# Isaac Brock Joins the Army

John Brock, after leaving the Royal Navy and returning to Guernsey, married Elizabeth de Lisle, daughter of the bailiff of Guernsey. John's brother, William, married Judith de Beauvoir of a long-established Guernsey family; another brother, Henry, married Susan Saumarez, sister of Admiral Sir James Saumarez.[1] In a society and time period when connections with important families could make all the difference between achieving a successful career and high office, Isaac was very fortunate. The other side of that coin was that he had to uphold the honour and dignity of the family name. This was an obligation that Isaac never forgot.

When Isaac was born on October 6, 1769, his mother, Elizabeth, had given birth to ten children — but three had died — and three more would be born subsequently. His father died in 1777, leaving Elizabeth with a large family. Fortunately, "They were left in independent, if not in affluent, circumstances."[2] Isaac had brothers in the army (John, Ferdinand, William, and Savery), and in business (Irving and William) while Daniel remained on the island, served in the Royal Guernsey militia, and eventually became the island's chief magistrate. Irving was also a writer and translator while Savery, after he left the army, married and settled in Guernsey. Isaac's sister, Mary, lived in England with her husband, Thomas Potenger. Another sister, Elizabeth, married John E. Tupper whose son, Ferdinand, wrote *The Life and Correspondence of Major-General Sir Isaac Brock, K.B.,* which provides a great deal of information about its subject.

Tupper writes about the young Isaac, "In his boyhood he was like his brothers, unusually tall, robust, and precocious; and, with an appearance much beyond his age, remarkable in his own family chiefly for extreme gentleness. He was, however, considered by his schoolfellows as the best swimmer and boxer in the school; and he used to swim from the mainland of Guernsey to Castle Cornet, a distance each way of nearly half a mile." In St. Peter-Port, Isaac attended Queen Elizabeth School, also known as Elizabeth College. At age ten he went to a boarding school in Southampton, England. At age fourteen, in order to learn French, he studied under a French pastor in Rotterdam in the Netherlands. Subsequently, he probably spoke and understood French capably and certainly read it, for his possessions included at least eight works (some of several volumes) in French along with a grammar of that language.[3]

When Brock was fifteen his family purchased a commission for him as an ensign in the 8th Regiment of Foot (also called the King's Regiment), where his brother John held a captain's commission. A young man would need access to money, either from his family or from a patron, to buy a commission, because it was expensive. The most junior officer rank was ensign and it cost £400. The price for a lieutenancy was £550, for a captaincy £1,500, for a majority £2,600, and for a lieutenant-colonelcy £3,500.[4] A glance at the pay for these ranks will show that a commission could not be financed from an officer's salary but needed another source. Annual pay and allowances for an ensign amounted to £96, for a lieutenant with up to six years service in that rank £119, for a lieutenant with seven years service £137, for a captain £192, for a major £292, for a lieutenant-colonel £310, and for a colonel £775.[5]

In Isaac's case, his brother William loaned the money — the loans amounted to £3,000 by 1811 (Chapter Five). Isaac next bought a commission as a lieutenant (1790), but in the same year gained the rank of captain because he had raised enough men to establish an infantry company. This was an independent company with his brother Savery as an ensign. However, Savery resigned the next year to enter a business apprenticeship under his brother William. (Savery would later serve as paymaster in the 49th Regiment.) Isaac purchased his majority in 1795, and in 1797 his commission as lieutenant-colonel. As ensign and lieutenant, his role was to assist a captain in command of a company; as major, he was "the regiment's senior officer for maintaining discipline";[6] and as lieutenant-colonel, he would usually command a regiment.

It was also a common practice to transfer from one regiment to another:[7] in 1791, Brock exchanged into the 49th Regiment, joining it in Barbados, and by 1797 he was its senior lieutenant-colonel, in effect its commanding officer. Roger Hale Sheaffe was a junior lieutenant-colonel. Both officers would later be closely identified with that regiment in the War of 1812.[8]

Although Brock purchased his commissions, the practice — which applied only in infantry and cavalry regiments — was producing fewer and fewer infantry officers for Wellington's army by 1812. One reason was heavy losses of officers in the fighting in the Peninsula, the reluctance of parents to buy commissions for sons in dangerous times, and the rapid increase in the army during the long wars with France. Another reason was reforms beginning in 1795, applied by the Duke of York, as commander-in-chief, as he tried to reduce the abuses of the traditional system. By 1812, over 60 percent of commissions in the infantry were granted free of charge while lesser numbers were awarded to "gentlemen volunteers" and to senior non-commissioned officers who had proven themselves worthy by deed.[9] However, there may have been a higher percentage of purchased commissions in the regiments in North America because they had not suffered heavy casualties before 1812. In any case, while Brock entered the army and rose under the old system, he proved fully worthy of his high officer rank.

During his earliest years in the army, Brock did not see action, for he was on garrison duty in England until 1790 when he moved to Guernsey and Jersey. Tupper tells an anecdote that took place soon after Brock joined the 49th. The regiment was cursed with "one of those vile pests of society — a confirmed duelist," who was, unfortunately, a dead shot. Brock refused to be intimidated by the other captain and so was challenged to a duel. Being tall, Brock knew that he would present an easy target at the usual distance apart of twelve paces. As they prepared for the duel, he demanded that they meet on equal terms. His answer was to produce a handkerchief and insist they fire across it at each other. Not surprisingly, his antagonist declined and soon after left the regiment.[10] Whether or not this actually happened, it suggests that from an early age Brock had acute insight into what others — particularly opponents — were thinking and how they might respond to determined action. He was to apply this trait very effectively in 1812 both before and after the war broke out.

A good deal of his time he spent in study but he also worked to develop prowess in boxing and swimming. His early enjoyment of reading for a purpose continued for the rest of his life. Twenty years later, Brigadier-General Brock spent a lonely winter in Fort George, Upper Canada. He wrote to his brother Irving,

> I hardly ever stir out, and unless I have company at home, my evenings are passed solus. I read much, but good books are scarce, and I hate borrowing ... should you find that I am likely to remain here, I wish you to send me some choice authors in history, particularly ancient, with maps, and the best translations of ancient works. I read in my youth Pope's Translation of Homer, but till lately never discovered its exquisite beauties. As I grow old, I acquire a taste for study.[11]

He had just passed his forty-first birthday.

In 1791, the 49th was sent to Barbados and Jamaica in the West Indies. These islands were unhealthy for European troops, who often fell sick from disease from which few of them recovered. The 49th continued to suffer from its experience even after it returned to England. European doctors did not know the real causes of those diseases and so lacked knowledge of what treatments would cure their patients or what medicines would be effective.[12] Captain Brock fell ill, but survived probably because of the skilful nursing of his servant, known to history only as Dobson. However, to fully recuperate Brock went home on sick leave and there soon recovered his health.

When he became senior lieutenant-colonel of the 49th, the regiment was quartered by the River Thames and crippled by disorganization owing to his predecessor's mismanagement. The regiment needed many new recruits to replace the men lost in the Islands as well as proper clothing and equipment. It is not surprising that disorganization became discontent in the summer of 1797 at a time when the Royal Navy was wracked by mutiny. He used a combination of conciliation and firmness, namely, courts martial of several officers guilty of gross misconduct, to re-establish the discipline of the 49th. For this he received the praise of the commander-in-chief, the Duke of York. Another test of his leadership came in 1800, when Brock returned from a brief absence and the men, who had been under Colonel Sheaffe's command, cheered. Brock rebuked them and confined them to barracks for a week. He showed decisively that he would maintain discipline rather than court popularity.[13] These were early demonstrations of a quality of leadership that would later be tested in Upper Canada.[14]

Brock's combat career really began with the expeditions to Holland (August to November 1799) and to Denmark (Copenhagen, March to April 1801). In 1799, under Sir Ralph Abercromby, an English force landed on the Dutch shore near the little town of Helder. Advancing southward, they fought against French and Dutch opposition until the beginning of October, when they were ready to assault Bergen. His regiment was in the right column, whose task was to attack Egmont-op-Zee. In a letter to his brother John, he told how, when the enemy threatened to turn his regiment's flank, he led a charge across the sand dunes that threw his opponents into disorder and forced them to retreat. He made light of a wound he received: "I got knocked down soon after the enemy began to retreat, but never quitted the field, and returned to my duty in less than half an hour."[15] Officers frequently wore cravats (usually made of silk) around their throats and in Brock's case the ball had penetrated a cotton handkerchief and a black silk cravat, but no further. This short, rather confused clash was his only experience of participating in combat before August 15, 1812.

The naval expedition to Denmark was intended to destroy the Danish Navy, thereby breaking a league of Northern Powers arrayed against Britain.[16] The commander was Sir Hugh Parker, but the victory was won by his second-in-command, Vice-Admiral Horatio Nelson, who took his ships almost under the guns of the Danish forts to get at the enemy's vessels. After some four hours of cannonading, it appeared that the battle was lost and Parker signalled the order to discontinue the action. The story is that Nelson put his telescope to his blind eye, thereby claiming he could not see the admiral's signal and so continued the fight. Brock did not witness Nelson's action but no doubt he heard about it as did the whole world. Isaac and his brother Savery, with the 49th, were on board the *Ganges* stationed next to Nelson's flagship *Elephant* and part of a line of ships bombarding the Danish batteries. According to Tupper, while Savery was pointing a gun "his hat was torn from his head by a grape shot." Isaac exclaimed, "Ah! Poor Savery is dead!" but, unwounded, Savery quickly jumped up to resume his task.[17]

The 49th was expected to land to storm the Danish batteries but the battle was won by sea power alone. Near the close of the combat, Brock accompanied Captain Fremantle to the *Elephant*. There he saw the admiral coolly send his famous message to the prince of Denmark. In it, Nelson demanded that the Danish vessels that had struck their flags cease firing or he would burn them without being able to save the men on board. After the letter had been written, he sent for wax to seal it. When the first messenger was killed he sent another, his explanation being that the message should be properly sealed so that there could be no hint of haste or fear on the part of the British. Nelson's calmness under pressure as well as his aggressive leadership may have influenced Brock's thoughts and behaviour when he commanded Upper Canada at the opening of the War of 1812. Nelson's success in Copenhagen harbour proved a major factor in ending the hostile northern coalition.

After a period in England, in 1802 the 49th was ordered to proceed to Canada. Early in July, Brock, with the first division of the regiment, boarded the *Tartar* for the voyage. During his brief exposure to fighting, he had caught glimpses of great leadership in Abercromby and Nelson. Although it would be a decade before he would again face combat, he would need qualities of foresight and leadership to prepare his troops and Canadians for a future desperate struggle. In the meantime, he would carry out a wide range of duties while yearning to return to Europe to join in the fight against Napoleon. It would be in battles that fame and promotion would be won, not in garrisons in far off colonies.

## CHAPTER TWO

# Early Years in the Canadas, 1802–07: From Regimental Commander to Commander of the Forces

A small fleet docked at Quebec, the capital of the Canadas and residence of the governor, on August 20, 1802, with the first part of the 49th on board two ships. On September 7, the second division under Lieutenant-Colonel Roger Hale Sheaffe arrived, and on September 11, the third division under Captain Charles Plenderleath. In that same month, Brock was in Montreal and concerned about the state of the barracks and of the hospital. He pushed for repairs to be made before the cold of winter descended.[1] Many military facilities were in disrepair because in peacetime soldiers were not required to perform fatigue duties (such as building repairs) unless paid extra. Whether or not Brock achieved some improvement is not clear, but the incident shows his concern that the men under his command be properly housed and looked after.

In February 1803, the commander-in-chief, Lieutenant-General Peter Hunter, ordered the 49th to the upper province in order to replace the Queen's Rangers, which was being disbanded.[2] York, the capital of Upper Canada, with a population between 300 and 400, had sixty to seventy wooden houses, surrounded by a few farms and large expanses of forest. Situated at the eastern edge of town, Government House served for the assembly and courts of justice. Near it was a blockhouse situated by a large marsh at the mouth of the Don River. Some two miles to the west were barracks, known as the "Garrison," situated on "a dry bank."[3] In midsummer, Brock wrote to Hunter's civil secretary, Lieutenant-Colonel James Green, about the large number of soldiers quartered in the eastern blockhouse and falling ill. If this continued he intended to move them all "to the Garrison," which so far was a much healthier situation.

Brock was soon to become acquainted with the great difficulties facing British troops in distant outposts, particularly close to the United States border. Early in August, eight men deserted from Fort George, where Sheaffe was in command, crossing the Niagara River to the American side. According to Sheaffe's official account, they were captured by native warriors and brought back to the fort. A different story was told by James FitzGibbon, in a letter dated September 27, 1845.[4] In 1803, FitzGibbon was a sergeant-major in the 49th at York and according to him the men deserted from York and crossed the lake to the American shore. He informed Brock and they took a party of men across the lake by bateau to Fort George. The deserters were caught the next day by a different party from the fort. Many biographers have repeated FitzGibbon's account, but its details may not be entirely accurate.

James FitzGibbon was born in Ireland in 1780, the son of a farmer and weaver. At age fifteen he joined a Yeomanry Corps (volunteers for local defence) and two years later was appointed to the rank of sergeant. In 1798 he was inducted into the Tarbert Fencibles, an Irish regiment raised for home service only, with the promise of appointment as pay-sergeant. His regiment was sent to England for garrison duty, and in August 1799 he was drafted into the 49th Regiment with the rank of sergeant. He served at Egmont-op-Zee as well as in the expedition against Copenhagen. At Egmont-op-Zee he was taken prisoner by the French and until he was exchanged in January 1800, he tried to learn the language.[5] Arriving in Canada with the regiment in 1802, he was already a confirmed admirer of Brock, who encouraged him to improve his education and loaned him books for that purpose. The colonel also obtained promotions for him without the purchase of commissions.[6] FitzGibbon admitted that he wrote the 1845 letter from memory so it is possible — indeed, probable — that he embellished the event, perhaps having in mind Brock's quick removal to Fort George when he learned of the mutiny there.[7] Whatever the truth about this action, what is clear is Brock's attitude toward desertion: it was a major crime and he would act against it as quickly and decisively as possible.

Scarcely had the deserters been captured when Brock learned of a conspiracy being plotted at the fort that if carried out would have been very serious indeed. Some twelve disaffected soldiers plotted to seize their officers, confine them to their quarters and perhaps even harm Sheaffe, plunder ammunition, and then desert to the American shore. Again, Brock rushed over from York, took command at the fort, arrested the conspirators, and sent them, as well as earlier deserters, to Quebec for trial. This conspiracy, he learned, had spread to troops at Chippawa, a small post above Niagara Falls, and at Fort Erie. All he could do in response was reduce the garrisons at those places. (Where he sent the men is unclear.)

He proposed other solutions such as removing the 49th from Fort George because troops there were tempted by the proximity to the United States to escape from the harshness of army life. However, since most posts in Upper Canada were near the American border, Brock turned to other proposals. He suggested strengthening the law against those who encouraged desertion, which was done by the Upper Canadian Legislature in 1804.[8] While he was on leave in England (1805–06), Brock proposed the creation of a veteran's battalion whose soldiers should be stationed at frontier posts. The British Army already had nine battalions of veterans and, possibly because of Brock's suggestion, in December 1806 a 10th Royal Veteran Battalion would be created to serve in North America.[9] Its members had served with other regiments but were still fit for garrison duty. The regiment would arrive at Quebec in the summer of 1807. Brock was an officer who gave some thought to the lives that soldiers led, often brutal, harsh, and lonely, and who tried to find ways of improving their lot.

An early example of his helping young soldiers was his encouraging FitzGibbon to get an education. Another example, out of many, is shown in a letter he wrote to his brothers on November 19, 1808. In it he explained that he had prevailed on Sir James Craig, the commander of the troops in the Canadas, to appoint Sergeant Robinson "to a situation in the commissariat at Sorel, worth 3s. 6d. a day with subaltern's lodging money and other allowances. He married a Jersey lass, whose relatives may inquire for him."[10]

Meanwhile, Brock had to deal with the deserters and mutinous plotters in accordance with normal practice of the period (i.e., by court martial).[11] The trials were held at Quebec and after being found guilty, seven men were shot in March 1804, one was pardoned, and the remainder transported to Barbados. When Brock received the news of the executions he ordered the garrison of Fort George under arms and read them the letter. Then he spoke to the men, "Since I have had the honour to wear the British uniform, I have never felt grief like this, as it pains me to think that any members of my regiment should have engaged in a conspiracy which has led to their being shot like so many dogs!"[12] His evident concern for his men, while still maintaining discipline, suggests one of his great gifts as a commander. It is likely that the men and officers of the 49th would long remember that emotional scene.

"Desertion from the British Army in North America was a problem of major proportions and incalculable costs. Nowhere else in the empire did so many men flee the colours so easily."[13] Along the Niagara River, British soldiers could be enticed by the apparent opportunities for land and employment in the United States as well as the apparent ease of crossing both above and below the Falls. Colonel John Graves Simcoe (first lieutenant governor of Upper Canada) had written about this problem in 1793 and it continued during the War of 1812.[14] In fact, forces on both sides of the border would be plagued by desertion (see the Underhill incident).

Whatever the general situation, the problems in the Fort George garrison had arisen under Sheaffe's command and so, inevitably, questions of his responsibility were raised. The prisoners complained about his "harsh and severe treatment" of them when on duty. Brock, refusing to put the major blame on Sheaffe, wrote to Lieutenant-Colonel Green that Sheaffe's "manner of addressing the men on the least irritation, must be allowed to be unfortunate, and to that failing must be attributed, in a great measure, the ill will which some men have expressed toward him. There is also another cause which ought not to be omitted," Brock went on, "whenever the command of the Regiment devolved by my absence on Colonel Sheaffe, he unquestionably required more from the non-Commissioned Officers than I knew was useless to expect from them. He did not sufficiently study the character of the men and his ardent zeal made him seek … after perfection where it is not to be found — Serjeants, for trifling errors, were too often reduced … He likewise perhaps was frequently tiresome in the exercise in the field by which the men became disgusted with what they should have taken delight to practice."[15] Brock mainly blamed "the temptations which are perpetually offered to the unwary soldier" by the proximity of the United States, but he also sought to save Sheaffe's career. General Hunter thought of showing open disapproval of Sheaffe's conduct, an action that would have checked the lieutenant-colonel's career or even have ended it. Brock disagreed and urged Hunter to act frankly: either tell Sheaffe he was unworthy of command and let him resign or treat him with confidence and hope he would change his behaviour. Brock accepted his junior officer's imperfections, which arose from zeal rather than from malice or incompetence. His argument saved Sheaffe's career, for Hunter wrote in the margin of Brock's letter that Sheaffe was "to proceed to York to take command there."[16] It would be interesting to know how Sheaffe felt toward Brock.[17]

There is anecdotal evidence of the contrast between Sheaffe's treatment of soldiers under his command and Brock's treatment. Here is how Tupper presents the contrast:

An old pensioner, who served many years in the 49th, and was at Fort George during the conspiracy, tells us that the men were displeased at objections being made to their visiting the town of Niagara; at their being allowed to fish only in their white trowsers; and at other petty sources of annoyance — moreover, that the four black holes were constantly full. He adds that

Colonel Brock, on assuming the command, allowed the men, in proper uniform, to visit the town freely; to fish in their fatigue dresses; and even to use their muskets to shoot the wild pigeons, which flew over in countless numbers, on condition that they provided their own powder and shot.[18]

This recollection suggests that while Brock was willing to allow the men a degree of latitude in their activities, he maintained rules so that the troops could be in no doubt that they were still subject to army discipline. Whatever the source of his leadership qualities, he demonstrated early in his army career that he was a very good leader of men. He also enjoyed Sheaffe's company, for when Sheaffe was at York and Brock at Fort George, Brock wrote that his absence, "deprives me of a favourite guest."[19]

Fortunately, Brock was able to enjoy some of the pleasures and social activities of Upper Canada. He engaged in what might be loosely described as horticultural activity when some fruit trees sent by General Hunter arrived at Fort George and Brock wrote to Green that he would take care of them and send them to York. In July 1803, he wrote to Green, "The house and garden and farm get on in the usual quiet and improving style," which raises the question of whose house, garden, and farm. Perhaps it was Green's. He sent gifts to Hunter of quails and, in February 1804, a saddle of venison and some fish. In January, Brock wrote about a large dinner party he had held "and in the evening there was a ball which was numerously attended." He invited officers of Fort Niagara's garrison to a dinner on January 18 but the invitation was declined. In February, he thanked Green for sending drawing paper, for "painting and drawing would help to pass the remaining weeks of winter."[20] No examples of drawings or paintings by Brock have been found, but there is frequent evidence that he enjoyed a good table and a well-attended ball.

During the summer of 1804, Brock sailed several times to Kingston, taking detachments of the 49th regiment there. In September he was in command of the garrison of Quebec City. He dealt with the usual minor garrison matters (e.g., quarters for prisoners, supply of gunpowder, and the need for more recruits). But what he really wanted was to return home, and by the summer of 1805 his request became an urgent demand because of "the confused state in which my private affairs are thrown in consequence of my absence and the likelihood of my suffering materially in a pecuniary way ..." What he meant by this is not clear in his correspondence or biographical writings. His wish was granted; he departed in October, leaving Sheaffe in command of the 49th regiment.[21]

Brock was well aware of events in Europe, where Napoleon continued to expand his conquests. In the month of Brock's departure for home, Horatio Nelson gained his great victory at Trafalgar at the cost of his life. Brock's world would feature British predominance on the oceans and Napoleon's expansion of his rule on the continent.

Brock also kept an eye on events in the United States. Early in 1806, resolutions were introduced in the House of Representatives to restrict British trade to the United States. During the debates, threats were made of confiscation, retaliation, and even invasion of Canada.[22] In April, Congress passed a non-importation act to exclude a list of British manufactures but held off its implementation until November. However, Anglo-American relations received a shock when a British frigate, *Leander*, cruising off New York City, fired across the bows of a merchant vessel to bring her to (perhaps to check for British deserters) and in doing so hit another ship, killing a man on board. The body was taken to New York for a public funeral, which was accompanied by anti-British popular demonstrations. President Jefferson ordered federal officials to arrest the *Leander*'s captain if they found him within their jurisdiction. The threat to Canada, where his regiment was stationed, seemed real to Brock, for he cut short his leave in June and by August was back in Quebec.

In September 1806, holding the brevet rank of colonel, Brock became the senior officer in the Canadas and, in consequence, commander of all the forces there. He exercised this role until Sir James Craig arrived in October 1807 and took over as both governor of British North America and commander of the forces.[23]

(Robert Milnes had served as governor until 1805 when he was succeeded by Thomas Dunn, not as governor but as civilian administrator of Lower Canada.)[24] With Craig were Lieutenant-Colonel Edward Baynes, as adjutant general — and a frequent correspondent with Brock — and Major William Thornton as secretary and aide-de-camp.[25]

Craig had joined the army in 1763, when he was fifteen — the same age as Brock when he had joined. Craig had a wide range of experience of combat in North America, Europe, India, and South Africa, where he was governor of Cape Colony for a time. His health had been poor for years and he was frequently ill during his term as governor and commander, which lasted until 1811. He would make great efforts to improve the defences of Lower Canada, but his political views and actions would cause serious problems. We need to look briefly at political developments during his term.

The economy of Lower Canada was experiencing great and rapid changes. Traditional agriculture was stagnating, while cutting and shipping of timber, shipbuilding, and commerce were expanding rapidly, largely because of the European war. The French-Canadian members who dominated the assembly represented farmers (habitants) as well as French-speaking professionals, small merchants, and shopkeepers. By 1810, this group was spoken of as the Canadian party with its newspaper, *Le Canadien*, and opposed was the British (or English) party with its newspaper, the *Quebec Mercury*. The English party consisted largely of wealthier merchants, bureaucrats, and seigneurs; it predominated in the appointed executive and legislative councils whereby it exercised great influence over governors. Disputes between the two parties arose over taxation (on land or on trade), whether to continue or to change the land system, the role of the Anglican Church versus the Catholic Church, who was eligible to sit in the assembly, and the freedom of the press to criticize the government.[26]

For all of his adult life, Craig was a military man who had risen to high commands and, consequently, was accustomed to receiving obedience. Ouellet argues that it was "Craig's authoritarian nature, revealing the military disciplinarian with little understanding of civilian life ... [that caused] the behaviour which earned him his reputation as a dictator." Napoleon's Continental System was straining Britain's economy and the United States seemed very threatening.

> Finding political disharmony in the territory under his jurisdiction, and interpreting political opposition as a threat to the security of the state, he committed the error of identifying the French Canadians and their aspirations with the French and their revolution. The military situation being what it was, with his highly developed sense of order and authority he determined that the power of the executive must be strengthened and social stability and political harmony imposed, by force if necessary. [27]

Instead of remaining aloof from political conflicts between the Canadian and English parties, Craig involved himself directly by supporting the latter against the former. He cancelled the militia commissions of the proprietors of Le Canadien and, denouncing it as "a seditious and libelous publication," seized its press and jailed its editors without trial. He dissolved the assembly in 1809, and again in February 1810, hoping to weaken the Canadian party, but an election later that year returned it to a majority — including the members still in jail. It was a clear defeat for the English party and, indeed, for Craig and his supporters. There followed a quiet session of the Legislature while Craig finished his term.

Brock was present in Lower Canada during most of this turmoil but there is no evidence that he got involved with politics. However, he did work closely with Craig on military matters and agreed with Craig's political views and actions. On occasion, in correspondence Brock expressed his sympathy for Craig. His clearest statement is found in a letter of February 19, 1811, to his brother Irving:

> Sir James Craig has triumphed completely over the French faction in the Lower Province. By their

41

conduct they have fully exemplified the character of their ancestors. The moment they found they could not intimidate by threats, they became as obsequious as they had been violent. The house of assembly passed every bill required of them; among others, one authorizing the governor-general and three councillors to imprison any one without assigning a cause. The state of the country makes such a measure highly necessary. Sir James has been very ill, and it is supposed that he cannot long survive the fierce and frequent attacks of his disorder. His death, whenever it comes, will be bewailed by all who possess the feelings of Englishmen in this country. He appears determined to keep me near his person, and I hardly know how to accomplish my grand object of visiting England in opposition to his wishes.[28]

Let us return to the year 1807.

Britain's impressment policy continued to produce conflict. The most serious incident occurred on June 21, 1807, when HMS *Leopard* fired upon the United States frigate *Chesapeake* before boarding it to remove suspected deserters. The gunfire badly damaged the frigate as well as killing some of its crew. In Norfolk, Virginia, where the battered *Chesapeake* lay, mobs rioted. Further north, public meetings denounced the "outrage" and pledged their support for strong government action. Jefferson swiftly issued a proclamation requiring all British armed vessels to leave American waters and forbidding all contact with them. He demanded satisfaction from Britain and ordered gunboats to prepare for action; in April 1808, Congress authorized an increase in the army of eight regiments.[29] Although at the time Jefferson talked about seizing Canada,[30] he relied mainly on economic pressure to bring about change in British policy. Thus, he imposed the Non-Importation Act, followed by the Embargo Act that closed American ports to foreign trade. Those measures proved ineffective.

Another serious incident occurred in May 1811. HMS *Guerriere* had seized an alleged deserter from an American brig and Captain John Rodgers was ordered to take his frigate, *President,* to cruise off the east coast. He spotted a warship, thought it was the frigate *Guerriere,* and proceeded to prepare for action. It turned out to be a much inferior sloop, the *Little Belt,* and after exchanging broadsides for some forty-five minutes, the *Little Belt* had suffered eleven dead and twenty-one wounded to one wounded on the *President.* The badly damaged British ship proceeded to Halifax. A court of inquiry in the United States concluded that the *Little Belt* began the fight by firing first. In his annual address to Congress, the president criticized British policy, "With this evidence of inflexibility, in trampling on the rights which no independent nation can relinquish; congress will feel the duty of putting the U. States into an armor and an attitude demanded by the crisis, and corresponding with the national spirit and expectations."[31] That belligerent talk reflected the feelings of many Americans while in Britain newspapers expressed outrage.[32] Even a settlement of the *Chesapeake* affair could not cool tempers. The two countries were moving ever closer to open war.

Back in June 1807, the *Leopard* and *Chesapeake* crisis brought on the real danger of an Anglo-American war that could mean invasion of the Canadas. Thomas Dunn and Brock were well aware of these developments, but it seems that only the colonel was worried about the state of Lower Canada's defences.[33] Brock told Dunn there were only 300 militia armed and instructed, while the walls of Quebec were so old and decayed that they were useless for defence. He asked for 600 to 1,000 men to be hired to work on the city's defences and a large call out of militiamen. He wanted the work and training of militia done before spring, when he expected the first American attacks might come.[34] Dunn and his executive council felt much less alarm and raised many objections — such as possible resistance to a call up of militia, the cost of paying the men, and the lack of arms — to Brock's requests. Brock attended a council meeting and then wrote a strongly worded letter (July 23) about the weaknesses of Quebec's defences and his surprise at the government's reluctance to call out the militia. The councillors may have had some concern about the loyalty of Lower Canada's population in case of an American invasion. Brock had no doubt that the people would resist vigorously but he was less certain of this if the invaders included French troops.[35] Although Dunn balloted one-fifth of the militia, Brock saw this as inadequate, so he kept his regulars concentrated at Quebec. He did achieve the completion of works enclosing the upper town and raised a battery of eight 36-pounders in the centre of the citadel to command the river and its opposite banks. All this made a small improvement to the defences.

Another indication of Brock's concern about defending the Canadas was his reaction to a proposal he received early in 1807 from the lieutenant of the County of Glengarry in Upper Canada. This proposal was made in the previous year when it seemed unnecessary, but now the threat of war appeared greater.[36] John McDonell suggested raising a corps of Highland Fencible Infantry from local inhabitants. (Fencible meant a regiment raised for service only in North America and the men were trained as regulars.)[37] That county was settled by Scots as early as 1784, with the 1803 addition of a large influx of Roman Catholic highlanders led by their priest, Alexander MacDonnell. He had been chaplain of a corps of Glengarry Fencibles in Scotland and when that regiment was disbanded in 1802, rather than struggle in poverty in the old country, many men and families emigrated to Upper Canada. In light of the shortage of troops in Lower Canada, it is not surprising that Brock heartily supported the proposal. Glengarry County is just over the Lower Canadian border from Montreal and Brock saw the corps as strengthening the defences of that city and even of Quebec. He also hoped that the corps "would hereafter become a nursery, from which the army might draw a number of hardy recruits."[38] The following year, Craig would order Brock to contact "the Glengarry people" but the governor, seeing too many difficulties to recruiting, cancelled the scheme. It would, however, be revived in 1811 and with support from Sir George Prevost as well as Brock, the regiment would be established.

Meanwhile, Upper Canada's lieutenant governor, Francis Gore, was concerned about apparent American threats to his colony, particularly what looked like warlike preparations at Detroit. He asked Brock to send weapons for the militia. Instead, Brock sent Lieutenant-Colonel Pye, deputy quartermaster general, to convey the commander's views to Gore, advise him on the defence of Upper Canada, and collect information for Brock. Brock made it clear that because of Lower Canada's defence needs, he was unable to send arms or men to the upper province. Dissatisfied with Brock's response, Gore travelled to Montreal for a face-to-face meeting. Brock continued his refusal to send troops and weapons, pointing out that he had sent 4,000 muskets to Upper Canada leaving only 7,000 for distribution in Lower Canada. He also made it clear that future responsibility for the defence of his province would rest with Gore, a burden that the lieutenant governor took on reluctantly.[39]

The British government had made it clear to Craig that its strategy for the defence of the Canadas was based upon the preservation of Quebec City because of its fortifications and its accessibility to the Royal Navy. Brock would have been aware of this focus on Quebec and that Craig had informed Gore of the government's strategic priorities, which meant that Upper Canada could expect little aid in the form of British troops. However, Craig suggested that Gore summon aboriginal leaders to a meeting to renew the traditional bond of friendship with the Crown. Gore, after making some changes in the Indian Department personnel, would organize meetings in 1808 for various native delegations at Amherstburg. At a public council in July, one of these leaders was the Prophet Tenskwatawa's brother, Tecumseh. These concerns and developments might seem remote from Brock's life, but in a few years they would become some of his most vital concerns.

Perhaps another reason that Brock could give little attention to Upper Canadian concerns was that he was distracted by a financial mess in the Commissary Department. A good deal of money flowed through this department because, while it was the army's financial office, it also handled buying, storing, and distributing the army's provisions and other supplies. John Craigie had been appointed deputy commissary general in 1781 and commissary general in 1784, but he had a lot of other business and political interests.[40]

For whatever reasons, his accounts for 1806 contained many unexplained expenditures. When Brock raised questions about them, he was met with obstruction by Craigie, who claimed that he acted under a special arrangement agreed to by Brock's predecessor and even had to the nerve to suggest that Brock lacked the authority to inquire into the commissary's affairs. That was certainly not the way

*Francis Gore, lieutenant-governor of Upper Canada, 1806–11 and 1815–17, painted by George Theodore Berthon.*

to respond to Isaac Brock. He continued to probe only to find an even worse situation. Craigie had received authority to draw £90,000 from the Treasury in Britain but had only paid a little more than half of this amount into the army's fund. (The army's bank in Canada was called the Military Chest.) Craigie refused, or was unable, to explain the discrepancy. While Craigie continued his obstruction, Brock reported to the British Treasury authorities that "no examination has occurred in his store account since the 24th of December, 1788. The account of fuel is likewise in arrear since the 24th of December, 1796, and the account of provisions since the 24th of June, 1800."[41] Brock drew up regulations for the commissary but Craigie refused to implement them or to provide full information on his accounts to the government. It turned out that he was using army funds for his own uses. As a result, he was dismissed as commissary general in 1808 and sentenced to repay the missing money to the government. This had not been done by the time of his death, shortly after.

The mismanagement of government funds and dissimulation by government officials appeared in other instances. Upon learning of these problems, Brock liked to act quickly and decisively. For example, in 1807, when he learned that the pay of the men in the Marine Department at Kingston was seven months in arrears, he sent an officer there to conduct an inquiry. In the same year, he ordered all commissaries at posts in Upper Canada to send their accounts in proper form to Quebec or face dismissal.[42]

He was also involved in another controversy in 1807. He was concerned that the troops, numbering almost 1,000 men, in quarters known as the Jesuit Barracks had no suitable area nearby for exercise or parade. He pointed out to President Dunn that due to the lack of such facilities, soldiers spent their time in taverns and often got into trouble. He wanted to use some empty adjacent land for a new officers' quarters as well as space for soldiers' recreation and parades, which officers could easily supervise. Previously, Dunn had agreed with Brock's suggestion, but in May refused to allow it. Brock was convinced that private interests (who had other plans for the vacant land) had produced Dunn's change of mind. He continued to refuse even though Brock made suggestions to accommodate other interests, but the colonel wisely kept his troops off the disputed land. This problem continued, for in 1811 Sir George Prevost sought the same improvement that Brock had suggested. In 1812, Prevost was given permission to proceed with barrack improvements.[43]

Another problem facing the garrison that Brock tried to solve was lack of proper hospital facilities in Quebec. His suggested plan for the construction of a hospital was not approved and the problem continued.[44] Brock had encountered difficulties upon his first arrival in Lower Canada. His persistent attempts to improve conditions for his soldiers was certainly laudable.

## CHAPTER THREE

# Brock: An Officer with Many Roles, 1808–10

Brock's career was flourishing, for as Colonel Brock he became commander of the forces in both Canadas on September 27, 1806, and began receiving the pay and allowances of a brigadier-general. In March 1808, he was sent to Montreal with the nominal rank of brigadier-general and this appointment was confirmed by the king to date from July 3, 1808.[1] A brigadier-general, or simply brigadier, might or might not be advanced to the rank of general.[2] In Brock's case, the eventual outcome was advancement to the rank of major general on June 4, 1811.

In Montreal, Brock was quartered in the Château de Ramezay (originally built in 1706 for Claude de Ramezay, governor of Montreal),[3] which was badly in need of repair. The government recognized the problem but was not willing to correct it. His friend in Quebec, Lieutenant-Colonel Thornton, tried to cheer him up: "I am sorry for your being the sufferer, but I can venture to assure you that, however unfavourable the building may be, you ought never to feel uneasy about your friends, for in your kindness and hospitality, no want of comfort can ever be felt by them: in this I am fully supported by the accounts from Montreal."[4] Brock also had helped Thornton and Frobisher to find accommodation in Quebec. At least Brock enjoyed the social life of Montreal, which was dispensed on a lavish scale by wealthy fur traders, for these were the prosperous years of the North-West Company. He did not enjoy the summer weather, complaining in July that it was much hotter than in Quebec.

Fortunately, by September he had been superseded by Major-General Gordon Drummond and was on his way back to Quebec. Drummond's father, Colin, had been serving as deputy paymaster general to the forces in Quebec when Gordon was born there in 1772. He came from a distinguished family in Scotland and entered the army as an ensign in 1789. He rose rapidly through the ranks, becoming the commanding officer of his regiment, the 8th Foot, in 1800 and a major-general in January 1805. He had seen action in the Netherlands and Egypt as well as having experience of staff duties. He sailed from England in May 1808 to serve on Craig's staff and in 1811, as a lieutenant-general, would serve briefly as commander of the forces.[5] Like Brock, Drummond would try to correct problems with barracks and hospital facilities for the troops.[6]

During this period of a little more than two years in Quebec City, Brock's military duties seemed to have been light. He sought leave to return to Europe, but Craig would not approve. Craig regarded Brock as one of his most dependable officers, shown by his making Brock a brigadier-general as well as his determination to keep him in the Canadas. There should be no wonder, given events in the United States. In April 1808, Congress authorized eight more regiments, five of them to be infantry and one each of riflemen, cavalry, and artillery. The government began moving troops to its frontier along the St. Lawrence River, ostensibly to enforce the trade embargo; as well, it was putting heavy armaments on ships being built at Oswego, a port on the southern shore of Lake Ontario almost across from Kingston, the major British naval base on the lake.[7] It is not surprising that those responsible for Canadian defence wondered about the Americans' real intentions.

An incident in May 1809 highlights how tense was the situation along the United States-Canadian border.[8] An American deserter, Isaac Underhill, a teacher in a school in Elizabethtown on the St. Lawrence River, was shot and killed by a band of United States troops who were trying to return him across the border. Captain William Bennett and some of his men of the Sixth Regiment of U.S. Infantry were on board an American schooner that was forced to shelter in a bay near Elizabethtown when they learned of Underhill's presence nearby. Bennett, on his own authority, sent men to arrest Underhill. He was shot trying to escape his would-be captors. The local justice of the peace, Henry Arnold, and other local people were outraged at this unauthorized invasion of their town and the killing of a man who was regarded as under the protection of British law. Upper Canadian authorities were unable to get Bennett extradited, but Arnold wrote to the Montreal *Canadian Courant* and other Canadian and American papers picked up the story. The United States government learned about Bennett's unlawful action and responded by apologizing to the Canadians, offering reparations, and court martialling their over-zealous officer. Bennett was found guilty of conduct unbecoming an officer but given only a reprimand. The author of the article assumes he received this light punishment because he was probably doing what was common practice along the frontier — namely, pursuing a deserter across the border and trying to return him to his home country. In other words, both British and American troops responded in this way to desertion — a serious problem for both their armies and naval vessels on the lakes. Despite this incident, and others along the Canadian-United States border, trade continued to flow and people moved back and forth for business or pleasure. It was something that the authorities could not stop or even really control. When war came, it was no easy task for governments to impose security to prevent desertion and spying along this border.

Whatever happened in North America, for army officers hoping for advancement and glory, the place to be was Europe in the struggle against Napoleon. The army was Brock's life and he accepted its discipline. If that required him to stay in the Canadas, he would make the best of it. He expressed this sentiment in a letter to his sister-in-law in London (William's wife) and asked her to call on the wife of Captain Thomas Manners of the 49th. This lady was the sister of the wife of James Ross Cuthbert, whom Brock described as his "most intimate friend, with whom I pass a great part of my leisure hours."[9] James had inherited the seigneury of Berthier from his father, was a militia officer, and was well-known as a supporter of the social hierarchy under British rule.[10]

A month later Isaac wrote to his brother, Irving, thanking him for sending out various articles that were needed. Everything had arrived but the cocked hat, and the lack of this caused him some inconvenience because, he complained, "from the enormity of my head, I find the utmost difficulty in getting a substitute in this country."[11] That hat took two years to reach Upper Canada, arriving after Brock's death! It may be seen in the Niagara Historical Museum.

In that same month, Craig told Brock he would be sent to command the troops in Upper Canada. Craig wanted him to move there without delay, as Major-General Baron Francis de Rottenburg was on his way from England to take command of the Quebec garrison.[12] Brock did not know if this move would be lasting or only brief and he was not pleased, for he would have to leave his garden "with abundance of melons and other good things." He had an unflattering opinion of the upper province: "Unless I take everything with me, I shall be miserably off, for nothing beyond eatables is to be had there; and in case I provide the requisites to make my abode in the winter in any way comfortable, and then be ordered back, the expense will be ruinous." [13]

Governor Craig felt it necessary to have an officer like Brock in Upper Canada so "that a scrutinizing eye may correct the errors and neglect that have crept in, and put all in order again."[14] It would seem that Brock had acquired a reputation of being able to clear up problems. Moreover, the governor had often urged to the British government the need to have a third general officer on the staff in Canada, particularly because he wanted to station an officer of that rank in the upper province. Colonel Baynes, who informed Brock of these circumstances, also mentioned Craig's admiration for the general: "If he liked you less, he might perhaps be more readily induced to let you go; as matters stand, I do not think he will."[15] The appeal to Brock's sense of duty left him no choice. He would have to give up his "grand object of visiting England," and the obstacle to his leaving was increased when in March he was informed that Craig's ill-health was forcing him to leave his post and return home (he would depart in June).[16] In Craig's view his departure meant it was even more necessary that Brock remain where he was. Craig knew that his friend would be disappointed and partly to soften the disappointment, as well as to show his esteem, he offered "as a legacy and mark of his very sincere regard, his favorite horse Alfred …"

No wonder Brock wanted to remain in Quebec, for social life there was lively. In the same letter quoted above, he wrote about "two frigates at anchor, and the arrival of Governor Gore from the Upper Province, have given a zest to society. Races, country and water parties, have occupied our time in a continued round of festivity." Brock had contributed in the form of "a grand dinner given to Mrs. Gore, at which Sir James Craig was present, and a ball to a vast assemblage of all descriptions." Lieutenant-Colonel Green wrote about the dinner and ball enjoyed by "as many Ladies as his [Brock's] rooms could conveniently contain." They danced in two rooms to the band of the 89th Regiment, "which unquestionably is the best Military Band I ever saw."[17] Knowing he was going to a much less sophisticated social setting, Brock commented cryptically in his letter, "Such stimulus is highly necessary to keep our spirits afloat." He concluded, "Heaven preserve you. I shall probably begin my journey upwards in the course of a few days." He was not going in a cheerful or optimistic mood. His next letter is dated Fort George, September 13, 1810. A new chapter — preparing Upper Canada for war — was beginning in his life.

At least he was able to take with him a long-time colleague as his military aide-de-camp (ADC), John Baskerville Glegg. He had entered the 49th Regiment June 1, 1797, as an ensign and was present in the same actions as Brock in 1799 and 1801. He had attended the Royal Military College between 1803 and 1805. Brock chose him as ADC in July 1810. He would serve at Detroit and, as a result, would be promoted to "Rank of Major in the Army" on October 7, 1812.[18]

He was in the thick of the fighting at Queenston Heights on October 13, for which Sheaffe would praise his services. After Brock's death, Glegg sought to become an aide to Prevost who agreed but there is no record of his taking up the post. He acted briefly as ADC to Sheaffe before serving as major of brigade to Generals Sheaffe, Rottenburg, Vincent, and Drummond. He returned to England and in 1826 went on half-pay. He served briefly as a captain in the Coldstream Guards in 1836 and died April 28, 1861, at Thurstaston Hall. Details of his life are lacking, but what becomes clear is he was a friend as well as an aide to Brock. [19]

Meanwhile, in Quebec City, what seems to have impressed most officers about the new garrison commander, de Rottenburg, was his wife, Julia, thirty years his junior. Colonel Baynes wrote to Brock, September 6, 1810, that Julia de Rottenburg "has made a complete conquest of all hearts. She is in reality remarkably handsome, both in face and figure, and her manners uncommonly pleasing, graceful, and affable." Several weeks later, Lieutenant-Colonel Thornton wrote to Brock enthusing over the baron's "*cara et dolce sposa*: she is young (twenty-three), fair, beautiful, lively, discreet, witty, affable — in short, so engaging, or rather so fascinating, that neither the courier nor my paper will admit of my doing her justice; however from what I have said it is necessary further to add and explain, that it is not my opinion alone but that of the public." This correspondence would hardly lift the spirits of an officer who enjoyed the company of women. Perhaps that is why on October 4, Baynes wrote to him, "The charms of Mrs. de Rottenburg have not effaced you from the recollection of your friends, who very sincerely regret your absence."[20]

CHAPTER FOUR

# Brock in Upper Canada, 1810–11

The colony of Upper Canada that Brock entered in September 1810 was a forested land with settlements that merely dotted the landscape from Cornwall in the east to Amherstburg in the west. The population numbered approximately 77,000, mostly clustered along the shores of lakes or banks of rivers. (By contrast, bordering New York State had over 959,000 inhabitants.) Kingston, with about 150 houses and 600 to 1,000 inhabitants, was regarded as the largest town as well as the main naval and shipbuilding centre on Lake Ontario.[1] York, the capital, had about 600 residents and, thirty miles across the lake, Niagara had perhaps 500 inhabitants. Inland, there was only Chatham and a few settlements along the Thames River.

Economically, the upper province was weak. It had practically no industry, only limited capital resources, and depended on lumbering and agriculture for most of its employment. The farms, however, could not be depended on to supply the need for food once the men were taken for military service. Moreover, the vital problem of providing for the many needs of the province from Lower Canada was made even greater by the poor and insecure communications.

In summer, travel was principally by schooner on the lakes and the upper St. Lawrence, bateaux on the St. Lawrence from Montreal to Prescott where the rapids ended, and canoes on smaller rivers.[2] Although water provided the fastest and cheapest means of transportation and communication, it was not without its problems, such as rapids in the St. Lawrence, the barrier of Niagara Falls, storms, and unmarked harbours. Roads in Upper Canada connected the main settlements along the St. Lawrence River and Lake Ontario, but spring thaw or rainfall turned them into almost impassible muddy tracks. They were little better when they dried, for travellers had to deal with ruts, holes, dust, tree stumps, and unbridged rivers. Travel during the winter, on snowy roads and frozen rivers, was somewhat easier but far from good. In February 1811, Brock wrote to his brothers that on his trip from York to Niagara he had travelled over the worst roads he had ever met. In December, Brock intended to send John Lane, the assistant commissary general, to Quebec, but, he wrote, "The roads are in so bad a state, that he cannot possibly travel for some weeks."[3]

Transportation difficulties made for slow and uncertain communications. A voyage across the Atlantic could take a month if all went well, but more likely six to eight weeks because of contrary winds or calms or fog or ice. Letters from England, by way of Halifax and Quebec, took from four to eight months to reach York; by way of New York City, the time was about two months. In 1810, the mail required about a month to go from Montreal to York, a direct distance of 350 miles. This time improved slightly before the war (e.g., Brock's letter of December 11, 1811, to the military secretary was answered from Quebec on January 7, 1812). In this same month, Captain Gray made the trip in only eleven days, taking six days from Montreal to Kingston and five from Kingston to York. During 1812, the speed of communications increased by the use of couriers and a post system along the St. Lawrence, so that letters between Montreal and York reached their destination in only a few days. A letter from Brock at Fort George, dated July 3, 1812, was answered on July 7th by Prevost.[4] From York to Amherstburg dispatches usually took six days and from York to St. Joseph's they ordinarily required two weeks since they had to go by the roundabout route of the lakes. [5]

Bringing people or goods from Europe or from Lower Canada was expensive, time-consuming, and subject to accidents. In wartime this supply route was vulnerable to attacks at sea, but the greatest exposure to enemy action was the section along the St.

Lawrence from Montreal to Kingston. If the Americans attacked here they would "cut off the Communication by Water between the two Provinces," wrote Gore in February 1809,[6] and everything to the westward would be lost.

Brock tried to make the best of living in Upper Canada, although it lacked the refinements and luxuries of Lower Canada. He was happiest when he was busy, as he told his brothers in September, "Here I am [Fort George] stationed for some time, unless I succeed in the application I mean to make shortly for permission to visit England. At present, Vincent, Glegg, and Williams, 49th, enliven this lonesome place. They are here as members of a general court martial, and are soon to depart, when I shall be left to my own reflections."[7] They did depart and, according to a correspondent who knew him well, although Brock "often sees ten or a dozen friends" at Government House, "unfortunately he is quite alone not an officer with him."[8] The writer, William Claus, mentions the absence of Captain Frederick Heriot, Colonel John Vincent, and Captain John Glegg. All these officers had long been in the 49th Foot and so shared experiences with their commanding officer — no doubt over a few bottles of wine.

As winter closed in, Brock's sense of isolation increased. He wrote to brother Irving in January 1811, "You, who have passed all your days in the bustle of London, can scarcely conceive the uninteresting and insipid life I am doomed to lead in this retirement." He passed much of his time alone in the evenings; "I read much, but good books are scarce, and I hate borrowing. I like to read a book quickly, and afterwards revert to such passages as have made the deepest impression and which appear to me the most important to remember...." He asked his brother to send him books of history, preferably with maps and translations of ancient authors, "As I grow old, I acquire a taste for study." For the first time Brock mentions his health, "I feel at this moment infinitely better, but am not quite the thing, without knowing what ails me." He thought about "directing my steps ... to Ballstown, a medicinal water of great celebrity, about twenty miles north of Albany [New York]." But a month later he cancelled the journey because his health was restored and, besides, he did "not admire the manners of the American people."[9]

He was an amazing man. Despite all the responsibilities on his shoulders and the increasing possibility of war with the United States, he remained a student of history and literature. And, although he wrote in January, "At present I live very abstemiously, and scarcely ever touch wine," he was not reclusive for he had a reputation for generous hospitality. He enjoyed the company of Colonel and Mrs. Murray, among others, and during the winter he held a ball. Another friend, Colonel James Kempt (the quartermaster-general 1807–11)[10] wrote that he had just received a letter from Mrs. Murray, "Giving me an account of a splendid ball given by you to the *beau monde* of Niagara and its vicinity, and the manner in which she speaks of your liberality and hospitality reminds me of the many pleasant hours I have passed under your roof."[11] (He also enjoyed the hospitality of others. At York, Lieutenant Governor Gore provided "an entertainment … to Brig. General Brock, the Members of the Legislative Council, and the House of Assembly, the Officers of the Garrison and the principal gentlemen of the Town and neighbourhood.")[12]

Brock's ambition and discontent were known by his friends. One of these, Colonel J.A. Vesey, wrote in April from London, "It is a pity that the 49th should be detained there so long, as it will interfere materially with the promotion of your officers. I fear you will have passed a lonely winter at Fort George, notwithstanding the addition of my friend Murray and his nice little wife to your society." Perhaps thinking of a cure for Brock's loneliness, Vesey, who had six children, wished one of them was a daughter old enough for Brock to marry. A month later, the colonel commiserated with Brock for the "stupid and uninteresting time" that he had spent in the colony.[13] His fellow officers' opinions of Upper Canada undoubtedly reflected Brock's thoughts.

Brock asked permission to return to England "on account of urgent private affairs requiring my presence," by which he meant financial affairs. On behalf of the commander-in-chief, Lieutenant-Colonel Torrens wrote directly to Brock, as well as to Governor General Prevost, giving permission as long as Brock could be immediately replaced by another officer, meaning one of equal rank. His command could be taken by Sheaffe because he was on the spot and had "strong claims to employment on the staff."[14] Brock's 1804 judgment of Sheaffe was being vindicated. The letter giving Brock permission to return to England arrived in Upper Canada in January 1812, but, to anticipate slightly, Brock turned down the proffered leave because he believed there was the strong possibility of war with the United States. If that occurred, his place was in Canada.

In the Ohio Valley and upper lakes, the aboriginal nations — angered by continued American encroachment on their lands — were drawing closer to war. At a very large gathering at Amherstburg in November 1810, Tecumseh spoke of their determination to defend their lands and their expectation of receiving aid from the Indian Department. Those officials, headed by Matthew Elliot (superintendent at Amherstburg), feared that the tribes "were on the eve of an Indian War," and the British would have to strive hard to restrain them.[15] No general conflict broke out, but native bands began sporadic raids against American settlements on the Wabash River.

LAC, C319

*Imaginary portrait of Tecumseh, artist unknown.*

When Tecumseh departed for the southern states to try to persuade tribes there to join his confederacy, Governor Harrison of
Indiana determined to undertake a campaign to destroy that confederacy's base of Prophetstown. He expected this action would finish Tecumseh's efforts to create a strong aboriginal union and would
also safeguard advancing American settlement. Harrison gathered a
mixed force about 900-strong of regulars and militiamen, including
experienced frontier fighters from Kentucky. During September and
October he led a force up the Wabash toward the Tippecanoe River.
On November 6th, they camped near Prophetstown. The tribes
gathered there feared they would be attacked and, with Tecumseh
absent, no leader was strong enough to restrain the most belligerent
warriors. Before dawn on November 7th, 600 to 700 warriors did
attack, but after a brief, fierce fight the natives were repulsed and
Harrison burned the deserted village.

When he returned, Tecumseh had even more reason to seek
British support against the Americans. While Americans rejoiced at
their success in the battle of Tippecanoe (and Harrison would use this
glorious victory to gain the presidency in 1840), their anger against
the British was further inflamed by claims that "the whole of the
Indians on this frontier, have been completely armed and equipped
out of the king's stores at Amherstburg."[16]

Brock recognized that because of the government's policy of
providing native tribes with weapons and other supplies, it had put
itself in a very awkward position in urging restraint. As he wrote to
Governor Craig, "Our cold attempt to dissuade that much injured
people from engaging in such a rash enterprise could scarcely be
expected to prevail," particularly as the Indian Department had provided them a "liberal quantity of military stores."[17] While muskets
could be used for hunting, "military stores" contains a suggestion of
other uses. Nevertheless, Brock's duty was to support Craig's policy.
Hence, in March 1811, he ordered Major Taylor, officer commanding
at Amherstburg, to dissuade the native warriors from launching war
but to do so carefully in order not to create resentment that might
threaten future alliance. Little did Brock know that in a few months he

would be responsible for maintaining the alliance without provoking conflict with the Americans.

The summer of 1811 saw many changes of command in the Canadas. Sir James Craig, because of his worsening health as well as his political difficulties, obtained approval to return to England[18] (see Appendix D). On June 19, 1811, he embarked from Quebec City, leaving Thomas Dunn in charge of the government of Lower Canada and Lieutenant-General Gordon Drummond in command of the forces in the Canadas.[19] Drummond moved to Quebec and Brock — a major-general as of June fourth — was given command of Montreal.

On September 14th, Sir George Prevost, the new governor-in-chief of British North America and commander of all His Majesty's Forces, arrived at Quebec.[20] The arrival of such an important personage required a good deal of ceremony, including the firing of salutes by guns on two ships and a reply by the "grand battery" on shore. He landed with "his lady, family and suite" at the king's wharf, where he was greeted by officers of the garrison and by the 8th Regiment, whose band played "God Save the King." He mounted his horse and, accompanied by officers, rode to the Château Saint Louis to be received there by the colours and band of the Royal Newfoundland Regiment. (Each regiment had a regimental flag with the colour of the cuffs and collars of the soldiers' coats and a union flag in the upper canton. The regimental colour and the king's colour — the Union Jack — had the regimental name or number enclosed in a wreath of roses, and thistles in the centre of the colour. They were carried into battle by ensigns guarded by two sergeants, the whole group known as the regiment's colour party. The colours provided a rallying point for the regiment amidst the smoke of battle but, naturally, drew enemy fire. It was an honour to carry and defend the colours and a great disgrace to have them captured.) Prevost had joined the British Army in 1779, and from 1794 saw active service in the West Indies. In 1795, his successful defence of Dominica against the French gained him promotion to the rank of major general and a baronetcy. He had political experience as lieutenant governor of St.

Lucia, governor of Dominica, and since 1808 lieutenant governor of Nova Scotia. There he had proven to be a pragmatic and conciliatory governor who avoided any serious quarrel with the elected assembly. The political crisis in Lower Canada raised the possibility of undermining popular support for the government in case of war with the United States. Prevost's political skill, along with his fluent bilingualism, help explain why he was chosen.

Meanwhile, Lieutenant Governor Gore of Upper Canada obtained leave to return to England and he departed in October 1811. Prevost's instructions from the British government were to combine the civil and military roles in Upper Canada, probably because it was the most threatened area of the colony in the event of war with the United States. Prevost decided to send Brock to Upper Canada as both military commander and civil administrator. The government's instinct was sound and no more a capable officer than Brock could have been sent. Brock's residence of about three months in Montreal ended as he departed for Upper Canada.

On September 30th, he met the members of the executive council, presented his appointment as commander of the forces in the province, and the orders of the Prince Regent "appointing the Officer Commanding the forces in Upper Canada to be a Member of the Executive Council."[21] The necessary oaths were then given in the presence of Gore, Chief Justice Thomas Scott, John McGill, the inspector general of public provincial accounts, Justice William Dummer Powell, and Prideaux Selby, the receiver general. On October 9th, the day after Gore departed for England, Brock began his term as president of the council that was to last just over a year. As administrator of Upper Canada, he headed the civil government and one of his most important tasks was to convene the Legislature, use his influence to have measures passed, and end a session by proroguing the Parliament.

As if the major general did not have enough on his mind, during that summer the Brock family was hit by a financial crisis. In 1810 and 1811, English trade and industry entered a period of depression that was part of a wider pattern of a severe shortage of credit in Europe and the United States.[22] William Brock was the senior partner of a London firm of bankers and merchants that declared bankruptcy in June 1811, partly owing to French seizures of ships in the Baltic Sea. William had advanced to Isaac about £3,000 for the purchase of his commissions and, being childless, had never intended to ask for repayment. Unfortunately, Isaac's name appeared in the company's books with the sum charged against him. But the family also suffered because William had been supporting his brother Daniel's business and, late in 1810, was forced to cut off those funds. There was a greater shock for Isaac. He learned that Savery had suffered financially and that he and William, both brothers connected with the firm, had quarrelled and become estranged because of the bankruptcy. In light of Isaac's strong affection for his family, it is not hard to imagine the sorrow he felt, and he expressed it in his letters. He wrote to Savery,

> I have this instance finished a letter to Irving. I attempted to write composedly, but found it impossible. The newspapers gave me the first intimation of the heavy misfortune we have all sustained ... I want to be at once apprized of the full extent of our misery. Why keep me in this horrid suspense?
>
> I write merely to say, for really my poor head cannot allow me to say more, that tomorrow I enter into the official duties of the president of this province. The salary attached to the situation is £1,000, the whole of which, I trust, I shall be able to save, and, after a year or two, even more.
>
> Yesterday was my first truly gloomy birthday I have ever passed. May you be happy.[23]

Weeks would pass before Brock could receive the latest news from his family. He wrote with uncertainty but he was prepared to act decisively. He asked Irving what was the size of the debt and whether or not he (Isaac) would have to sell his commissions. He intended to sign over his salary, urging Irving to "pay over as fast as you receive it, unless indeed want among any of you calls for aid; in that case make use of the money, and let the worst come. I leave everything to your sober discretion." As a major-general, Brock was supposed to receive an annual salary of £456/5/0. It was not easy for Brock to give up this money, for he explained that he had spent £300 or £400 on "outfits" and so could not send any sums that year. As president of the council — in effect, lieutenant governor of the province — he had to maintain a certain image, which meant: "Much shew and feasting are indispensable to attract the multitude, especially in a colony like this, where equality prevails to such a degree that men judge of your disposition, of your frankness, by your frequency of the invitations they receive. At present, all classes profess great regard and esteem for me; but although I hope they may, I cannot expect such sentiments will continue long." He was too critical of both Upper Canadians and of himself. It is not clear if Brock did drastically curtail his expenditures; no complaints have come to light in the records. All evidence indicates that he was regarded with respect and even affection by most of the population.

That Isaac had many true friends is clear from a letter written to him by William:

> You have received, or will receive shortly, a letter from our assignees, desiring to be informed in what manner the debt, which appears in our books as owing by you, is to be liquidated … it amounts to something over £3000 … Some reports had, but very erroneously, been circulated that they [the assignees] had already commenced legal steps against you; and upon this report a young gentleman lately arrived from Canada, a Mr. Ellice, called upon Charles Bell to enquire if it were so, and told Bell that rather than anything unpleasant should happen to you, he would contrive to pay the debt himself, so great was his esteem and friendship for you.[24]

William had just learned of Brock's appointment and hoped his brother would not quit "his enviable situation, for a mere major-general's appointment in Europe." The family had lost heavily. William, Savery, and Irving became dependent upon small incomes while a brother-in-law, John Tupper, lost between £12,000 and £13,000, enormous sums for the time, but at least, he escaped total ruin. No further correspondence about this family crisis has been found, but the brothers would become reconciled. On October 13, 1812, William wrote to Savery that Isaac wished William and Irving to become reconciled, and so William "went up to day on seeing him and shook hands. He then showed me two lines which he had just received from Isaac. It is satisfactory to me that we shook hands before I was aware of the contents." [25]

The fact that Edward Ellice was willing to take on the Brock family debt out of esteem and friendship for Isaac tells a good deal about the regard for the general in English-Canadian civilian society. Born in 1783, Ellice was still a young man when he took over leadership of his father's widespread business enterprises upon his death in 1805. Edward is described as "a prominent merchant-banker and shipowner in the City [London], trading in furs, fish, sugar, cotton, and general merchandise in North and South America, the East and West Indies, and Europe." He was well educated (he had received his Master of Arts in 1800), well connected socially and politically in Britain, for he had married Lady Hannah, daughter of Charles, 1st Earl Grey, a leading figure in the Whig aristocracy, and wealthy — he inherited his father's Scottish estate as well as the large seigneury of Beauharnois. One indication of his financial strength is the fact that in 1813, despite the financial strains of years of warfare, he was able to borrow £150,000 from the Bank of England to aid his business. Until his death in 1863, Ellice played important roles in Canadian and British politics and business. Brock would have met him in Lower Canada and obviously impressed him, for bailing out a financially distressed army officer was probably something rarely done by a shrewd businessman.

Brock's complaint about the high level of expenditure that was expected of him and the resultant strain on his income was not an unusual situation. Officers were expected to maintain an expensive style of living that could, a times, strain their income. They were required to maintain a mess and that expense required a substantial private income of £200 to £300 above his pay. According to one historian, officers' pay was low compared to professionals of similar social status and even with some extra payments, officers were "abysmally paid."[26] An extra allowance was given for taking command of a garrison but there were deductions that sometimes surprised the officer. In February 1812, Major Donald Macpherson, commander of the garrison of Kingston, wrote that he understood in taking on the command he would receive a daily allowance of five shillings, which would be reduced by deductions to four shillings and nine pence. To his surprise he found that that amount would be reduced even further because it was subject to income tax. From an endorsement on the letter, it appears that the deductions remained.[27] Brock, too, watched his expenses carefully. In February he wrote to the military secretary (Noah Freer) that he had learned he was being charged £20 for his "portion of the expense of a canoe employed in taking Governor Gore and myself to York." He asked that Prevost "may consider this sum a fair public charge."[28]

While trying to cope with the family's financial problems, Brock had to deal with administrative matters of the Upper Canadian government. After assuming both civil and military command, one of his first concerns was the management of the Indian Department. The accounts of that department had fallen into arrears and Craig had appointed a deputy commissary general to bring the accounts up to date. But this officer, John Lane, was stationed at Fort George and the deputy storekeepers at different posts were required to send their accounts to the storekeeper general at Lachine in Lower Canada before they were sent to Lane at Fort George. Clearly, the system was seriously inefficient and Brock, typically, suggested that it be simplified. Either the storekeeper general should move to Upper Canada or his role in dealing with the accounts should be taken on by Lane. Prevost preferred to keep control in Quebec by ordering Lane to move there, where all future Indian Department accounts were to be sent. Brock disagreed with this change on the grounds that their examination in Upper Canada would be easier and quicker because that was where the accounts originated. His concern for efficiency was in this instance not shared by Governor Prevost.[29]

Prevost may have been influenced in his decision to post Brock to Upper Canada by reports about the poor condition of the forts along the Niagara frontier and of their supplies. Lieutenant-Colonel R.H. Bruyeres (commanding the Royal Engineers) reported in August 1811 on forts George, Chippawa, and Erie.[30] Fort George was "very much out of repair," Fort Chippawa contained only a blockhouse and storeroom "enclosed with a line of picketing very much decayed," and Fort Erie was to a great extent "unfinished and weak." None of these forts could provide effective defence. This gloomy analysis was confirmed by a report in September from Major-General George Glasgow (commanding Royal Artillery) to Prevost. Fort George, the principal fortress for the frontier, had only twenty-one gunners and three artillery officers, and Glasgow wrote about the lack of horses and drivers for the artillery and powder magazines unfinished and unprotected. He concluded that no post in Upper Canada was safe or strong.[31] This information would have been provided to Brock.

The threat of American hostilities continued to grow. President Madison, in his annual address to Congress, appealed for an increase in the country's military forces (see Chapter Three). In January 1812, the House of Representatives voted to increase the regular force by 10,000 men and authorized the president to raise up to 50,000 volunteers and to repair all naval ships.[32] The men in charge of the defence of the Canadas could not disregard these ominous actions. Brock undertook to gather information and to plan for the defence of his province. In December 1811, he sent a sweeping review to Prevost suggesting "precautionary measures ... to meet all future exigencies."[33]

He believed there had existed "a general opinion ... that, in the event of hostilities, no opposition was intended," but that view was changing because a strong regiment and military stores had been sent to Upper Canada and "a military person" had been appointed to administer the government. The regiment referred to was the 41st, which had been sent to Upper Canada in the summer to relieve the 100th (it was to go to Bermuda, but Prevost kept it in Lower Canada). Brock had recently visited Niagara and had found "the principal inhabitants" determined to defend "their property and support ... the government." But Brock also pointed out that Prevost needed to act for those people: "Look with confidence to your excellency, for such additional aid as may be necessary, in conjunction with the militia, to repel any hostile attempt against this province." He went on to general observations and for a military commander with no experience as a political leader they demonstrate a remarkable grasp of political realities. He knew there were many "improper characters who have obtained extensive possessions, and whose principles diffuse a spirit of insubordination very adverse to all military institutions ... It is certain that the best policy to be pursued ... [if war came] will be to act with the utmost liberality, and as if no mistrust existed; for, unless the inhabitants give an active and efficient aid, it will be utterly impossible for the very limited number of the military ... to preserve the province." He had perhaps learned from the example of Craig's mistakes in Lower Canada not to act as a high-handed martinet but to understand public opinion and work to change it.

After this introduction, Brock wrote about each area of the province. Significantly, he first reported on "the district of Amherstburg." He saw the greatest American threat there, but he thought it the place where "active operations," if undertaken, "must defer any offensive attempt on this province, from Niagara westward." The Americans, fearing attack from native warriors, would be compelled to send large forces to that frontier. In order for the British to obtain "an active co-operation on the part of the Indians," they would have to show them that "we are earnestly engaged in the war," and the way to do that was to seize Detroit and Michilimackinac.[34] In other words, if war came, act aggressively rather than wait to be attacked.

Brock anticipated the opening moves of the war and the capture of those two American posts would have precisely the effect

Painting by Peter Rindlisbacher

*Amherstburg Shoreline, 1804. In the shipyard on the extreme left of the painting is the schooner* General Hunter, *with its framing in the early stages of construction. Near the ship, naval personnel can be seen, as well as a group of redcoat soldiers from the 49th Regiment near the shore. There are partially de-rigged schooners in the center and right of the painting. A small American coasting schooner can be seen navigating around the down-bound raft in this narrow stretch of the Detroit River. There are many small craft operating along the waterfront, such as a lug-rigged skiff, a sprit-rigged boat, and a native canoe.*

he expected. He put the strength of the local militia at 700 men, too few for offensive operations. If a rupture seemed imminent, he proposed to reinforce Amherstburg with 200 regulars from Fort George and York, which would clearly indicate to both natives and militia that the government would resist an attack. Another vital need was to upgrade Fort Amherstburg. He sent Captain M.C. Dixon of the Royal Engineers to Malden in spring 1812 with the task of making improvements. On July 8th, Lieutenant-Colonel Thomas St. George, the commanding officer, reported to Brock, "We are hard at work at the Fort and have done a great deal since you left us … [Walls had been strengthened and twenty cannon mounted.] In short, every exertion possible is made by us."[35]

From Amherstburg to Fort Erie, Upper Canada depended for its defence on a naval force, but it consisted of only a ship and a schooner "of bad construction, old," and badly in need of repair. Brock reported that the Americans had two vessels "both in perfect readiness for any service." Whatever the disparity of force, when it came to the test the British would prevail by using their vessels effectively and by capturing the American brig. However, Brock pointed out that if Fort St. Joseph's were to be maintained and (in the event of war) Michilimackinac attacked, "many vessels" would have to be hired or purchased.

He mentioned that the Americans were already manning a war-ship at Sackets Harbor on Lake Ontario. Indeed, a recruiting party had come to Buffalo and "a petty officer" even had the nerve to cross the border to seek recruits. The magistrates were informed but the American escaped. It seems Brock had sources of information on the other side.

Next he dealt with the Niagara frontier, where he believed the main invasion attempt would come "with a view to conquest. All other attacks will be subordinate, or merely made to divert our attention." He estimated that nearly 3,000 militia and 500 native fighters could be collected along this line and, together with the regulars, they would provide and effective defence against anything but a very large force. Besides urging the need for regular troops, he pleaded for gunners, drivers, and horses to complete the Car Brigade. This was a volunteer corps of farmers who employed their horses in drawing field guns for the army. He also wanted a body of cavalry and reported that he had already received offers "from many respectable young men" to form a troop. All they needed from Lower Canada were swords and pistols.

Brock dealt finally with Kingston and the eastern end of Upper Canada. He believed the militia from the Bay of Quinte to Glengarry County to be the most dependable in the province. Those from the Bay could be stationed at Kingston, but from the town eastward the men would prefer to remain to protect their property against raids from the American shore. Brock expected that the Americans would likely raid across the St. Lawrence and so it would be best to have the militia watching American movements since, whenever

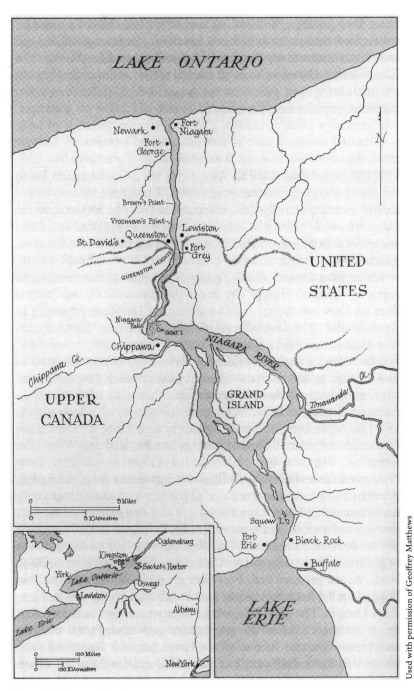

Map of the Niagara Frontier.

Used with permission of Geoffrey Matthews

the men were needed elsewhere, they could be moved quickly. He praised Richard Cartwright, "the senior militia colonel at Kingston," but because of that post's distance from York or Fort George, Brock urged the appointment of a regular officer "of high rank" to direct any operations there. Major Donald Macpherson of the 10th Royal Veteran Battalion would take command at Kingston.[36]

He concluded by assuring Sir George, "It will ever be my utmost pride to meet your views and to merit your approbation." When it came to actual campaigns in 1812, Brock would not always conform exactly to Prevost's wishes, for the governor preferred passive defence whereas the major-general believed the best course was to attack first. In this letter of December 2nd, before he was swamped by the necessities of warfare, Brock showed his ability to outline a strategic vision. It is clear, also, that Brock expected Upper Canada to be defended vigorously whatever difficulties that involved.

The very next day, Brock returned to the most serious problem in terms of defending Upper Canada. He wrote to Prevost, "My first care, on my arrival in this province, was to direct the officers of the Indian Department at Amherstburg to exert their whole influence with the Indians to prevent the attack which I understood a few tribes meditated against the American frontier." He believed these efforts had failed and that the natives faced destruction. Probably he was referring to their defeat at Tippecanoe, where their casualties were fewer than those of the Americans and neither their forces nor their spirit were destroyed.[37]

What is unusual is that Prevost used Brock's letter in an unexpected way. He sent an extract of it to the British minister in Washington, A.J. Foster, so that he could use it to counter any charges that the British government was inciting native people against the United States. As well, Prevost enclosed an extract in a dispatch to Liverpool pointing out that Brock had anticipated Liverpool's directions, dated July 28, 1811, to officials in Canada to do everything possible to restrain the Indians.

It was obvious that one of the major considerations for the defence of Upper Canada was the role of native nations. There was no unanimity among the Six Nations on the Grand River about supporting the British should war break out with the United States. The Iroquois in New York State had no choice because they lived on reserves surrounded by American settlements. For a variety of reasons — mainly concerns about their own safety — the New York Iroquois sought to persuade the Iroquois on the Grand to adopt a neutral stance in the event of war. British abandonment of native allies in 1783 (Treaty of Paris) and 1794 (Battle of Fallen Timbers) was remembered, not least among the Six Nations. On the Grand there were pro-American, pro-British, and neutralist factions. There was also discord between followers of John Norton, also known as Teyoninhokarawen, who favoured strong links with the British Army, and Deputy Superintendent-General William Claus, who sought to uphold the Indian Department's influence. Brock's efforts to gain aboriginal support for the defence of Upper Canada would be complicated by these many divisions and personal animosities among the Six Nations. These difficulties and the roles of Norton and Claus will be dealt with in later chapters.[38] In effect, the British found themselves between a rock and a hard place because their influence depended largely upon supplying natives with provisions, including weapons and ammunition. To cut off those supplies would remove any chance of restraint on their warriors' actions. At the same time, the Americans believed that the British were providing the means for frontier warfare, if not actually encouraging attacks on settlers. "From the American perspective, the reality on the ground was a degree of co-operation between Britain and Natives that was a threat. As a consequence, defeating the Natives was, in part, to the Americans a way of hitting Britain, whether or not the two powers were at war."[39]

The distribution of "presents," rewards, and payments to native peoples was a recurrent theme before and during the war. There were both practical and symbolic reasons for this British policy. The army gave supplies to the Six Nations to persuade them to take up arms in defence of Upper Canada, and to western nations because their warriors could not support their families when on campaigns. In June 1812, on behalf of the Grand River people, Norton requested a

LAC, C128832

*Major John Norton, Teyoninhokarawen. Watercolor on ivory, 1805, by Mary Ann Knight.*

"regular stipend" for warriors, "otherwise want [would] oblige them to return to their usual occupations for the Support of their families." Brock replied that "he saw clearly the propriety of my remark," at the same time adding that he thought "Goods might answer the purpose better than money."[40] Although the Iroquois were being influenced by "the cash economy," gifts of goods were of greater importance. Great quantities of these were given, including thousands of guns, gun locks, pistols, brass kettles, knives of various kinds, gunpowder, lead, shot, flints, "lances" or pikes, swords, pipe tomahawks, blankets, buttons, cloth, clothing, body paint, jewellery, shoes, coats, saddles, shawls, silk handkerchiefs, shoes, coats, medals, silver gorgets, ear bobs, and vermilion dye.[41] Providing these goods, as well as large supplies of food, seriously strained — and sometimes overwhelmed — supply routes to Upper Canada. The strain on the British finances was also heavy, for the cost of presents rose "from £60,000 in 1811 to at least £125,000 in the last year of the war. During the war, £350,000 were required for presents alone."[42] These presents and payments came from a long tradition and had symbolic importance. In Benn's words, "Native peoples saw gifts as rewards for past assistance, as manifestations of the giver's power, as expressions of affection towards friends in need, and as compensation for not being able to hunt, trade, or farm while on campaign."[43] The distribution or exchange of gifts represented friendship, the sharing of what each party had. The refusal by the British or their inability to provide supplies might be interpreted as denial of friendship or the ending of an alliance. Brock would be aware of this problem but the real crises in the British-native alliance would come after his death.

In eastern Upper Canada, in the district of Johnstown, the little village of Elizabethtown perched on the north bank of the St. Lawrence River. Although by 1810 it had a courthouse and jail, the place had far less importance than Prescott, a few miles downriver. (Prescott would have a garrison and Fort Wellington erected nearby during the war.)[44] However, there is a story of a dramatic event taking place in Elizabethtown in 1811, before Isaac Brock had taken over the government or had won any victories. The account presented by Fryer has Brock proceeding up the St. Lawrence River, passing Prescott. As he approached the village of Elizabethtown, he heard the sounds of a quarrel. It was a bitter fight over changing the name of the village as a consequence of the government making it the district seat and centre for a courthouse. Two prominent families, the Buells and the Joneses, wanted different names that would honour their families. Brock, after eating a meal in the local tavern, listened to the claims of the two factions. Then he proposed the solution of naming the village after him, and so much was the townspeople's respect for the general, that they did just that.

*Brock's monument in Queenston.*

The story seems to have originated in family tradition and appeared in an early history of Leeds and Grenville Townships. The author includes a cautionary footnote: "Some discrepancy exists between this and other accounts."[45] Evidence for this account is elusive. In the Journals of the assembly and of the Legislative Council of Upper Canada, both for 1812, there are four references to Elizabethtown and none to Brockville.[46] The *York Gazette* of February 25, 1812, refers to Elizabethtown. Letters written in July 1812 refer to Elizabethtown, while Colonel Lethbridge, writing to Brock on August 10, mentions Brockville but on August 30 writes about an "affair at Elizabethtown."[47] The change of name can be seen occurring in November of that year, for on the 15th Reverend William Smart delivered a homily, "Death and Victory: A Sermon Occasioned By the Death of Major Gen. Brock, Who Fell In the Battle of Queenston, Upper Canada, on the 13th Day of October, 1812: Preached at Brockville, Elizabethtown, November 15th 1812." On the first page is a letter to Reverend Smart, requesting him to print the sermon. The letter writer was Lieutenant-Colonel Levius Sherwood (1st Leeds militia), who signed "Com. at Brockville."[48] By December, the ambiguity over the name had been replaced by certainty, as in reports of the Alien Board the reference is to residents of Brockville.[49] Hence, from late in 1812 the usage of Brockville in place of the former Elizabethtown became popular. Another problem with the claim for the change of name in 1811 is the fact that Prescott was the transfer point for passengers and cargo when travelling up the St. Lawrence, so it would be unusual, indeed unlikely, that Brock would stop at Elizabethtown. Local lore is that some people gave the village the name of Brockville after hearing about the Battle of Queenston Heights and the next step was a petition of June 1813 to the Legislature.[50] The records of the Legislature are incomplete and the petition may be in the missing gap. What is not in doubt is that in March 1818 a bill was moved in the assembly "to establish and confirm the names of the new Towns of Brockville, Belleville and Toronto."[51] What happened to that bill is unclear and it was not enough for the inhabitants of Brockville. They petitioned in 1819 to have the town incorporated. A bill was introduced and read, but two years later there was another petition making the same request and another bill was brought forth.[52] Brockville's status was definitely established in January 1832, when it gained a president and board of police. Whatever the official standing of the town, before the end of 1812 its name stood for a permanent tribute to the "Hero of Upper Canada."

## CHAPTER FIVE

# 1812: Preparations for War

Early in 1812 the question of Brock's leave was at last settled. In January he had been given permission to leave but by the next month he had changed his mind, chiefly because it looked like he would see action. Prevost was probably very pleased to read Brock's letter, "Being now placed in a high ostensible situation, and the state of public affairs with the American government indicating a strong presumption of an approaching rupture between the two countries, I beg leave to be allowed to remain in my present command."[1]

Signals coming from the United States were certainly ominous. In the newly elected 12th Congress, a group of young Republicans gained control of the House of Representatives and so strongly urged war with Britain that they became known as "War Hawks." Their leader was the speaker, Henry Clay, from Kentucky, who in February 1810 had boasted, "The conquest of Canada is in your power. I trust I shall not be deemed presumptuous when I state ... that the militia of Kentucky are alone competent to place Montreal and Upper Canada at your feet." [2] Other well-known members were John C. Calhoun, William Lowndes, Felix Grundy, and Peter Porter (see Appendix D). As explained in Chapter One, both Britain and France, in pursuit of their economic warfare, seized neutral ships. Between 1807 and 1812, the French actually detained more American ships than did the British. Perkins writes, "From the end of 1807 onward there was little to distinguish between the two foes of American commerce." Secretary of State James Monroe prepared a report in July 1812 that showed France and her allies had seized 469 American ships compared with 389 detained by Britain.[3] Yet, anti-British sentiment remained so strong in the House of Representatives that French seizures were not mentioned and it was Britain that was condemned.

In Europe, Napoleon's Continental System still impeded British trade to the Continent, in spite of the system of licences and despite the decision by the czar of Russia to open the Baltic ports to trade. As well, the important American market was closed in March 1811 by President James Madison's application of Macon's Bill Number 2. Britain's economic woes were increased by a crop failure and growing unemployment in the cities. Manufacturers and others appealed to Parliament to repeal the orders-in-council, but any change was delayed by the assassination of Spencer Percival, the prime minister who had decided on repeal. By the time his successor, Lord Liverpool, announced that the Orders would be suspended on June 23, 1812, it was too late for the news to reach the United States and to influence the decision of Congress or the president. Moreover, Britain retained the practice of impressment and right of search while the War Hawks continued their pressure for war. Even if President Madison had known about the repeal, it is unlikely that he would have been able or willing to back down on the decision for war.[4]

The United States had a population of almost 7.5 million and its settlers were advancing rapidly into New York, Pennsylvania, and Ohio, thus bringing them closer to Canadian border. The American economy was better prepared for war than in 1775, because both agriculture and industry were more developed so that, for example, there was no need to depend on foreign suppliers for weapons and ammunition. What was lacking was preparation and planning. As one historian puts it, "As so often in military history, resources were less important than the ability to utilize and direct them."[5] This would be precisely the situation at the outset of the War of 1812. American leaders expected a quick and successful invasion of the Canadas

Lossing, 176

*James Madison.*

because of their small population and paucity of regular troops above Montreal. The planners seemed not to realize that offensive warfare was very difficult along the Great Lakes frontier and particularly if a campaign involved mutual support by separately advancing forces. Distances were longer than they appeared to the planners in Washington and maps could not convey the exhausting obstacles to movement presented by forests and bogs.

In the spring of 1812, plans were formulated for a potential war against their northern neighbour. President Madison and his secretary of war, Dr. William Eustis, approved a plan devised by General Henry Dearborn that proposed simultaneous attacks on the Canadas.[6] One thrust would be toward Montreal, in order to gain control of the St. Lawrence River, a second would aim at the Niagara River, and the third would be an invasion from Detroit eastward into Upper Canada. It would have made more strategic sense to attack Montreal and gain control of the St. Lawrence River because that would have cut off manpower and supplies to Upper Canada, which could not resist for long on its own resources. What resulted, in effect, were poorly prepared and uncoordinated attacks almost entirely against Upper, rather than Lower, Canada.

Yet Eustis (and Madison) had received sound advice in January from General John Armstrong, who later in the year would replace Eustis as secretary of war. In a lengthy letter, Armstrong laid out what his country would need to launch a successful war against the Canadas.[7] He listed war materials, magazines, the different kinds of troops required, but above all those were two great needs. He urged the government to secure naval ascendancy on the lakes, for who-ever had it would "win the game," and "for the successful invasion of the Canadas (the great operation of the war, because that only by which Great Britain can be brought to a sense of justice) you must rely on a regular army." He recommended at least 10,000 regulars with additional militia forces. He pointed out the need to obtain information about British forces and posts. He wanted Detroit to be strengthened because of the British and native threat to west-ern territories, but warned that this step "would be positively bad unless your naval means have an ascendancy on Lake Erie." On strategy, he also had sensible advice. The Canadas relied on the St. Lawrence River for supplies and communication with Britain. Capture Montreal, which commanded both the St. Lawrence and Ottawa Rivers, and the result would be "Kingston, York, Fort George, Fort Erie and Malden, cut off from their common base must soon and necessarily fall." Echoing Brock's advice, Armstrong urged an attack via Lake Champlain "rapidly and audaciously" supported by diversionary moves against the Niagara frontier, toward Kingston, and from Vermont to threaten British posts on the Sorel River. Good advice but difficult to carry out given the difficulties of transportation and communications in those areas. It is hardly necessary to say that almost none of this advice was heeded in 1812.

While the president was commander-in-chief, the planning for and execution of war were the responsibilities of Secretary of War Eustis. His capabilities were limited and his tasks were not helped by that fact that he "and eight clerks were expected to carry out the duties of chief of the general staff, Quartermaster-General and commissary general, as well as supervisor of pensions, Indian Affairs and Land Warrants."[8] In 1812, two major-generals and nine brigadier-generals commanded the army. These generals were all elderly veterans of the Revolutionary War, appointed more for political reasons than for demonstrated military ability. Furthermore, promotion came through seniority.[9]

In January 1812, Henry Dearborn, a major-general of the militia of Massachusetts, was appointed to the same rank in the regular army and commander of the Northern Department. Born in 1751, he had served in the American Revolution, later as Jefferson's secretary of war, and from 1809 as collector of taxes for the Port of Boston. It was because of his political prominence, rather than his military abilities, that he received his military command.[10]

William Hull, the fifty-nine-year-old governor of the Michigan Territory, had served as a junior officer of Massachusetts troops in the American Revolution but had since followed a political rather than military career. He was in Washington in early 1812, and may have been lobbying for a military appointment. Hull later claimed that when Eustis and President Madison asked him to take command of the North-Western Army he declined. But, in April, he accepted the command because the only suitable alternative officer was too ill.[11] Like Armstrong, Hull urged the government to create a naval force "sufficient to command Lake Erie" before it declared war. Without it, Michilimackinac and Chicago would fall to the British and their native allies. He also pushed for an army "on the Niagara river to assist and co-operate with the Army at Detroit," which was the capital of Michigan territory. In June, believing that the government would take those steps, Hull began to assemble his army in Ohio for the march to Detroit.[12] His advice was not followed and his prophecy of failure would be amply fulfilled.

For the command on the Niagara frontier, Governor Daniel Tompkins of New York recommended Stephen Van Rensselaer,[13] but as late as June 27 the appointment had not been made. His appointment would be based upon political considerations, which would have effects on the campaign on the Niagara Frontier. Realizing his limitations, Stephen insisted that his cousin, Solomon Van Rensselaer, should be his chief of staff.[14] Solomon had battle experience and had served as New York's adjutant general of militia. A problem that would create great difficulties for campaigns in 1812 (and in later years) was the fact that when militia and regulars served together, whoever held the higher rank commanded both. In effect, a militia officer of superior rank to a regular had the right to command regular troops. In both Hull's and Van Rensselaer's campaigns, this arrangement caused ill-feeling and even refusal to co-operate — much to Brock's benefit. In the Canadas, regular officers outranked their counterparts in the militia and every effort would be taken to make sure that a militia officer did not command regulars.

Between December 1811 and April 1812, "Congress enacted a war program,"[15] which was more impressive on paper than in reality. Measures were passed to increase the regular army to 35,000 men, to raise 50,000 volunteers for a year's service, and to authorize the president to call out 100,000 militia for six months' term. Despite offering an increased bounty, by June the army numbered less than 12,000 regulars.[16] The quality of that army would be severely criticized by the superintendent of the medical department of the northern army (Dearborn's command). He complained of the "bad policy of the government" in offering too small an inducement to recruits with the result that "the army was composed of that description of men, who were habitually indolent, or who could find no other employment."[17] Republican majorities refused to strengthen the navy, leaving it with only five frigates, seven brigs, three ships, and 165 gunboats.[18] The United States had done nothing to prepare its naval forces for warfare on the United States-Canadian border. There was only one commissioned warship on the Great Lakes: the sixteen-gun brig *Oneida* at Sackets Harbor on Lake Ontario. On

*General Stephen Van Rensselaer.*

Lake Champlain, Lieutenant Sidney Smith of the U.S. Navy commanded two grounded gunboats that he managed to get floating.[19]

North of the border, professional soldiers were in charge of governments and they set about systematically preparing the means to defend their colonies.[20] They asked for help from Britain, but realized that little could be spared as long as the widespread war with Napoleon continued.

While the Americans were raising large numbers of troops and proposing even more, it seemed that the forces available in British North America — just over 10,000 — would be too few to mount an adequate defence. About half of these troops were in Lieutenant-General Sir John Sherbrooke's command in the maritime colonies. It was the Canadas that were directly threatened and there Prevost had just over 5,700 regulars from a variety of regiments: the 8th (King's) Regiment; the 41st, 49, and 100th Regiments of Foot; the 10th Royal Veteran Battalion; the Royal Newfoundland Regiment of Fencible Infantry and the Canadian Fencibles; as well as 450 Royal Artillery gunners.[21] No wonder Sir George decided to revive the proposal to raise a fencible corps in Glengarry County of Upper Canada. He authorized Captain Macdonell of the 8th Foot to raise it. He began recruiting in February 1812 and efforts soon spread to Scottish and Acadian settlements in the Atlantic colonies. Brock suggested raising two further companies in Upper Canada and Prevost agreed so that the number of men increased to 600.

The bulk of manpower for defence would have to be provided by the militia and Prevost worked on strengthening that force. Out of Lower Canada's population of 270,000 to 300,000, there were some 49,500 men between the ages of sixteen and fifty able to bear arms. Prevost gained a great deal from the Legislature that met from February to May. It voted a generous £60,000 for training and arming the militia and authorized the governor to embody militiamen when invasion was imminent rather than only after it had occurred. The assembly passed a new Militia Act that authorized Prevost to embody 2,000 bachelors, aged eighteen to twenty-five, for ninety days of training. In the event of an invasion, their service could be extended to one year.[22] While the men of this Select Embodied militia would be paid the same rate as British regulars, they could not be compelled to join a regular regiment. Recruiting began in April 1812, and by May, four battalions had been raised. In September, a fifth battalion was created and in February 1813 a sixth. The governor also took up Charles-Michel de Salaberry's suggestion to raise a volunteer militia force called the Provincial Corps of Light Infantry, or Voltigeurs Canadiens. He was an experienced regular officer in the 60th Foot and aide-de-camp (ADC) to Major-General de Rottenburg.[23] De Salaberry came from a distinguished French-Canadian family and he appointed most of his officers from prominent Lower Canadian families. It proved difficult to obtain sufficient officers; by June only 309 men had joined — well short of the authorized goal.[24] Prevost, therefore, suspended recruitment.

Other measures that Prevost took would impact Upper Canada's defence. The two main regiments in his garrison, the 41st and the 49th, were due to return to England but Prevost was told that in the event of war he could keep them as well as those being sent as replacements — namely the 103rd and the 1st, or Royal Scots. He also kept the 100th Regiment, which was to have gone to Nova Scotia. By retaining all these regulars, Prevost was able to send troops, as well as arms and ammunition, to Upper Canada. (In May, he would send units of the 41st and the Royal Newfoundland Regiment and, after the outbreak of war, parts of the 10th Royal Veterans and of the 49th.)[25] He requested all kinds of military stores from England, and some would be sent, but they would take time to arrive and even more time to reach the upper province. He approved the building of another warship on Lake Erie. To ease the serious shortage of trained officers in Upper Canada, he sent Captain Andrew Gray, acting deputy quartermaster-general; Captain M.C. Dixon, Royal Engineers; and, later, Lieutenant-Colonel Christopher Myers, Colonel Robert Lethbridge (inspecting field officer of militia), Lieutenant-Colonel John Vincent, and, in August, Major-General Sheaffe.[26]

Another shortage occurred in both Canadas, this time of specie — money in the form of coin. In April, Brock wrote to Freer, Prevost's military secretary, about the "inconvenience to which the public service has already been exposed owing to a scarcity of specie," which would only get worse, and, in the event of war, "the almost total impossibility ... of getting a sufficient supply to defray the ordinary expenses of Government." He had acted by consulting "some of the principal Merchants as to the practicability of introducing ... a paper currency," and the response seemed positive. He even went into details about how much would suffice (up to £15,000) and the range of notes (five shillings to £10).[27] By July, Brock had to report that the project was going nowhere. Prevost dealt with the specie shortage by persuading his assembly to approve a paper currency called army bills. To achieve this solution he had to employ his political skills, winning the support of francophone politicians and clergy to overcome the popular distrust of paper money. The army bills would provide a stable currency for both Canadas during the war, although they did not solve all of Upper Canada's financial problems.[28]

In Upper Canada, Brock had about 1,000 regulars (most stationed at Fort George) to defend an extensive territory, sparsely populated and with only seven fortified positions.[29] Early in February, Brock asked Prevost for reinforcements for both the 41st at Amherstburg and the 49th on the Niagara frontier, as well as a regiment for Kingston, additional companies of the "Newfoundland Regt to act as Seamen and Marines," and "an addition of 100 Seamen to the Lakes." He requested more artillery, materials to build gun boats, and changes in commands of the Provincial Marine.[30]

It was clear that Brock had no choice but to rely on militiamen and native warriors to bolster the province's defences. To improve the militia he would have to meet the elected legislative assembly and persuade them to amend the existing militia law, giving him stronger powers. We have seen that Brock was not tolerant of challenges to his authority when he believed he was carrying out his duty and that he had sympathy for Governor Craig's authoritarian political outlook. Would Brock, in his role as administrator of Upper Canada, act as a martinet or could he find the arts of negotiation and compromise? (Prevost was setting a precedent in the political setting of Lower Canada, with great success.) It is remarkable how Brock proved able to work within the political limitations of his position while, at the same time, he provided decisive military leadership. What he faced in the elected assembly was a body of men, most of whom were not interested in military affairs and unwilling to accept the administrator's decisions without question. There were critics of the executive but no organized or systematic opposition. This fifth Parliament, elected in 1808, contained more members willing to criticize government actions than any previous assembly.[31]

Brock began preparations for his first meeting with the assembly before the end of 1811. As he wrote in his letter of December 2 to Prevost, in order to obtain active support from Upper Canadians they would have to be convinced that the government would provide the resources to resist American invasion. Furthermore, he proposed to demonstrate his trust in the people, even if he could sense among them "a spirit of insubordination." In early February, a little more than a week after the Legislature's session had begun, Brock analyzed the attitudes of many members,

> The most powerful opponents to Governor Gore's administration take the lead on the present occasion. I, of course, do not think it expedient to damp the ardour displayed by these once doubtful characters. Some opposed Mr. Gore evidently from personal motives, but never forfeited the right of being numbered among the most loyal. Few, very few, I believe, were actuated by base or unworthy considerations, however mistaken they may have been on various occasions.

In other words, Brock saw personal motives rather than ideology under opposition, even in the case of the government's leading opponent, Joseph Willcocks. Hence, he believed he could persuade many of those members to support any proposals he "may think necessary to recommend for the peace and defence of the country [Upper Canada]."[32] He would try but with limited success.

Critics of previous lieutenant governors had become an opposition group in the assembly from about 1806, and during 1809 Willcocks appeared to be the leader of that opposition.[33] He first won election to the assembly in 1807. The next year, he was elected for the constituency of 1st Lincoln and Haldimand. He lived in Niagara, where from 1807 to June 1812 he ran a newspaper called *Upper Canada Guardian; or, Freeman's Journal*. In the paper, as well as the assembly, he criticized arbitrary actions by appointed government officials, which led Gore and his supporters to label Willcocks as seditious and even as a rebel. In a house of twenty-three members, his group numbered nine and he gained two more supporters during the session of February to March 1812. Brock faced a strong and experienced opposition that would be very concerned about any increase in government power or any threats to civil rights.

The militia system of Upper Canada, dating back to Simcoe's act of 1793, required all males sixteen to sixty years of age to provide military service when called upon by the government.[34] Brock was well aware that the men's attendance at annual June militia musters was usually low and their standard of training poor. He sought to improve the attendance, training, and arming of the militia by introducing a "militia supplementary act," as well as three other measures, all mentioned in his letter to Baynes of February 12.[35] These measures were: "suspension of the habeas corpus — a copy of the act now enforced in the Lower Province. An alien law. The offer of a reward for the better apprehension of deserters."

On February 3rd, Brock opened the fourth session of the fifth provincial Parliament. In his opening address to the Legislative Council and the House of Assembly, he deplored American warlike preparations but spoke of his confidence in the militia, reminding members that money and improved instruction were needed to make it an effective force (see Appendix B).[36] His proposal to strengthen government power by suspending habeas corpus was defeated by a small majority, an outcome he attributed to the influence in the province of recent American settlers. (Habeas corpus was and remains a strong protection against arrest and detention without trial.)[37] The assembly did stiffen the law for the apprehension of deserters from the army, voted £5,000 for the militia, and passed a supplementary bill by ten votes — Joseph Willcocks voted against. The members limited the new act to one session, thereby showing they were still reluctant to give their new administrator all the authority he wanted. In writing to Prevost, Brock expressed his disappointment in his closing address of March 6: "The exigencies of the time alone authorize me to give my assent to the amended militia Bill, for under circumstances of less urgency its very limited duration would oblige me to reject it."[38]

The supplementary act of 1812 provided for two types of militia: sedentary militia, liable for call up in event of invasion, and flank companies — that is, militiamen who were to be trained and equipped like British regulars. Each battalion or regiment would have two companies of up to a maximum of one hundred men, made up of volunteers. If not enough volunteered, men under the age of forty could be balloted. The training of these companies would be up to six days a month, which was much more intensive than that received by the sedentary militia. The act provided for the replacement of one-third of the men in a flank company after six months of service, a second third after seven months, and a final third after eight months. militia officers were required to take an oath of allegiance and the same could be imposed on the other ranks. To prevent confusion over command, any regular lieutenant-colonel would have authority over all militia colonels and lieutenant-colonels. Finally, the act provided for annuities of £5 to a widow of a militiaman killed or who died on active service and £9 to a militiaman who became disabled and incapable of earning his livelihood.[39]

A month later, Brock sent instructions for organizing and training flank companies to twenty-five officers commanding militia regiments to prepare them for "future exigencies" and, he hoped, to demonstrate that militiamen could be trained to a high level of efficiency.[40] He urged the officers to arrange training for localities that would cause the least "material inconvenience" to the volunteers. Printed rules would be sent to them as soon as possible and they would contain "the most simple and ... the most useful movements" for the training of the militia. Brock's sensible instructions and advice show that he had a sense of how Upper Canadians regarded military training: "It is my earnest wish that the little the men have to learn may be acquired by way of a pastime and not looked upon in the light of an irksome restraint." He expected that many residents would be familiar with the use of a musket so that for them training sessions could be reduced to three times a month. Believing that it was important for the men to know why he was embarking on this new effort, Brock wrote, "The chief object of the flank companies is to have constantly in readiness a force composed of loyal, brave and respectable young men," who could be called upon by the government in an emergency to provide an example to the rest of the militia force. He informed the officers that "arms and accoutrements" would be issued to the flank companies and, knowing how easily muskets could disappear, he instructed them to lodge the weapons in depots.

Brock ordered clothing for these volunteers so that they could appear in uniform, but, knowing it would some time before the uniforms arrived, he suggested each man provide himself with a short coat of dark cloth, pantaloons, and a round hat. It would be November before pantaloons, shoes, jackets, shirts, stockings, and blankets for flank company militiamen began to arrive on the Niagara frontier.[41] In York, residents were asked to subscribe to funds to provide flank companies there with clothing.

He soon received reports on how the formation of flank companies was being received; results were mixed. In the 2nd Lincoln regiment, out of 550 men 522 volunteered for flank companies; in the 3rd Lincoln, 206 men out of 211. However, in the 1st Lincoln, "a great number" did not volunteer and most of those were "people from the United States," recently arrived.[42] The results in these regiments in the Niagara District were mixed, a situation that would be common across Upper Canada.

There were many reasons why men volunteered or refused to serve and they should be looked at briefly. Gray points out, "The majority of the men enrolled were relatively recent arrivals from the United States, who had no particular affection for the Crown," and, even if they did, had to devote a great deal of their energy to establishing their families and homes on the frontier. Often, "local circumstances dictated the willingness of men to turn out and to remain on duty."[43] In other words, a farmer could not be away from his farm for any length of time during planting and harvest times. In May, Prevost wrote to Liverpool that "it might not be prudent to arm more than 4,000" of the 11,000 men eligible for militia service, referring to Upper Canada.[44] His impression contrasted somewhat with Brock's observations. Brock had travelled about the province and came away with the impression there was widespread determination "manifested by all ranks" to defend Upper Canada in the event of war with the United States. By early May, he counted about 2,000 men in the flank companies and believed the number would increase if he had "sufficiency of Arms for them." Noting that these volunteers received no compensation, he made a proposal to the executive council, which it accepted. It approved an appeal to the British government that in the event of war the family of "every soldier, Regular and militia ... [and] every mariner employed on the Lakes, who may be killed" should receive "a portion of the Waste Lands of the Crown." [45] Brock thought it important to publicly demonstrate his confidence in the flank companies. As a result, Aeneas Shaw, adjutant general of the militia, issued a Militia General Order on May 25 that began, "The very satisfactory reports made to the President by the officers commanding corps of the spirit and zeal manifested by the men in volunteering ... for the flank companies has afforded His Honor the most lively gratification and confirmed ... [his] opinion ... of their determination to defend bravely their country" and to emulate the loyalty of their fathers. Consequently, he announced he had petitioned the British government for permission "to allot to the wives and children of such soldiers, militia and marine who may be killed in the present contest a portion of the waste lands of the Crown" and to provide relief to those disabled "for whom no provision is otherwise provided."[46]

After the war began men would have even more reasons to avoid militia duty or leave without permission for their homes. In areas threatened by invasion, or where native warriors and other troops were concentrated, they might feel they needed to protect their families and property against foraging. If they left their homes, they might fear there would be a threat from a "resident disloyal element."[47] They might also believe the Americans were certain to win or, if they had grievances, they might even sympathize with the invaders.

May would see a good deal of activity along the river as militia and regular forces moved in, set up encampments, and went through training.[48] There and elsewhere in the province volunteer units, encouraged by Brock, appeared. (An exception was Brock's rejection of a proposal by a black man, Richard Pierpoint, a former member of Butler's Rangers, to "raise a corps of Men of Colour on the Niagara Frontier."[49] However, late in the summer, such a unit would be formed. See Chapter Eight.) Rifle companies were authorized in a Militia General Order of May 25, and the 1st York Militia and 1st Oxford each raised a company. There were Troops of Horse in the Johnstown District, some of whom served in Kingston's garrison, and in response to offers by "many respectable young men" who would provide their own horses, two troops of Niagara Light Dragoons were authorized in June.[50] These cavalrymen would provide speedy communication between Forts Erie and George. Artillery companies were raised in Kingston and from the 1st and 2nd Lincoln militia.[51] A Car Brigade to draw field guns was made up of militiamen using local farmers' horses.

To summarize, Brock's legislative program and his public announcements show careful preparation of the militia for defence of the province, although he could not be sure of its effectiveness until the contest commenced. He repeatedly demonstrated a concern for militiamen's needs, moods, and feelings. His efforts were not always successful, but provide a sharp contrast with how the militia was being treated on the United States side of the border.

Before going there, let us return to Brock's preparations to defend Upper Canada.

Native warriors could be a formidable force, for the number of warriors in the Great Lakes region has been estimated at 10,000.[52] Of this number, "more than eight thousand were so-called Western Indians mostly residing in the United States." There were about

450 Wyandot near Detroit, 850 of Tecumseh's Shawnee along the Wabash, and 600 Chippaways (Ojibwa) and Ottawa on Lake Huron, to mention only a few. In Upper Canada, there were about 1,590 native warriors scattered from the Grand River to the St. Lawrence River and into Lower Canada. Brock might not have known all these numbers, but he was certainly very aware of the value of aboriginal warriors to his defensive plans.

In January, he wrote to the military secretary about the importance of sending "Indian presents" (meaning supplies and provisions) early in the year to Amherstburg in order to supply the large numbers of aboriginal families that regularly gathered there.[53] Writing to Prevost in February, Brock returned to his much repeated theme that he must have a strong military force at Amherstburg so that he could act offensively in that area in the event of war. As he had written previously, he believed "the Indians in the vicinity would in that case willingly co-operate with us and other Indians would follow their example."[54] He also feared that as a result of American work on the fort at Detroit it would be too strong to carry by assault. On this point he may have been correct, but when the time came that fort's strength was never tested.

As commander of the forces, Brock had scope to act on his own initiative and did so in February by writing to Robert Dickson, a fur trader of many years who had numerous contacts among tribes in the upper lakes region. Born in Scotland, Dickson was married to the daughter of a chief of the Santee Sioux and was known as the "Red Headed Man." In his confidential note, Brock asked Dickson what co-operation might be expected from "you and your friends." Brock wanted to know numbers of warriors, what supplies and equipment they might need, and when could they meet.[55] Dickson was well acquainted with aboriginal discontent with the Americans. He sent a reply that reached Brock at Fort George in July, saying he would lead a force of 250 to 300 warriors to Fort St. Joseph. There, they would play a crucial role in the opening of the war in the northwest.

In May, Brock attended a council held on Grand River tract and found a serious division of opinion over supporting the government among the Six Nations. Benn writes, "He met with a cold response when he suggested that the Iroquois form three companies of warriors and rotate one each month to the Niagara Peninsula to help guard the border."[56] One chief demanded that the government settle Iroquois land claims before they would provide warriors. Disagreements going back many years over the sale of Grand River lands seriously divided the Six Nations, and the dispute involved both William Claus and John Norton. Brock could not resolve that disagreement, and when asked if he would provide assistance against American encroachment on native lands he replied, "It is out of my Power, while we are at peace, to interfere."[57] In the event of American invasion, Brock would oppose them by force, but even then, he could not be certain of Iroquois support.

Early in June, a deputation of Iroquois from New York State arrived at the Grand River to plead for neutrality in the event of war.[58] They pointed out the great disparity of population between the United States and Upper Canada, the probability that the province's recent settlers would welcome American invaders, and the British failure to support aboriginals in previous wars. Both Claus and Norton replied, arguing that neutrality would not protect

*Powder magazine in Fort George, the only building remaining from the original fort.*

native peoples from attack if the Americans invaded. They were also supported by other Grand River leaders, and, according to Norton, "an apparent Majority" promised "should the Enemy invade us suddenly" their warriors would support the king. This statement might have encouraged Brock, but when the people of the Grand River learned of the declaration of war, Norton writes, "A small party only repaired to Niagara, and many of these not the most steady men."

Discussions with aboriginal nations were akin to diplomatic dealings, for they affected Anglo-American relations as well as Upper Canada's security. It is not surprising that Prevost, on the one hand, agreed with Brock's "line of conduct" toward aboriginal nations but, on the other, repeatedly warned him to exercise "the utmost caution."[59]

About three weeks after the declaration of war, Brock received a letter from "the Commander on the American side," asking permission for a delegation of Onondagas to cross the border to meet with "their Brethren."[60] The New York Onondaga and Seneca delegates hoped to persuade the Grand River peoples to accept neutrality. Brock would not allow those delegates to travel to the Grand River, where they might gather intelligence; instead, the meeting was held in Queenston. The principal speaker for the New York Iroquois, Arosa (also known as Silver Heels), lamented the miseries that both peoples would suffer from engaging in war, and pointed out that his people were in the power of the Americans. He expressed their determination to remain apart from the fighting. He entreated the Six Nations to adopt neutrality. Their delegate's reply was to regret the separation of the Iroquois, but reminded those from New York that "the King ... does not desire to invade the Americans," but, if they invaded Upper Canada, "We cannot be passive Spectators — we must share the same fate with him." Brock must have remained uncertain about the degree of support he would receive from the Grand River.

The British had the great advantage of possessing armed warships on the Great Lakes. These were manned by the Provincial Marine, which was essentially a transportation service for the army under the control of the governor of British North America. The

Royal Navy had established a naval force on inland lakes against the French during the Seven Years' War and continued it during the Revolutionary War. Afterwards, the small flotilla came under army control (commanded by Quartermaster General Lieutenant-Colonel Pye) and became known as the Provincial Marine or Marine Department. The army commissariat paid for ships and men, who were drawn from the army, merchant ships, and, in times of war, from marine corps. The Marine Department had stations at Quebec, Kingston, and Amherstburg, the latter two had dockyards and served as bases for the Lake Ontario and Lake Erie squadrons, respectively. Two reports — one dated December 7, 1811, and the other January 29, 1812 — described the conditions of the Marine and recommended changes.[61] On Lake Champlain there was only the hulk of a vessel (floating, but incapable of going to sea). On Lake Ontario there were four vessels, although only three were seaworthy, namely, the *Royal George*, *Earl of Moira*, and *Duke of Gloucester*. The *Royal George* (twenty guns) had been launched in 1810 but not commissioned until 1811, and was the largest warship on the lake. The *Earl of Moira* (ten carronades) had been launched in 1805 and would require extensive repairs to make it seaworthy. The *Duke of Gloucester* (six guns) launched in 1807 was the smallest of the three. It was used by the civil government, which would be left without a vessel if it was taken for military service. To solve the problem, the schooner *Prince Regent* (ten guns) would be launched at York in July 1812.

Lieutenant-Colonel Pye believed that Kingston was highly vulnerable to attack because of its location close to the American border. He recommended moving the naval establishment to York because it was safer and easier to defend. That was the beginning of using York as a shipbuilding centre; it was a role that would not last long.[62] The American capture of the provincial capital in April 1813 brought about the destruction of a ship on the stocks and a naval storehouse. No more ships were built there during the war.

On Lake Erie the British had the brig *Queen Charlotte* (sixteen guns) and the six-gun schooner *General Hunter* "falling fast into

Painting by Peter Rindlisbacher

*Lake Erie Patrol, 1812. Ships are* Lady Prevost, General Hunter, *and* Queen Charlotte.

decay." In December 1811, Lieutenant-Colonel Pye recommended it be replaced and during the next summer the *Lady Prevost* (twelve guns) would be launched. This fleet was responsible for controlling not only Lake Erie but also Lakes Huron and Michigan.

Brock and Gray wanted changes made to prepare the Marine for war. On Lake Ontario the elderly John Steel was replaced by forty-seven-year-old Hugh Earl, who had twenty years experience in the service. (He would be replaced in 1813 by Commodore Sir James Yeo, Royal Navy.)[63] In March, Prevost promised to send "a strong detachment of the Newfoundland Regiment, selecting their seamen and artificers" to proceed to York.[64] The commander of the Lake Erie fleet was eighty-five-year-old Alexander Grant, who had served in the army as long ago as the Seven Years' War. Brock wanted him replaced by Lieutenant George Hall, which was done in March. The general hoped this younger Provincial Marine officer would be both more vigorous and more efficient.[65] More seamen were enlisted but there remained a lack of experienced officers.

As administrator, Brock had to deal with other political issues aside from preparing for war. One that really tested his ability to act in a political rather than military role arose from attacks in the assembly on Robert Nichol. Nichol had a varied career until he established a forwarding business in Fort Erie around 1803; soon after, became acquainted with Brock. Slowly, his business prospered, in part because he supplied the British garrisons at Fort Erie and Fort George. Although FitzGibbon described him as a "mean looking little Scotchman, who squinted very much," a friendship developed between Nichol and Brock. While in command at Fort George, Brock had often invited Nichol to dine with him. Nichol was well informed about Upper Canada and, at Brock's request, he prepared a report on the province's resources.[66] In later years, Brock also came to regard Nichol as a political ally because of his opposition to Joseph Willcocks and other government critics.

In 1811, Willcocks initiated an assembly investigation into Nichol's handling of public funds as a road commissioner. A committee condemned Nichol for misapplying funds, but in February 1812 another committee, after carefully examining vouchers that he had presented, reversed this decision. Nichol, however, had criticized the assembly's conduct, prompting twelve members to vote that he was guilty of contempt, for which he was jailed. He applied to Chief Justice Thomas Scott for a writ of habeas corpus, which gained him release from jail and led to a vote in the assembly condemning Scott "of a violent breach of the privileges of this House."[67] Brock expressed his annoyance at the assembly's conduct in writing to Prevost, "The inordinate power assumed by the house of assembly is truly alarming, and ought to be resisted, otherwise the most tyrannical system will assuredly be pursued by men who suffer themselves to be led by a desperate faction, that stop at nothing to gratify their personal resentment." By that "faction" he meant "Mr. Willcocks and his vile coadjutors."[68] Brock was equally annoyed at the assembly's censure of Scott but, since it was the last session prior to a general election, he thought it unwise to intervene by dissolving the house before it took that action. He believed — and he was told by Scott's friends — that the government's critics wanted his interference in order to give them an issue in the coming election. Clearly, Brock exercised cool judgment that helped to soothe tempers rather than exacerbating the situation into a crisis (a contrast to Sir James Craig's earlier actions in Lower Canada).

Brock demonstrated his confidence in Nichol by appointing him that February as lieutenant-colonel in command of the 2nd Norfolk militia, and in June as quartermaster general of the militia. Nichol would be of great assistance to the general when he gathered his forces to capture Detroit.[69]

Glancing ahead at Nichol's career, he became a leader of the opposition in the House of Assembly, a move that Tupper attributes to vanity, "which ... impelled him ... to soar far above mediocrity. Lest he might be thought servile and dependent in consequence of his having a pension."[70]

As administrator, Brock seems to have been regarded as a man of integrity and honesty who was unfortunately surrounded by the bad advisers left behind by Lieutenant Governor Gore. At least, this was the view of William Firth (attorney general from 1807 to 1812) and Dr. William W. Baldwin (a civilian doctor who also practiced law), both of whom had been critics of Gore. Their view seems not to have affected Brock's policies or their outcome, partly because the threat of war was too dominant.[71] A surprising responsibility that fell on the general was to appoint a clergyman to the Church of England benefice of York. The position became vacant in the summer of 1811 and the bishop of Quebec, Jacob Mountain, had authority over Upper Canada. He offered the post to Reverend John Strachan, who was teaching in Cornwall. Strachan turned down the appointment, chiefly because it did not include the position of bishop's official, or representative, which was worth £150 in salary a year. Mountain proposed appointing someone else but Brock, having taken on the government, refused on the ground that York needed a clergyman of established reputation. The bishop had never had a nomination rejected before, which was shocking enough. More shocking was that Strachan changed his mind and accepted the appointment from Brock, whose offer came with the added position of chaplain of the garrison, which included additional salary. The bishop had not been consulted by Strachan, another breach of procedure, and Mountain expressed his great displeasure in a letter to Brock. Several letters passed between the two strong-willed men. After Brock curtly informed the bishop that he failed to understand the bishop's attitude, Mountain sent a conciliatory reply and expressed his great respect for the general. In July, Strachan became "the officiating minister of the Church of England at York." Brock, thus, was responsible for bringing to York a man who would play a leading religious and political role during the war and even more so afterwards.[72]

Brock dissolved Parliament in May, hoping in the ensuing election to obtain a more loyal — and agreeable — assembly.[73] He was not pleased to see Willcocks easily re-elected along with a number of his supporters. In a house of twenty-five members, eighteen were new. Among them was the recently appointed attorney general, John Macdonell, who was to become Brock's provincial aide-de-camp. Brock's experience with this house will be looked at in the next chapter.

Amidst preparations for war and political work, Brock still enjoyed outdoor activities and social life. Baynes complained of the severe January cold in Quebec City, while envying the "milder climate" of Brock's post. He thought Brock "fortunate" because he could indulge in, as Baynes wrote, his "pastime in shooting wild pigeons," which gave him "a very great advantage over us in these respects."[74] In February, Brock gave a ball.[75] In March, Baynes again reported severe winter weather at Quebec, which was hard on Lady Prevost's health. The colonel also sent greetings from his own wife and from Mrs. Cator.[76]

On the first of June, President Madison sent a message to Congress requesting a declaration of war. His four reasons were impressments, violation of American neutral rights and territorial waters, "pretended blockades," and orders-in-council.[77] These were issues of Maritime rights. But Madison also drew attention "to the warfare, just renewed by the savages, on one of our extensive frontiers," which was clearly an appeal to western interests. In the House of Representatives the vote on June 4 was seventy-nine for to forty-nine against. Opposition in the

House came from New York, Connecticut, Delaware, Rhode Island, and some from Massachusetts, Vermont, and New Hampshire. In the Senate, debate was prolonged with proposals being made that would have limited the conflict to naval warfare or only to privateering, or would have delayed a declaration for weeks or months.[78] Finally, on June 17, the Senate voted nineteen to thirteen for war and the president signed it the following day. The close votes in both houses and the Senate's delay indicated how seriously divided the nation was on this measure, as well as concerns about lack of preparations for war. These problems would bedevil American war efforts until at least 1814.

Before going on to describe and analyze campaigns, we need to look at the defenders' strategic ideas because they greatly influenced the distribution of resources and how the commanders behaved. The British government instructed Prevost not to commence offensive operations "except it be for the purpose of preventing or repelling Hostilities or unavoidable Emergencies."[79] The traditional strategy of commanding British generals in the Canadas had been to concentrate the forces at Quebec on the assumption that as long as that fortified city held out, if invaded the rest of the colony could be reconquered after reinforcements had arrived from the home country. Prevost's knowledge of the resources he had available, as well as his own inclination, favoured a defensive strategy. He believed that he had too few troops and the fixed defences, aside from those at Quebec City, were too weak to risk attacks on the United States or to effectively defend the territory above that city. He stated this view very clearly in May 1812: "Quebec is the only permanent Fortress in the Canadas ... To the final defence of this position, every other Military operation ought to become subservient, and the retreat of the Troops upon Quebec must be the primary consideration." Any American invasion ought to be resisted but "done with caution, that the resources, for a future exertion, the defence of Quebec, may be unexhausted."[80] Furthermore, he believed the Canadas would derive no benefit from attacks on the United States. Prevost observed that public opinion in the United States was sharply divided over the decision for war and, therefore, he considered "it prudent to avoid

103

every measure which can have the least tendency to unite the people of America. Whilst disunion prevails among them, their attempts on the British American Provinces will be feeble." Hence, he informed Brock, "Our present plans are all defensive."[81] It is not surprising that Prevost regarded the vast expanse of Upper Canada, with its scattered population of mostly recent American immigrants, as indefensible. Another side of his outlook was a tendency to seek agreement with American commanders, partly in hopes that Britain and the United States would settle their differences diplomatically. That was what lay behind the truce he made in August with Major-General Dearborn. Prevost's belief in a passive defence can be seen in his somewhat fretful comments on the capture of the American Fort Michilimackinac and his advice (in September) to Brock about withdrawing from Detroit and Amherstburg in order to strengthen the defences of the Niagara frontier. These examples will be dealt with in later chapters.

Brock never denied the importance of Quebec to the defence of British North America, but he showed a different understanding than Prevost of what might be accomplished and how British success might affect American behaviour. The situation in 1812 was different from what it had been in 1807, when Brock was commander of the forces in Lower Canada and denied weapons and manpower to Gore for the defence of Upper Canada. Then, the threat to Lower Canada was greater because there was widespread support in the United States for hostility toward Britain, and Quebec's defences were in very bad condition. He believed the British had the advantage of better quality troops and leaders than the Americans, as well as the valuable assets of naval forces on the lakes and potentially large numbers of native allies. He did not believe that attacks against the United States would unite its people behind the war, because their divisions were so deep. In fact, he saw positive advantages in vigorous defence (which might include offensive action) because it would delay a conquest of Upper Canada, giving the British time to marshal their strength, boost Upper Canadian morale, and would probably distract the Americans from attacking Lower Canada. In terms of practice, Brock believed in audacity, which he had demonstrated in his charge during the attack on Egmont-op-Zee and which he advocated repeatedly in correspondence with Prevost. (See his letters of December 2, 1811, and February 6, 1812.) A typical example of his argument was given in a letter of February 12 to Colonel Baynes: "The assurance … of England co-operating in the defence of this province, has infused the utmost confidence [among the people]." He ended his letter mentioning "a project which I consider of the utmost consequence in the event of hostilities," that being the capture of Detroit and Michilimackinac immediately upon the outbreak of war. If this was not done, "not only the district of Amherstburg, but most probably the whole country as far as Kingston, must be evacuated. How necessary, therefore, to provide effectually the means of their capture." And the means he proposed was to arrange for the North West Company to transport a small body of the 49th and a detachment of artillery by canoe, from Montreal to St. Joseph's Island, to seize Fort Michilimackinac.[82]

Prevost's actions did not entirely coincide with his expressed beliefs, for, as detailed above, he sent troops, officers, and supplies to help Brock defend his province. Prevost was able to spare some of these resources because he had kept the 100th Foot instead of transferring it to Nova Scotia and because reinforcements (103rd and 1st Foot) had begun to arrive from overseas. In effect, his troop strength in Lower Canada increased.[83]

# CHAPTER SIX

# War Breaks Out in the North and West

The problems of campaigning against the Canadas appeared even before the outbreak of war. New Englanders, particularly in Connecticut, Massachusetts, and Rhode Island, opposed the conflict and refused to help the war effort. This widespread opposition would make it very difficult to raise manpower and logistical support for offensives against the lower St. Lawrence River front (Montreal and Quebec cities). Instead, the earliest American campaigns were directed toward the west (Detroit and the Niagara frontier). This strategy was the result of frontier Americans' desires to end native resistance and to gain the rich farmlands of Upper Canada, as well as the belief that most of its residents, recent immigrants from the United States, would either support or else not resist an invasion. These attitudes probably explain why a greater number of the army's new regiments and officers came from the western regions.[1]

A significant difference between the two sides is shown by how each notified its posts of the declaration of war. News of the declaration was dispatched by fur trade associates in New York City to merchants in Montreal, who immediately sent word to Prevost at Quebec.[2] He acted swiftly by cancelling the recall to Europe of the 41st and 49th Regiments and the transfer of the 100th Foot to Halifax. Regular and fencible regiments were positioned south of Montreal, under the command of Major-General Baron de Rottenburg. The news reached

Kingston early in July and resulted in the immediate call-out of militia there, as well as along the St. Lawrence River. Supplies of arms and ammunition were sent upriver and Colonel Robert Lethbridge was sent to take command at Kingston. He was to be responsible to Brock, but knowing the difficulties of keeping in touch with that energetic general, Prevost gave Lethbridge a degree of discretion while stressing that he was not to start hostilities.[3] Brock received the news of the declaration on June 26th, at York, and immediately sent word to Fort Amherstburg and Fort St. Joseph. The commanders at both posts knew of the state of war before it was received by their American counterpoints opposite. The British commanders took full advantage of their prior knowledge.

Colonel Philetus Swift at Black Rock, near Buffalo, complained that the British knew of the declaration "almost two days before us." Other American officers echoed this complaint and it appeared in newspapers.[4] Those officers also expressed nervousness at the extent of defensive preparations across the border. For example, at the end of June, Major-General William Hull worried that the British had "at least 1,500 regular troops ... together with a considerable body of militia well disciplined and completely armed" and could call upon about 400 "savage warriors," whereas his side had only 1,300 "effective men."[5] Little did the letter writer know of Brock's struggles to raise and train the militia, and to gain native support.

In a letter dated June 28, here is an American view of how the news of the war was received on the Niagara frontier:

> The news of the war reached the British at (Niagara) Fort George on the 24th by express, two days before it was received at our military station. General Brock, the British Governor, arrived at Fort George the 25th. Several American Gentlemen were there on a visit, which were treated very politely by the Governor, and sent under the protection of Captain Glegg, his aid[e], to Fort Niagara with a flag. The news of the war was very unwelcome on both sides

of the river. They have been for six years in habits of friendly intercourse, connected by marriages and various relationships. Both sides were in consternation: the women and children were out on the banks of the river, while their Fathers, husbands, sons, etc., were busily employed in arming. It was said Captain Glegg also bore a summons for the surrender of Fort Niagara, but this was contradicted by Captain Leonard commanding that post, who said the message was merely to inquire if he had any official notice of the war; and that he answered in the negative.[6]

It would not have been surprising if Brock did have the nerve to demand the surrender of Fort Niagara. He might have if he had known how unprepared his opponents were. It was not until June 23, four days after he had learned of the declaration, that New York Governor Daniel D. Tompkins appointed a militia brigadier-general, William Wadsworth, to command the troops at Black Rock and vicinity. General Wadsworth was not happy, for he "had no experience of actual service. My knowledge of the military art is limited; indeed, I foresee numberless difficulties and occurrences which will [be] present to which I feel totally inadequate."[7] He was not the kind of commander to inspire his troops, and they had plenty of troubles. At the end of June, Tompkins complained of lack of arms, ammunition, and camp equipage. These shortages continued into July. Indeed, conditions seem to have worsened as Wadsworth reported a lot of sickness among the troops and increasing discontent among the militia. "They were called out at a moment's notice," he wrote, "and could make no preparations for themselves and found very little made for them." Supplied with only a little bread, they could not make any more because they had no camp kettles.[8] Although the number of American regulars and militia arriving at the Niagara frontier increased over these weeks, their conditions remained bad.[9] Furthermore, in these same letters, the militia generals reported on strong defensive works being erected on the

Canadian side of the Niagara River, whereas, in contrast, Fort Niagara was in such a decayed state that its commander estimated he could defend it for no more than one hour against a determined attack.

Nevertheless, General Peter Porter (one of Henry Clay's War Hawks) believed there was so much discontent among the Upper Canadian militia that they could not be relied upon even to defend the province. He urged an invasion soon because, "Our standard once planted on their shores, and supported by a respectable force, I have no doubt that most of the inhabitants would seek protection under

*Governor Daniel Tompkins, 1774–1825, frontispiece D.D. Tompkins,* Public Papers of Daniel D. Tompkins. vol. 1 *(1902). Tompkins was governor of New York State 1807– 16 and vice-president of the U.S. 1817–25.*

Courtesy of Special Collections, James A. Gibson Library, Brock University

it." His view may have been widespread for it appeared in the press.[10] The Americans may have been aware that Brock was worried about his militia's reliability, for they were obtaining information by various means from the opposite side.

A more realistic appraisal of the situation was made by Governor Tompkins. Writing to the navy agent in New York City, he pointed out that British naval superiority on Lakes Ontario and Erie kept American vessels confined to ports and also prevented military stores from proceeding to Detroit. He was informed there were strong British garrisons "assisted by Indians and militia" on the frontiers of New York and, unless effective defensive and offensive measures were taken (getting naval forces on the lakes, sending more troops and supplies, and gaining possession of Montreal), his state was under threat and no successful invasion of Canada could be undertaken.[11]

After learning of the declaration of war, whether or not he thought them dependable, Brock called out the militia. He instructed those along the St. Lawrence to be ready to meet an attack. On the Niagara frontier he put the experienced Colonel Henry Procter in command of the troops between Niagara and Fort Erie and Colonel Claus in command of the militia from Niagara to Queenston.[12] He ordered out the Car Brigade, the Provincial Cavalry, and the flank companies of the Lincoln militia all to reinforce the 41st Regiment along the river. To stress the seriousness of the situation, the order stated, "The troops will be kept in a constant state of readiness for service, and Colonel Procter will direct the necessary guards and patrols, which are to be made down to the bank and close to the water's edge."[13] It is not likely he expected an immediate invasion threat, but his action clearly demonstrated both to Americans and Canadians that he would defend the province.

About 800 men turned out, "Very cheerfully, but already shew a spirit of impatience," which was because of lack of supplies such as "blankets, hammocks ... kettles ... [and] tents."[14] However, a "car brigade has been completed ... with horses belong to gentle-men who spared them free of expense." But many of the militiamen, being farmers, became concerned about getting in their harvest, and by mid-July Brock decided he had to allow half of them to return to their farms. Their home visits would be short-lived.

From the beginning of June, General Hull had begun a march from Urbana, Ohio, overland toward Detroit, some 200 miles distant. He led three regiments of Ohio volunteers and a regiment of regulars, a force totalling 2,075 men.[15] His advance was "plagued by almost continuous rain, by the near mutiny of Ohio volunteers ... and by friction resulting from the fact that their colonels [D. McArthur, J. Findlay, L. Cass] outranked the lieutenant-colonel [James Miller] commanding the regulars."[16] On June 18, the same day as the declaration of war, the secretary of war wrote two letters to Hull, but only in one did he mention the declaration. That letter was sent not by a speedy express but by public mail, so that it travelled very slowly, reaching Hull on July 2nd. (The other letter, sent by express, reached Hull on June 26.) The previous day, Hull's weary army had reached the shores of Lake Erie and, in order to hasten his movements, he hired the schooner *Cuyahoga*.[17] When he took this action he probably did not know of the declaration of war, for he loaded the unarmed schooner with sensitive cargo. It was to carry to Detroit his heavy baggage, medical stores, sick men, and his army's muster rolls, as well as his correspondence with the War Department. The schooner was captured by Lieutenant Frederic Rolette, an officer of the Provincial Marine, and six seamen in an open boat.[18] Hull's correspondence was taken swiftly to Brock at Fort George. He learned of the strength of Hull's force — larger than he had thought — as well as his despondency and fears.

Captain Charles Roberts at Fort St. Joseph — which overlooked the strait between Lakes Huron and Superior — learned of the declaration of war on July 8.[19] His garrison consisted of a small detachment of Royal Artillery and one company of the 10th Royal Veteran Battalion. Some fifty miles to the southwest, a small stockaded fort on the American island of Michilimackinac dominated the strait between Lakes Huron and Michigan. Located on a major fur-trade route, it was strategically and commercially important. Brock's aim was to catch the Americans off guard by seizing the island, but he

*Painting by Peter Rindlisbacher*

*The capture of the* Cuyahoga *provided Brock with valuable information about General Hull's army and its condition.*

had to take other considerations into account —Prevost's repeated commands to restrain the natives and to take no action that would give the Americans a pretext for hostilities. Brock would later inform Prevost that he had relinquished the thought of "offensive operations" and "attended only to defensive measures." His definition of defensive measures differed significantly from Prevost's.[20]

On June 26 and 27, Brock ordered Roberts to attack Fort Mackinac if practicable.[21] Both letters arrived on July 8, but four days later there came two more, dated June 28 and 29, ordering a suspension of hostilities. Roberts also received Prevost's instruction from Colonel Baynes to protect the post, assist the North West Company, and, if necessary, retreat. On July 15, yet another letter (dated July 4) from Brock authorized Roberts to use his own discretion. He read the major-general's mind, for he was already gathering forces for an attack.

Hull's original orders were to march to Detroit and provide protection against aboriginal tribes. When his army reached the town, he was greeted by a seventeen-gun salute.[22] On July 9, he received orders to invade Upper Canada and issue a proclamation. He delayed because some of the Ohio militiamen refused, claiming they had the constitutional right not to serve outside the United States. Three days later, under pressure from the rest of his army and in need of supplies, Hull crossed the St. Clair River and occupied the village of Sandwich (now Windsor). He made himself comfortable in the brick house of Lieutenant-Colonel François Baby, a prominent politician and militia officer. Baby subsequently would seek damages of £2,450 from the Americans, without success, but in 1824 would receive compensation of £444 from the British government.[23] The invasion had been unopposed and it looked like Upper Canadians would offer little resistance. "The Americans were giddy with success," writes Borneman, who quotes Hull's ADC, Lieutenant Robert Wallace: "The British cause is very low in this province and their militia and Indians are deserting by hundreds. Our Flag looks extremely well on his majesty's domains."[24]

With news of Hull's invasion of Upper Canada, Brock had no choice but to recall those militiamen. He could not meet all their needs, but because they were "so clamorous for their pay ... [he]

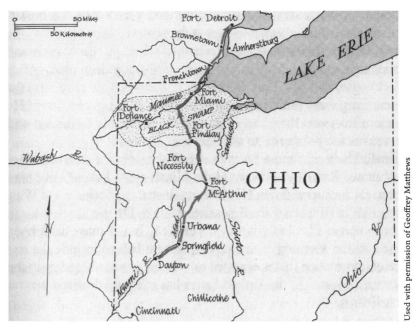

*Hull's march to Detroit.*

Used with permission of Geoffrey Matthews

directed Mr. Couche to make the necessary advances. This has drained him of the little specie in his possession."[25] In other words, Brock was short of money for the men and for supplies.

The village of Sandwich contained the district jail and courthouse but was much less important than Fort Amherstburg and the town of Malden, to the south.[26] Malden contained perhaps 150 houses and a public storehouse, because the town was the major Upper Canadian port on Lake Erie. There was a small dockyard nearby "guarded by blockhouses," while the channel in front was sheltered by Bois Blanc Island, which also contained blockhouses and batteries. "A few hundred yards to the north ... stood [the fort], the most important British fortress west of Lake Ontario." It has been described as "an irregular pentagon, with bastions at the five corners, and embrasures ... surrounded by a deep ditch and two rows of heavy pickets and supported by a small redoubt close to the riverbank." A road from Malden to Sandwich crossed by a bridge over the Canard River, eight miles north of the fort and a formidable barrier for an army moving overland. Hull still had some way to go before he would occupy territory of any significance.

Nevertheless, on July 13, Hull issued a proclamation describing his arrival as a liberator, bringing "the invaluable blessings of civil, political and religious liberty." He promised protection for those who remained at their homes and pursued their "peaceful and customary avocations." Those who resisted would "be considered and treated as enemies and the horrors and calamities of war will Stalk before [them]." He warned about fighting alongside native allies, "No white man found fighting by the side of an Indian will be taken prisoner; instant destruction will be his lot" (see Appendix C).[27] While this proclamation may have encouraged desertions from the militia, it also had contrary effects among many Upper Canadians, according to Michael Smith, an American-born resident living on the main road from Sandwich to Fort George. In his book about the province, published in 1813, he wrote, "I believe almost every one of them [militiamen passing on the road] that saw or heard of this proclamation, treated its contents with contempt. People are hardly ever so willing to do wrong from the advice of others, as of their own accord."[28] militiamen, if ordered to do so, could not avoid marching with their aboriginal allies. Smith believed if Hull had marched "with haste from Sandwich to Fort George, the province would ... have been conquered without the loss of a man." Speedy or decisive action was not Hull's style.

Hull expected that he would need to embark on a regular siege of the recently strengthened Fort Amherstburg. Most of his Michigan militia remained at Detroit, along with about one hundred Ohio militiamen who refused to cross into Canada. This refusal by militiamen to serve outside of the United States would occur again in later campaigns, much to the discomfort of commanding generals. Hull's force of about 400 regulars and 800 militia, although dwindling in numbers, was still larger than the forces he faced. On July 14, he held a Council of War — usually called when the commander could not decide what action to take — and it voted to delay the assault on Fort Amherstburg until heavy guns could be brought from Detroit and placed in position for a bombardment. He later wrote that it would take "at least 2 weeks" to make the travelling carriages for 24-pounders and mortars.[29] He was wasting valuable time that the defenders would use to their advantage.

While Hull was proclaiming his triumph and preparing to advance, a very different scene was being acted further north. On the morning of July 16, Roberts embarked his force of 150 fur traders and forty-five of the 10th Royal Veterans, as well as some 400 native warriors led by Dickson and John Askin Jr. (storekeeper for the Indian Department on St. Joseph's Island)[30] on the company's schooner *Caledonia* and in canoes. They landed early in the morning of July 17 on Mackinac Island, where the American commander, Lieutenant Porter Hanks, knew only rumours of gathering forces at St. Joseph's Island. After Roberts' men had hauled a 6-pounder gun to the top of a hill overlooking the fort, he called upon Hanks to surrender. The worried lieutenant knew that his fort could not withstand a siege and he feared that after losing a battle the enemy's native forces might massacre all the prisoners. He capitulated on terms that included parole for his garrison (except for three deserters from the British Army).[31] Parole meant the men promised not to serve against the British until they were released from that promise. Subsequently, the arrival of those parolees at Detroit would help to undermine General Hull's confidence there. This bloodless victory yielded large supplies of arms, ammunition, and provisions — according to one author, all valued at £10,000.[32] As well, Roberts moved his base to the captured fort, which he regarded as a stronger position from which to control the area.

Native support for the expedition had included Ojibway, Ottawa, Sioux, Menominee, and Winnebago members, but a large group of Ottawas had sat out, waiting to see who won. Roberts, worried about the uncertainty of Ottawa support as well as the "debilitated" condition of his Royal Veterans, pleaded for more regular troops.[33] Brock was aware of this fragility of native support and believed that the best antidote was to attack boldly. The strategy would be amazingly successful against General Hull.

Hull sent foraging parties up the Thames River, to both secure badly-needed supplies of flour and to seek out residents willing to join the Americans. Among those who offered their services to the invaders were Ebenezer Allan, Andrew Westbrook, and Simon Z. Watson. Brock reported to Prevost on these American raids, referring to Watson as "a desperate character" who was leading twenty men and meeting little resistance.[34] From Brock's point of view, the situation was bad and it became worse.

On July 21, Hull reported large desertions of Canadian militia: "About sixty came in yesterday. I send them to their homes and give them protection." The commander at Amherstburg, Lieutenant-Colonel St. George, verified this problem, writing to Brock that so many militia had departed that he had "not more than 471 in all this morning — and in such a state as to be totally inefficient in the field."[35] Two militia regiments, the 1st and 2nd Essex, were mustered in the area. Each regiment was composed of two flank companies. One historian has written, "They remained more of a paper organization than a spirited and competent fighting unit" and, besides, the men seemed to be more concerned about their crops than about defending the province.[36] (Their concern might be justified because a few local residents joined American patrols that in their search for supplies were not above plundering farms.) St. George could only depend on his tiny force of 300 men of the 41st Regiment, a detachment of Royal Artillery and Royal Newfoundland Fencibles. There were about 400 native warriors with various leaders, Tecumseh the most forceful of them.

Brock now sought to influence public opinion by issuing a proclamation in reply to Hull's (see Appendix C). Brock condemned the "unprovoked declaration of War" and, following his invasion of Upper Canada, Hull's insult to its residents "to seek voluntarily the protection of his government."[37] Brock asked, "Where is the Canadian subject ... that has been injured by the government in his person, his liberty, or his property?" He urged the people to "cooperate cordially with the King's regular forces to repel the invader," and pointed out, in no uncertain terms, that Canadian freeholders were bound by oath to defend their king and country. He asserted that Britain would never abandon Upper Canada, even if it were conquered. He denounced the "unjustifiable threat" that no quarter would be given to native warriors or their white allies and asked, "By what new principle are they to be prevented from defending their property?" If the American invaders feared native warfare, "Let him retrace his steps ... [for the aborigines] are men, and have equal rights with all other men to defend themselves and their property ..." He made clear his attitude and policy, but Upper Canada's defenders were more influenced by his actions.

The natives would fight alongside the British as allies not as subjects, and fought according to their own norms and values. They were heavily dependent on the British for weapons and supplies, including food and clothing. The British-native relationship has been described as "symbiotic" because each needed the other for their mutual benefit.[38] Matthew Elliott, district superintendent of the Indian Department, and his agents cultivated the support of many diverse groups such as the Shawnee, Wyandot, Kickapoo, Chippewa,

Menominee, Fox, and Sauk. Indian leadership was a loose alliance between a war chief and his followers so that a leader, such as Tecumseh or Roundhead, could not simply issue orders to their warriors as a European officer could to his troops. This was a situation that British authorities had to recognize and accept. Brock proved to be amazingly capable of winning native support.

Hull assembled a council of natives and sent agents to Tecumseh and to the Grand River in attempts to win native support. He reported that warriors were returning to their villages and the influential Wyandots had held councils to persuade the nations to remain neutral. On July 18, Hull sent a message to the Six Nations promising them security for their lands and rights if they would take no part in fighting.[39] This message, as well as the neutral stance of native groups in the Detroit area, strengthened the sentiment of those on the Grand River who wished to avoid taking sides. It is not surprising that flank companies of the Norfolk militia refused to move to Amherstburg, partly because their distrust of the natives on the Grand River made them reluctant to serve at a distance from their homes. (Another reason usually cited was their hostility to their commander, Colonel Thomas Talbot, who controlled land granting in the area and acted "like a feudal baron.")[40] Brock sent Captain Chambers with fifty men of the 41st Regiment to Moraviantown on the Thames River to help defend against incursions by Hull's forces. Brock also wanted to add militiamen to Chambers's detachment, but their reluctance to leave their homes, as well as the very weak support promised by native warriors, had "ruined the whole of [Brock's] plans" to resist Hull's invasion.[41]

Norton was well aware of Brock's problems with militia and native forces, but he would do what he could to limit the invaders. As soon as he heard of Hull's invasion, he proposed to collect as many warriors as he could and employ them "to prevent the enemy from drawing supplies from the River Thames."[42] With Brock's approval, Norton began to collect warriors but found there was widespread reluctance among the Iroquois to leave the Grand River, giving the reason that they were "occupied … in Harvest." Perhaps more important, they were worried about the threat of Hull's army being able to advance to their territory. Benn suggests another motive for sending warriors to the mouth of the Grand River, ostensibly to guard against an American water-borne attack. He describes this move as "a sham" because the Provincial Marine controlled the waters and the Americans had no naval force on Lake Erie. The "point of the exercise," Benn concludes, was to show solidarity with the British while keeping open the possibility of departing to their homes or of joining the invaders if Hull succeeded in defeating Brock.[43] Norton and his party of warriors demonstrated both their loyalty and usefulness by chasing away a number of Americans who had penetrated up the Thames River and by encouraging militiamen to help defend the province.

The news of the capture of Michilimackinac brought more warriors to Norton's side. He received a fresh supply of ammunition and a letter from Colonel Procter "requiring [them] to join him at Sandwich with all possible expedition ... in consequence of General Hull's having retired to Detroit." The situation in that area was improving for the defenders.[44] Norton and his men would arrive the day before Brock.

Under unceasing pressures to manage the province's government and to defend against both actual and potential invasions, an angry and suspicious Brock lost his temper about his aboriginal allies. Although he was well aware that the tribes below Lake Erie had been reduced to desperate straits by the loss of their lands, he criticized the natives as unreliable allies.[45] (Black points out, "Although the Natives were not always reliable allies, they were allies, and, allowing for different cultures and styles of fighting ... no more unreliable than other allies.")[46] In August, writing to Baynes, Brock gave full reign to his fears. He believed that if he were forced to retreat, the Indians would "then shew their true disposition. And as human nature in all instances in which it determines to forsake and act against a benefactor is found infinitely more rancorous and cruel, everything horrid must be expected to be committed." He, therefore, advocated an extremely harsh measure against them as soon as the government was in a position to carry it out — expulsion from the Grand River tract. He even repeated this suggestion at the end of the month, although he had received crucial native support in the capture of Detroit.[47] There is no evidence that his suggestion was seriously considered by any higher authority. His rancor was the result of specific and short-lived frustrations and he acted toward those allies in a manner that demonstrated trust. His comments at times about elected members of the assembly and even the people of Upper Canada were just as harshly critical.

Yet Brock tried in another, unusual way to win Six Nations' support. He asked Willcocks to go to the Grand River to attempt to persuade the natives to help defend the province against American invasion. What prompted this steadfast opponent of some of Brock's most important measures in the assembly to undertake the mission has never been fully explained. (Brock invited him to dinner, which may have softened Willcocks's animosity.) Nor is it clear why Willcocks had influence with the Six Nations. He would delay his mission because of illness and would not complete it until after Brock had defeated Hull. Willcocks would claim that his efforts had succeeded, but whether it was his influence or John Norton's, or the result of Brock's victory, is an open question.[48] Whatever the reason, a good-sized native warrior force would travel to Fort George in September.

Brock's August appointment of James Givins as a provincial aide-de-camp may also have been intended to increase Brock's influence with aboriginal residents. Givins's career in government and military service in Upper Canada went back at least to 1775 and in the Indian Department to 1797. (In that year he was appointed assistant superintendent of Indian affairs for the Home District, and he continued as a prominent official of the Indian Department until his retirement in 1837.) At the same time, Brock gazetted him a major in the militia.[49] He would accompany Brock to Detroit and fight at Queenston Heights. Givins's "finest hour," according to his biographer, "came on 27 April 1813 when ... he assisted in the defence of York against the invading Americans."[50]

Now that the province was invaded and militiamen in some areas were deserting while others were refusing to march against

Hull, Brock began to lose confidence in that force and in the general attitude of the population. He was also prevented by his political duties at York from acting to lead the campaign. It was at this time of crisis that he showed his finest quality as a leader, simply by not giving way to despair. He expressed his determination (as well as political skill) in a letter to Prevost: "Most of the people have lost all confidence — I however speak loud and look big."[51] He was prepared to take the initiative and act positively, a course that could lead either to great success or disaster. Yet, Brock had a pretty sound sense of the incapacities of his opponents. He set out to strengthen the forces at Fort Amherstburg. He sent Henry Procter, the lieutenant-colonel of the 41st Foot, to supersede St. George as commanding officer at Fort Amherstburg. Procter had more than thirty years service in the army and was highly regarded by Brock, who in his annual inspection of the regiment the previous year had commended both him and his men.[52]

Hull sent probing patrols out from Sandwich. On July 16, an American force approached the bridge over the Canard River. They found it guarded by a small detachment of British and native forces. After an exchange of shots, the detachment withdrew except for two sentries of the 41st, who continued to resist the American advance. One, John Dean, was badly wounded and taken prisoner while the other, James Hancock, fell mortally wounded.[53] (He would be the first soldier killed in action in this war.) The Americans had control of the bridge and Colonels Cass and Miller urged Hull to allow an immediate advance against Fort Amherstburg. Hull refused, mainly because he believed that an infantry assault without the support of heavy artillery would produce unacceptably high casualties.[54] He put his men to work building carriages for the guns but progress was very slow. There were a few skirmishes along the river later, but the Americans did not advance beyond it. According to John Richardson, a young volunteer in the 41st Regiment, the fort could not have sustained a siege for long. In his account of the war, he described its weak defences, including its wooden buildings, which could have been easily destroyed by a few "missiles."

Instead of sending boats down the Detroit River, or throwing another bridge across the Canard where the defenders were not posted, Hull used up more time in "daily skirmishes" at the partially destroyed bridge.[55]

Hull sent pleas to his government for reinforcements and an escort for a supply train approaching from Ohio. Colonel Procter, who had reached Amherstburg and taken command, sent Captain Adam Muir with men of the 41st, a few milita, and Tecumseh with a small force of warriors to ambush the Americans. At Brownstown, on August 5, they scattered the American relief force and captured both supplies and official dispatches to and from Hull. (The correspondence was taken to Procter, who would give the papers to Brock when he arrived.)[56] Hull had expected action on the Niagara frontier to divert Brock's attention, and warned the secretary of war of the consequences of "delay at Niagara." In order to protect his communications with Ohio to the south, he might have to withdraw his troops from Upper Canada.[57] British control of the river and lake constituted a continuing serious threat to Hull's supply route. He heard no good news about the Niagara frontier; instead, all the reports he received were bad.

Hull learned of the loss of Michilimackinac from friendly natives and it was confirmed on August 2nd, when the paroled garrison reached Detroit by schooner. News of the British victory in the north persuaded the Wyandots to switch from neutrality and support the British side. This change indicated to Hull that more tribes of the Northwest would join the British unless he could capture Fort Amherstburg. Thus, they added to the strength of the native forces already present under Tecumseh as well as those coming from the east under Norton (Iroquois, Ojibway and Ottawas).

A Council of War called by Hull on August 5 voted to assault Fort Amherstburg immediately and he agreed. Then he received news that Brock was coming westward with reinforcements. Hull changed his mind and withdrew most of his forces to the American side on August 8. He wanted to withdraw south from Detroit to either the Maumee or Raisin Rivers, closer to his bases of supply and reinforcements. The colonels of the Ohio militia flatly refused. The following day, he sent

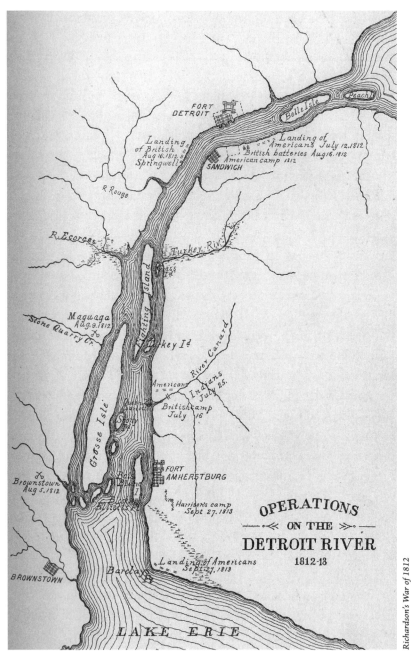

*Map of operations on the Detroit River.*

out yet another force to protect another supply train. This escort was ambushed near the village of Maguaga by Captain Muir with a force of 150 regulars and militia along with warriors led by Tecumseh.[58] The Americans put up a spirited resistance, forcing the regulars and militia to retreat to boats and the Canadian shore while the Indians dispersed into the woods. However, instead of proceeding to meet the supply train, the escort rested overnight and returned to Detroit. On August 11, Hull ordered the rest of his men out of Sandwich to Detroit.

Meanwhile, although he was anxious to proceed to western frontier, Brock was very busy in York. On July 27, he called a special session of the Legislature in an effort to get measures he thought necessary for the security of the colony. He again sought amendments to the Militia Act and the suspension of habeas corpus.[59] He quickly became disappointed with the members, for on the following day he wrote Prevost, "The repeal of the Habeas Corpus will not pass — And if I have recourse to the Martial Law I am told the whole armed force will disperse."[60] In fact, he despaired that most of the population seemed to be expecting "a change taking place soon" (i.e., the American conquest would succeed). On the 29th, he was still pessimistic about the assembly, for although "I have assembled the Legislature for the express purpose of amending the [militia] act, I much fear nothing will be done. Your Excellency will scarcely believe that this infatuated House of Assembly have refused by a majority of two to suspend even for a limited time, the Habeas Corpus."[61] He planned to go over to Fort George and return to York on August 1st, hoping to see a change of attitude as a result of the news of the capture of Fort Michilimackinac. It was true that the legislators refused to approve suspension of habeas corpus, but they did strengthen the Militia Act's provisions to ensure obedience to orders and voted £10,000 for the militia. On August 3rd, Brock met the executive council and described a situation that could hardly have appeared gloomier. American invaders were poised to advance further into the Western District where, he believed, the militia was in a "perfect state of insubordination." Some persons in that part of Upper Canada had even begun to negotiate with the enemy.

Meanwhile, as Brock saw it, assembly members were wasting time for they "had consumed eight days in carrying a single measure of party." He sought the councillors' advice about proroguing the house and proclaiming martial law. The next day they unanimously recommended those actions and on August 5th Brock ended the session.[62] His closing address was curt although he thanked the members of the assembly for "the liberal grant of all the monies at [their] disposal" assuring them it would be "faithfully applied" to the defence of the province. He made it clear that his pressing interest was to lead his forces to meet Hull's invasion, "That you may not unnecessarily be detained from your homes, I hastened at a moment's preparation to meet you," to assent to the bills passed and to "close the present Session of the General Assembly."[63] He would never meet the provincial Parliament again.

We need, at this point, to deal with the issue of martial law. Imposing it meant the suspension of civil courts and replacing them with military law and courts. That would put enormous power into the hands of army officers not answerable to the Legislature of Upper Canada. It was an issue that had to be handled with great delicacy because, first of all, Brock was uncertain about the basis of his authority to impose martial law even though the executive council had approved. Secondly, he saw difficulties in putting it into practice. He explained to Prevost that his "civil office" authorized him to convene courts martial for trials of militiamen and inflict the sentence of death "whilst in regard to the military my power is limited to the mere assembling of a court." He requested from Prevost equal authority over each service.[64] Another question he had was whether or not militia officers could sit alongside regular officers on a court martial. Prevost suggested that Brock had the authority to impose martial law based on his king's commission under the circumstances of the invasion of the province, but he was unwilling to actually authorize such a drastic measure. Instead, he advised the president to obtain the opinions of the "first law characters" of Upper Canada and then proceed as he judged best. In effect, he seemed to leave Brock to make up his mind on this own.[65] Later that month, the governor sent him a warrant to strengthen his authority over courts martial, but Brock (and Prevost) never did impose it. Two of his successors, namely Baron Francis de Rottenburg and Lieutenant-General Sir Gordon Drummond, would do so. The former would impose partial martial law in the two eastern districts in order to procure supplies from the farmers for the army. Drummond would rescind this proclamation, but in March 1814 would decide he had to impose it again in order to procure "provisions and forage" for the troops.[66] Although these civil and military commanders acted cautiously and for specific, limited purposes, they came under severe criticism from many residents of the province.

Let us now return to the summer of 1812.

Prevost's response to Roberts's victory was a mixture of commendation and emphasis on strictly passive defence. On August 12 he wrote to Brock, pleased with Roberts's "zeal and promptitude." But he fretted, "At the same time, I must confess, my mind has been very much relieved by finding that the capture took place ... subsequent to Brigadier-General Hull's invasion of the Province, as had it been prior to it, it would ... have afforded a just ground for the subsequent conduct of the enemy, which I now plainly perceive no forbearance on your part could have prevented."[67] A reservation about waiting for the other side to act before making a move was not a tactic that made sense to Brock. He and many others could see widespread positive effects of Roberts's victory.

An unfortunate consequence of the capture of Michilimackinac occurred far to the southwest, outside Fort Dearborn. Acting on Hull's orders, Captain Nathan Heald evacuated the fort on August 14th. He led out a group of regulars, militiamen, women and children, and thirty Miamis allies. They were suddenly and unexpectedly attacked by 500 local Potawatomi warriors under Blackbird, who had heard of the British capture of Fort Michilimackinac and, later, of Hull's withdrawal from Upper Canada. The Miamis fled, but all the militia, twenty-six of the regulars, two women, and twelve children were killed and the survivors were taken by their attackers. Some of these prisoners later escaped or were ransomed by the British. It appeared to natives of the Northwest, who had long opposed American expansion, that the British were the stronger party in the war. They burned Fort Dearborn and, after hearing of Hull's surrender, the tribes began to carry out frontier raids in September against Pigeon Roost Creek, Fort Harrison, Fort Madison, and Fort Wayne.[68] None of these attacks was authorized by Brock or by the British Indian Department. Indeed, they created both great fear and anger in the frontier states and territories. In response, more militiamen would be raised in Ohio and Kentucky, and Harrison would lead a force to the relief of Fort Wayne while Brigadier-General James Winchester would be authorized to march a force of regulars to Detroit. The memory of the massacre near Fort Dearborn strengthened both anti-British and pro-war sentiment throughout the frontier. The shadow of a small conquest proved to be very long.

CHAPTER SEVEN

# Brock Goes to War

Encouraged by Roberts' capture of Michilimackinac, all the members of the flank companies of York militia volunteered to accompany Brock to Amherstburg. He took only one hundred men because he could not leave York undefended. As well, he was able to send Lieutenant-Colonel Christopher Myers, in whom he had great confidence, to command the Niagara frontier.[1] Later that month, Major-General Sheaffe would arrive there and take charge.

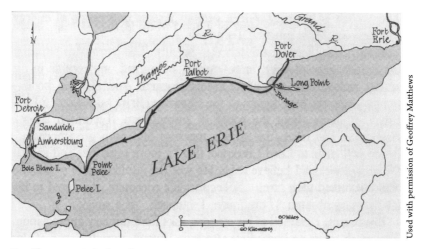

*Brock's passage to Amherstburg.*

Early on August 6, Brock and the militiamen left York bound for Burlington Bay. From there, Brock went to the Mohawk Village on the Grand River to seek support from the natives. They held a council and promised to send sixty warriors in a few days. On a wet and windy August 8, Brock departed from Port Dover, on Lake Erie, where the flank companies of the Norfolk militia had volunteered to join him along with Lieutenant-Colonel Nichol, quartermaster general of the militia. They also took along a 6-pounder gun. With 250 militiamen and fifty soldiers of the 41st, they embarked in a motley collection of small boats and were joined on August 9th by sixty volunteers from Queenston. They rowed all day but awoke the next morning "Wet and cold ... some of us lay in boats and some on the sand." They "set off early but the wind blew so hard we were obliged to put into Port Talbot." While the rain continued, "most of us set out to get something to eat, being tired of bread and pork. Five of us found our way to a place where we got a very good breakfast, bought some butter and sugar and returned." The flotilla battled strong winds and incessant rain the following day and Brock was so determined to keep going that they "continued our voyage all night, which was very fatiguing."[2] He expected the men to follow the light in his boat:

> General Order, Head Quarters, Banks of Lake Erie, 15 miles south west of Port Talbot, August 11th, 1812, 6 o'clock p.m. The troops will hold themselves in readiness, and will embark in the boats at twelve o'clock precisely. It is Major-General Brock's positive order that none of the boats go ahead of that in which is the Head Quarters, where a light will be carried during the night. The Officers commanding the different boats will immediately inspect the arms and ammunition of the men, and see that they are constantly kept in a state for immediate service, as the troops are now to pass through a part of the country which is known to have been visited by the enemy's patroles. A Captain, with a subaltern and thirty men,

will mount as picquet upon the landing of the boats and a sentry will be furnished from each boat.... A Patrole from the picquet will be sent out on landing to the distance of a mile from the Encampment.

The enemy was not capable of threatening his force as much as he feared but his concern for his men's safety made good sense. His General Order on the following day repeated this theme:

It is Major-General Brock's intention, should the wind continue fair, to proceed during the night. Officers commanding boats will therefore pay attention to the order of sailing as directed yesterday. The greatest care and attention will be requested to prevent the boats from scattering or falling behind. A great part of the Bank of the Lake when the boats will this day pass is much more dangerous and difficult of access than any we have passed. The boats will therefore not land, excepting in the most extreme necessity, and then great care must be taken to choose the best places for landing. The troops being now in the neighborhood of the enemy, every precaution must be taken to guard against surprise.[3]

While British troops were trained to follow their officers without question, militiamen were much less likely to follow Brock simply because of his rank. One incident during this voyage suggests why he gained his followers' confidence in his leadership. The boat Brock was in hit a rock,

Oars and poles were immediately employed to shove her off; but quickly seeing this could not be imme-diately done the General jumped overboard and ... everyone else in the Boat was overboard instantly. The Boat consequently floated at once, was shoved from the Rock and the people getting on board again she proceeded on her way. He then took his liquor case and gave each man a Glass of Spirits to prevent injury from their wet clothes.

I was told from time to time after by many Gentlemen then accompanying that Expedition, that his simple act of his had the most animating effect upon all under his Command.[4]

What an inspiring gesture, giving the men a little shot of liquor. Brock later wrote a note praising the "cheerfulness and constancy ... displayed by these Troops under the fatigue of a long journey ... and during extremely bad weather." Whether or not the troops ever read this note, they would have been aware of his good opinion of their efforts.[5]

He arrived at Amherstburg just before midnight on August 13, whereupon some native warriors fired a *feu de joie*. Immediately, Brock asked Colonel Matthew Elliott, district superintendent of the Indian Department, to tell the men not to waste ammunition. That night, or early the next day, he met Tecumseh and the two were immediately impressed by each other. Tupper describes how Tecumseh turned to his followers and exclaimed, "This is a man!"[6] Captain Glegg's description shows that the British were also impressed,

Tecumseh's appearance was very prepossessing ... in height five feet nine or ten inches; his complexion, light copper; countenance, oval, with bright hazel eyes, beaming cheerfulness, energy, and decision. Three small silver crowns, or coronets were suspended from the lower cartilage of his aquiline nose; and a large silver medallion of George the Third ... was attached to a mixed coloured wampum string, and hung around his neck. His dress consisted of a plain, neat uniform, tanned deer-skin jacket, with long trousers of the same material ... and he had on his feet leather moccasins, much ornamented with work made from the dyed quills of the porcupine.[7]

Brock already knew from papers captured on the *Cuyahoga* something of Hull's attitude and the forces he commanded. From the correspondence that Tecumseh had captured at Brownstown on August 5th, Brock learned of dissension among Hull's officers as well as his increasing despondency. Brock realized that he would have to act quickly before Hull received reinforcements, which were supposedly on their way.

The next morning, Brock consulted Elliott, Tecumseh, and other chiefs about plans for the capture of Detroit. He also assembled his principal officers to consult their opinions about crossing the river. "Lieutenant-Colonel Nichol, the quartermaster-general of the militia, eagerly seconded the general, telling him that, as he had resided for some time at Detroit, he knew every feature of the town and fort, and that he would lead the troops to any point selected for the attack.

"*The Meeting of Brock and Tecumseh,*" by Lorne K. Smith. A highly imaginitive depiction.

Library and Archives Canada, Acc. No. 1997-229-1

Upon this the general said: 'I have decided on crossing, and now, gentlemen, instead of any further advice, I entreat of you to give me your cordial and hearty support.'"[8] Another story is that when Brock asked Tecumseh about the territory he would be invading, the warrior, "taking a role of elm bark, and extending it on the ground, drew forth his scalping knife, and with the point presently edged upon the back a plan of the country, its hills, woods, rivers, morasses and roads — a plan which ... was fully as intelligible as if a surveyor had prepared it."[9] Whether or not this happened, it does suggest that Brock and Tecumseh co-operated closely and planned carefully for their attack on Hull.

Brock also issued an order to the troops, congratulating them on the American retreat across the river. He praised Procter's "judicious measures" and the "judicious management of the Indians" by Elliott and Major McKee (another Indian Department agent). He admonished the militia for "the numerous desertions" but softened the criticism by saying that he was "willing to believe that their conduct proceeded from an anxiety to get in their harvests" rather than from pro-American sentiments. He requested from militia commanders the names of militiamen who had remained on duty so "that immediate measures may be taken to discharge their arrears of pay." Here was a tangible reward for loyalty. He reminded the troops that they still faced the task of driving away the enemy.[10]

The bridge over the Canard had been repaired after Hull's withdrawal and Captain Matthew C. Dixon, Royal Engineers, and Captain Hall of the Provincial Marine had begun constructing batteries on a high part of the riverbank opposite Fort Detroit. When that battery of three guns and two mortars was complete, Brock demanded Hull's surrender, beginning with a bold statement followed by a warning that played on American fears of massacre: "The force at my disposal authorizes me to require of you the immediate surrender of Fort Detroit. It is far from my inclination to join in a war of extermination, but you must be aware that the numerous body of Indians who have attached themselves to my troops will be beyond control the moment the contest commences."[11] Hull refused, replying, "I am prepared to meet any force which may be at your disposal...." His words would prove braver than his actions. Brock's response was to order his artillery to bombard Detroit. The American artillery replied but with no effect. A militiaman from Queenston wrote, "We are told we are to attack them (the Americans) to-morrow, and we all appeared well agreed and in high spirits."[12]

Brock organized his force of 300 regulars and 400 militia into three brigades. The first, under the command of Lieutenant-Colonel St. George, consisted of fifty men of the Royal Newfoundland Regiment and Essex and Kent militiamen; the second, under the command of Major Peter Chambers, consisted of fifty men of the 41st and all the York, Lincoln, Oxford, and Norfolk militiamen; the third, commanded by Major Joseph Tallon, consisted of 200 of the 41st. Colonel Procter had overall command "under the orders of the Major-General."[13] (He had thirty Royal Artillery men but did not specify their brigade.) The next day, Brock gave specific orders about the intended crossing: "The troops will be in readiness to embark at McGee's Point at three o'clock to-morrow morning. Colonel Elliott will proceed during the night to the eastern shore of the River Rouge, and upon communicating with the Major-General the troops will immediately commence crossing ... and land between River Rouge and Spring Wells. Colonel Elliott will place the Indians in a position to take the enemy in flank and rear should he be disposed to oppose the crossing." He did not forget the comfort of the troops: "The officers of the commissariat will make the necessary arrangements to supply the troops ... on the opposite shore with provisions and every article required.... During the operation of the troops in the field each man will receive one gill of spirits per day. The number for which provision is to be made may be calculated at two thousand."[14]

All was not well in Fort Detroit. The Ohio colonels, Lewis Cass and Duncan McArthur, along with other men from that state, were plotting to remove Hull from command and replace him with McArthur. It appears that Hull was aware of this conspiracy but was afraid there would be mutiny if he acted against the ringleaders.[15] Instead, he ordered Cass and McArthur to take a detachment to meet the supply column that, fearing attack by native warriors, had not advanced beyond the River Raisin. Late on August 14, they took 350 of the best Ohio militia on their mission but the same night received a message from Hull to return to Detroit. They sent no reply to Hull and, making no haste to get back, were not present to help resist Brock's crossing. Besides the absence of these forces, Michigan militia were beginning to desert. Another worry that preyed on Hull's mind was his responsibility as governor of the Michigan Territory for the safety of the civilian population. Hull, therefore, concentrated his forces, both regular and militia, in and about the town and fort, while most of the women and children took shelter in a root cellar in an orchard. Just south of Fort Detroit, at Spring Wells — the likeliest spot for the British crossing — he had posted Colonel Snelling with a gun. His orders were to remain unless compelled by superior force to retreat and to inform Hull of enemy movements. Yet, without orders, Snelling withdrew from that position "before daylight" on August 16, leaving the landing place unguarded.[16]

On the night of August 15–16, about 600 warriors, led by Tecumseh and Elliott, crossed the river. Many began circling through the woods around the fort giving the impression of much larger numbers. Early the next morning, Brock's little army of 700 men began the crossing. Richardson, a participant, described the scene:

> A soft August sun was just rising as we gained the centre of the river, and the view … was certainly very animated and exciting, for, amid the little squadron of boats and scows, conveying the troops and artillery, were mixed numerous canoes filled with Indian warriors, decorated in their half-nakedness for the occasion, and uttering yells of mingled defiance of their foes and encouragement of the soldiery. [They could see and hear] … the flashes and thunder of the artillery from our batteries … [at Sandwich].[17]

The troops had with them two 3-pounders and three 6-pounders and were also supported by the guns of *Queen Charlotte* and *General Hunter*. At Major Thomas Evans's suggestion, Brock also provided some 300 militiamen with cast-off red tunics of the 41st to give the appearance of being regular troops.[18]

After landing at Spring Wells, Brock's intention was to form up his troops and, together with native allies, block Hull's communications to the south — the source of supplies and reinforcements. In his later report to Prevost, Brock explained his "intention of waiting in a strong position the effect of our [artillery] fire upon the Enemy's Camp, and in the hope of compelling him to meet us in the field." In the open, Brock believed his forces would have the advantage. However, when he learned from scouts "that Colonel McArthur ... had left the garrison three days before with a detachment of five hundred men, and hearing soon afterwards that his Cavalry had been seen that morning three miles in our rear, I decided on an immediate attack."[19] It was a bold response, for Detroit, with about 150 houses and 700 inhabitants, was surrounded by a sturdy palisade of pickets. Behind it, on high ground, loomed the fort with a parapet eleven feet high and twelve feet thick ringed by a twelve-foot deep dry ditch and two rows of cedar pickets.[20] Guns commanded the road that approached the main gate and other guns and mortars inside the fort fired back at the British batteries. It was a very strong defensive position. Meanwhile, British artillery had found the range and rounds began landing inside Fort Detroit. Several officers were killed including the unfortunate Lieutenant Hanks.

Brock's force "moved forward by sections, at nearly double distance, in order to give our little force a more imposing appearance."[21] Soon the men could see on the road at the town's gate two 24-pounder guns, their gunners standing by with their matches burning. Whether loaded with round shot or canister (a tin can loaded with small balls), the fire from these guns could have slaughtered the approaching column. Brock made a prominent target astride his horse for his tall stature and brilliant uniform marked him as the commanding general. So worried was Lieutenant-Colonel

Nichol, who was riding beside him, that he urged Brock to let the troops led by their officers precede him. Brock thanked Nichol but refused, stating that he would never ask the men to go "where I do not lead them."[22] He had a strong sense that Hull would submit to the bluff. Although his troops were probably still beyond artillery range, Brock was taking a great risk.

The view presented to Hull was that of an army predominantly of British regulars, supported by a large number of native warriors, and with artillery that commanded the fort and town. He may have believed that Brock's force was three times greater than his and he did not know if the detachment under Cass and McArthur was close enough to support his defence. Richardson believes that the appearance of confidence in the advancing troops, as well as the effective British artillery fire, intimidated Hull into refusing to allow the guns to fire. One historian argues that overnight Hull's will to resist faded as he increasingly feared a possible massacre by native warriors and as his confidence in his army dwindled. "Thereafter, possibly under the influence of alcohol and narcotics combined with the effects of his earlier stroke, his behavior became increasingly disordered; his speech became indistinct, he dribbled incessantly, and he took to crouching in the corners of the fort."[23] (American fear of massacre of captives by native warriors had a history dating back at least to the warfare of the 1750s when exaggerated accounts of the wanton and brutal slaughter of men, women, and children were reported in colonial newspapers. Later corrections were disregarded or forgotten.)[24] The source for these descriptions of Hull's erratic and desultory behaviour seems to be the testimony of some officers at Hull's later court martial (especially Major Snelling) while other officers had less critical recollections. Many, however, agreed that the general was sitting in the "safest place in the fort."[25] Without consulting anyone, Hull ordered the gunners not to fire. He sent an officer to cross the river with a flag of truce to seek a brief cessation of hostilities and also ordered a white flag raised in the fort. An officer described the chaotic scene: "I saw Captain Hull on that morning … take a dirty towel to fix as a flag of truce on one of the boarding pikes, which I thought too dirty; he then brought out a table-cloth or a sheet, which I thought would be too large, and said it should not go up, as the American ensign must be lowered, and the enemy might suppose we had surrendered."[26] General Hull overheard this conversation but said nothing. He had much to worry about, as he later wrote, "What was ... decisive in my mind, was my situation, even in the possible event of success over ... [Brock's] white force," because, "It would in this case have become a war with savages, who would have been aided by all the remaining forces of Upper Canada, and the navy on the lake."[27] Perhaps he became haunted by the words of his own July proclamation, which threatened "a war of extermination" if native allies joined the British. His fear was personal — his daughter and her children were in the town — as well as general for the civilian population.[28] He had no means to gain control of the water, he had no information of the whereabouts of Cass and McArthur, and, isolated within the fort, he would soon run short of provisions. The officer with the flag of truce returned to the American side because only Brock could approve a ceasefire and Hull then sent Colonels J. Miller and E. Brush to "accept the best terms which could be obtained." (Brush commanded the Michigan militia.)

Meanwhile, the British column had approached to within less than a mile of the fort when Brock ordered the men to wheel to the left, through an open field and orchard, where they had cover to protect them from enemy guns. He also consented to Norton's request to lead his "party ... to the left, to examine some inclosures and a ravine that might conceal an ambuscade."[29] The general then went up to a rise in the ground to reconnoiter the fort when he learned that Hull had sent out a white flag. Brock dispatched Colonel Macdonell and Captain Glegg to find out what it meant. Glegg rode back to inform the major-general that Hull proposed to surrender the fort. Brock gave his instructions and Glegg returned to join Macdonell in negotiations with the Americans.

For the next hour, Brock's troops lounged, perhaps eating their cold breakfasts, while a few officers "were provided with an excellent breakfast by the people of the farm-house" nearby. Suddenly, one of

Brock's ADCs rode out from the fort with the news that a capitulation was agreed. Brock ordered the troops to advance through fields toward the fort, but the official surrender took place only after the American garrison had evacuated the fort. Guards were then mounted on the ramparts and Richardson "(at that time a young volunteer armed with a musket taller than myself) had the honor of mounting my first guard at the Flag Staff."[30]

Hull surrendered Detroit and his entire command — 2,188 men, including the detachment under Cass and McArthur.[31] (They subsequently complained that they would have fought rather than surrender, but they were not burdened with Hull's responsibilities. In fact, when Hull was offering to surrender, McArthur's men were cooking and eating oxen instead of hurrying toward Detroit.)[32] With his troops outnumbered by prisoners, Brock sent the 1,600 Ohio volunteers home on parole, escorted by native warriors, while Hull and his 582 regulars were sent eastward to Quebec City.

The capture included thirty-nine carriage guns, fifteen wall pieces, 2,500 muskets, 500 rifles, and abundant quantities of shot, powder, and flints, all of which would significantly add to Upper Canada's defences. Also taken were "three floating batteries," merchant schooners and bateaux, the American baggage train of more than one hundred wagons and pack-horses, and the brig *Adams*, which, renamed *Detroit*, was added to the Provincial Marine's strength. Finally, Hull's military chest "containing about six thousand dollars in money and a hundred packs of valuable furs belonging to the government" joined the spoils.[33] The supplies that could be sold were valued at $200,000 (£4,000) and the proceeds would be distributed among the capturing army. Each man would receive at least four pounds and Brock £214.[34] His success showed the crucial importance of control of the lakes, for Brock could move himself, troops, and supplies swiftly while denying that advantage to the enemy. Hull's failure was "a colossal disaster for the United States: in one blow its strategic plans were shattered, and the whole middle western frontier was now open to Indian depredations far worse than might have occurred at Detroit, as several previously neutral tribes now took up the tomahawk."

"Ironically," Latimer points out, "Brock's victory and his subsequent act of detaching Michigan Territory from the United States virtually guaranteed that the war would continue; just as Britain was seeking a peaceful solution, Brock's success removed any chance of a diplomatic breakthrough."[35]

*Major General Hull surrendering to Major General Brock. Hull, on right, hands his sword to Brock.*

LAC, C16404

On the following day after "breakfasting ... with Tecumseh [and others] at an inn in Detroit," Brock put his subordinates to work writing.[36] The general issued a General Order to the troops that included the terms of the capitulation and a proclamation to the inhabitants of Michigan (see Appendix D). In the General Order, Brock expressed his satisfaction "with the conduct of the Troops" praising the "steadiness and discipline of the 41st Regiment, and the readiness of the Militia to follow so good an example." He also praised the Royal Newfoundland Regiment "for their steadiness in the field, as well as when embarked in the King's vessels." He had good words for the militia who had accompanied him to Amherstburg expressing his admiration "at the conduct of the several companies of Militia who so handsomely volunteered to undergo the fatigues of a journey of several hundred miles to go to the rescue of an invaded district." His officers were commended, and the native warriors,

> The conduct of the Indians under Colonel. Elliott, Capt. [Thomas] McKee, and other officers of that department, joined to that of the gallant and brave Chiefs ... has since the commencement of the war been marked with acts of true heroism ... Two fortifications have already been captured from the enemy without a drop of blood being shed by the hands of the Indians; the instant the enemy submitted, his life became sacred.[37]

Norton was proud to record in his journal, "The Americans can have no pretence for accusing the Indian Allies of cruelty in this Instance."[38] Norton proposed to remain in the area, especially because he was being joined daily by more warriors. Brock's thoughts, however, had already turned to the American threat on the Niagara frontier and he "urged" Norton to lead his fighters there.

In his proclamation of August 16th to the inhabitants of Michigan, Brock informed them that the territory had been ceded to Britain but he assured them "that the laws heretofore in existence shall continue in force until His Majesty's pleasure be known, or so long as the peace and security of the said territory will admit thereof; and … they shall be protected in the full exercise of their religion, of which all persons … will take notice, and govern themselves accordingly."[39] All persons, particularly militiamen, were to deliver up their weapons. Colonel Procter would govern the territory.

In four days, Brock had accomplished what his opponent with a much larger army had failed to do in over a month. It was an astonishing achievement under any circumstances and even more because it was totally unexpected. He owed a great debt to Tecumseh and his warriors, and Brock would pay him a tribute, writing to Lord Liverpool, "A more sagacious or a more gallant Warrior does not I believe exist."[40] There is a story that Brock took off his crimson sash and presented it to Tecumseh, who in return gave him an elaborate multi-coloured sash called a *ceinture fléchée*. The next day Tecumseh was not wearing the sash and he explained to Brock that he had given it to the Wyandot chief, Roundhead, out of respect for an older warrior who had faithfully supported the cause of native unity. The story is odd and it might be true, but a careful investigation has shown there is no contemporary evidence for such an exchange. The story first appeared in print in 1818 and its source is unknown.[41]

The regulars and militia volunteers had performed effectively and the artillery, as well as Provincial Marine, contributed significantly. There were many parts to the force that defeated Hull and conquered Detroit, but it was Brock's leadership that brought them together to make a winning combination.

Brock also benefitted from the fact Hull's invasion was not supported by attacks elsewhere across the frontier, for example across the Niagara River or the St. Lawrence above Montreal. Across the border from Lower Canada, there was no serious threat. The American commander, General Dearborn — known as "Granny" to his soldiers — was gathering his forces very slowly and, as late as July 28th, inquired of Eustis who was to command operations in Upper Canada.[42] Such uncertainty at that level did not bode well for American planning and, in fact, Dearborn did not act aggressively until November. When, eventually, Van Rensselaer would attack across the Niagara River against Queenston, he was not supported by invasions upriver or by naval forces on Lake Ontario nor by diversions elsewhere on the frontier. The news swept eastward by official and unofficial channels. Captain Glegg took dispatches and the colours of the Fourth U.S. Regiment to Prevost. An urgent message was sent from Fort George to Kingston to send up three companies of the 49th and a detachment of the Royal Newfoundland Regiment so that the garrison at the fort would not be outnumbered by the arrival of prisoners from Detroit.

General Hull and other prisoners sailed from Detroit for Fort Erie with a guard of York militia on the vessel. On August 28, a victory parade came from the fort down the Queenston road in full view of Americans on the opposite bank. John Lovett, secretary to General Van Rensselaer, expressed the deep humiliation all felt,

> Yesterday I beheld such a sight as God knows I never expected to see ... I saw my countrymen, free-born Americans, robbed of the inheritance which their dying fathers bequeathed to them, stripped of [their] arms ... and marched in a strange land by hundreds.... Before and behind, on the right and on the left, their proud victors gleamed in arms and their heads erect in the pride of victory. How many of our unfortunate brethren were in this situation, I know not ... I think the line, including wagons, pleasure carriages etc., was half a mile long, scattered. The sensations this scene produced in our camp were inexpressible; mortification, indignation, fearful apprehension, suspicion, jealousy, dismay, rage, madness. [43]

This author also expressed widely held views of condemnation directed at the unfortunate General Hull,

> From his officers ... it appears that there was through the whole army a very great disaffection towards

Hull. Cowardice is pretty generally imputed to him. Many allege corruption ... I saw a gentleman who was present when General Hull alighted from his carriage at Fort George, hale, corpulent, and apparently in high spirits, and hence will he ever return? I saw a gentleman who had this day seen one of Hull's captains, who openly and roundly asserted that Hull

*Portrait of Sir George Prevost, by Baptiste Roy-Audy.*

Château Ramezay Museum Collection, 1998.573

145

was a *coward*, that as soon as the first gun was fired he sat down with his back against a solid protection.

Hull proceeded to Quebec City and would return on parole to the United States in October. In January 1814, he would face a court martial, charged with treason and cowardice. He would be found guilty of cowardice and neglect of duty and would be sentenced to

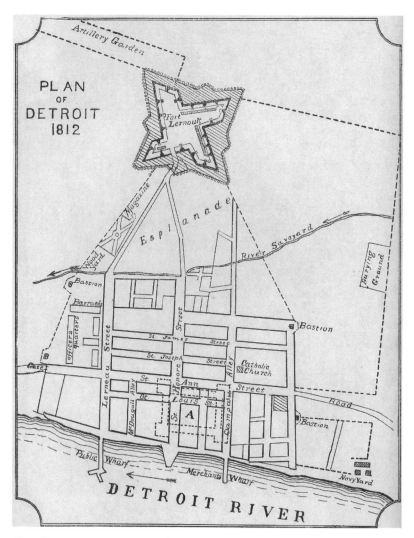

*Plan of Detroit.*

death, but President Madison would pardon him on the grounds of his service during the War of Independence. One historian considers him "the scapegoat for the failures of others as well as his own ..."[44]

Brock with his ADCs and members of the York militia returned from Detroit to Fort Erie on the *Chippawa*. During the voyage he discussed "the coming campaign with several officers of the militia"[45] These included Captain Peter Robinson of the 1st York militia and, according to Tupper, among other remarks, the general is said to have observed to Robinson: "If this war last, I am afraid that I shall do some foolish thing, for if I know myself, there is no want of courage in my nature — I hope I shall not get into a scrape." It seems that Brock thought that the Americans on the Niagara frontier were still so disorganized and unprepared that he could make a quick strike at Fort Niagara. The capture of this major enemy base would be a serious setback to American plans and their troop's morale. His opportunity never came.

Further east, on August 1, Sir George Prevost had received dispatches from London informing him that the orders-in-council had been repealed and that the British minister in Washington, Augustus J. Foster, was trying to open peace negotiations. Prevost wasted no time sending Colonel Baynes, his adjutant general, to negotiate a truce with General Dearborn whereby both sides would take only defensive measures. This fitted in with the governor's defensive strategy as well as his hope (and the British government's) that the war could be ended by diplomacy. The agreement made on August 9 did not apply to Hull, over whom Dearborn claimed to have no authority. In early August, both Dearborn and Prevost wrote to their governments of the advantages each was gaining from this ceasefire. President Madison rejected Dearborn's armistice and instructed him to resume military operations; the armistice would end on September 4.

Before the *Chippawa* reached Fort Erie, it was met by the *Lady Prevost*, which carried dispatches informing Brock of Prevost's armistice with Dearborn. This meant that Brock would have to abandon any plan he might have had to attack Fort Niagara. One of his great fears was that his native allies would "naturally feel disheartened and suspicious of our intentions. Should hostilities recommence I much fear the influence the British possess over them will be found diminished."[46] He hoped for peace, but did not expect it.

When Brock arrived at Fort Erie, August 23rd, he learned of yet another truce, this one made by Sheaffe with Major-General Stephen Van Rensselaer. Sheaffe knew of the capture of Detroit and, seemingly thinking to prevent an American counterattack from Niagara, agreed with Van Rensselaer that no troops or supplies could be sent further inland than Fort Erie. The American commander had not yet heard of the fall of Detroit. He probably hoped to impede Brock's campaign in that direction. Prevost, not knowing of Brock's capture of Detroit, was very displeased by Sheaffe's truce because it might prevent Brock from reinforcing Amherstburg. The commander of the forces told Brock of his annoyance but to avoid embarrassing Sheaffe would not repudiate it.[47]

A few days after the armistice with Dearborn, Prevost informed Brock that he was sending Major William Ormsby with three companies of the 49th, "protecting a considerable supply of ordnance and ordnance stores," along with £2,500. Major Heathcote, a company of the 49th, 110 men of the Royal Newfoundland Regiment, and fifty of the Royal Veterans with "an additional supply of ordnance stores and camp equipage for 500 men" were to leave the following day. As soon as enough bateaux had been collected, Colonel Vincent was under orders to take members of the 49th and Royal Artillery with guns to Kingston. Prevost also planned to send army bills to Brock.[48] This aid was to strengthen Brock's defences not provide the means for attacks.

The ceasefire enabled Prevost to send men and supplies upriver unmolested by the enemy but, at the same time, it also opened the main waterways to American shipping. The schooner *Julia* had been trapped at Ogdensburg along with several other schooners. All were able to sail to Sackets Harbor where they were soon armed and added to a growing naval force. On September 5th, the commander at Sackets, Lieutenant Melancthon Woolsey, informed the secretary of the navy, "It is with pleasure I inform you that all our Merchant vessels have succeeded in getting up out of the River. [W]e can now muster eight or nine fine schooners — two of them can carry two thirty two pounders, one two twenty fours and the rest will average eight light guns each...."[49] In effect, the Americans were able to use water transport on the St. Lawrence and Lake Ontario without fear of British interception. The British, because of their control of the lakes, did not benefit in the same way from the truce. Malcomson's judgment is no exaggeration: "Clearly, the armistice gave the Americans a reprieve when their fortunes were barely afloat.... Inadvertently, he [Prevost] assisted the American army on the frontier."[50] More important, he had allowed the Americans to create a fleet on the key lake where a new commander, Isaac Chauncey, was soon to take an active role.[51]

Brock was surprised and perhaps "disheartened and furious" by both truces. There is a trace of annoyance in his letter to his brothers: "A cessation of hostilities has taken place along this frontier. Should peace follow, the measure will be well; if hostilities recommence, nothing could be more unfortunate than this pause..."[52] His assessment was prophetic.

On September 24th, Brock arrived at Fort George where he was greeted "by the principal inhabitants of the Town and vicinity in carriages and on horseback as a testimony to their respect for our gallant Chief." After arriving at Government House, he made a short speech of thanks to the assembled crowd.[53] He quickly got down to business, ordering improvements to the fort's defences, such as mounting guns captured at Detroit on the bastions, and having more batteries erected around the town. The truce enabled him to give militiamen a break from duty. He allowed up to four-fifths of the flank companies "to return to their homes, but the men [were] ... to hold themselves in readiness to return at a moment's notice." He also ordered a "general inspection" of the Home, Niagara, and London District militia regiments, required full reports on their manpower, and directed drill "once in every week." He was also to take stronger action against militiamen of doubtful loyalty.[54]

After completing these arrangements he sailed to York, accompanied by General Sheaffe. There, one newspaper commented, "His Honor seems to enjoy a state of health that promises many future years of useful service to his King and Country."[55] Little more than seven weeks later, he would be killed in battle.

After a brief stop in the capital, Brock headed to Kingston. During that voyage he wrote to his brothers,

> You will have heard of the complete success which attended the efforts I directed against Detroit. I have received so many letters from people whose opinion I value, expressive of their admiration of the exploit, that I begin to attach to it more importance than I was at first inclined. Should the affair be viewed in England in the light it is here, I cannot fail of meeting reward, and escaping the horror of being placed high on a shelf never to be taken down.
>
> Some say that nothing could be more desperate than the measure; but I answer that the state of the province admitted of nothing but desperate remedies. I got possession of the letters my antagonist addressed to the secretary at war, and also of the sentiments which hundreds of his army uttered to their friends ... I crossed the river, contrary to the opinion of Colonel Procter ... etc.; it is, therefore, no wonder that envy should attribute to good fortune what ... I must say, proceeded from a cool calculation of the *pours* and *contres*.
>
> It is supposed that the value of the articles captured will amount to 30 or £40,000; in that case my proportion will be something considerable....
>
> A cessation of hostilities has taken place along this frontier. Should peace follow, the measure will be well; if hostilities recommence, nothing could be more unfortunate than this pause. I cannot give you freely an account of my situation — it is, however, of late much improved. The militia have been inspired, by the recent success, with confidence — the

disaffected are silenced. The 49th have come to my aid, besides other troops. I shall see Vincent, I hope, this evening at Kingston. He is appointed to command of that post — a most important one. I have withdrawn Plenderleath from Niagara to assist him. Plenderleath is sitting opposite to me, and desires to be remembered.[56]

Brock was also happy that his success would help his family. After mentioning the possible value of his share of the captured articles, he continued,

If it enable me to contribute to your comfort and happiness, I shall esteem it my highest reward. When I returned Heaven thanks for may amazing success, I thought of you all.... Let me know my dearest brothers, that you are all again united. The want of union was nearly losing this province without even a struggle, and be assured it operates in the same degree in regard to families.

He thanked his brothers for their letters, which had been brought to him by Major Smelt and Captain Brown of the 103rd regiment at Quebec. He was gratified to receive a letter from Richard Potenger, son of his sister Marie, and urged him to continue to study for the priesthood. He had previously received a letter from a relative by marriage, Sir Thomas Saumarez at Halifax. He mentioned the loss of "two valuable military friends, lamenting, "I begin to be too old to form new friendships, and those of my youth are dropping off fast." In spite of the heavy burdens of command and political responsibility in wartime, he remained a warm-hearted person with strong interest in his family and friends.

In this letter he also mentioned some movements of officers. Lieutenant-Colonel John Vincent was put in command of Kingston and Brock had sent Major Charles Plenderleath from Niagara to assist

Vincent. Brock's cousin, James Brock, was remaining there with the 49th rather than acting as Brock's private secretary, probably because the latter's "salary [was] a mere pittance." He mentioned Sheaffe being sent to the upper province and continued, "There never was an individual so miserably off for the necessary assistance. Sir George Prevost has kindly hearkened to my remonstrances, and in some measure supplied the deficiency." Fryer believes Brock's attitude to Sheaffe "had softened," although Brock had long been supportive of Sheaffe and there seems no reason that his view would have changed at this time.[57]

Brock was aware of the wider and immediate effects of his victory at Detroit. Upper Canada was saved from conquest, at least for the time being. All the captured weapons and supplies made invaluable additions to the province's military stores. As one group of militiamen succinctly put it, "Here, for the first time, we got a supply of good arms."[58] Perhaps they exaggerated but they were reflecting an attitude of increased confidence.

Many Upper Canadians could scarcely believe that General Hull and his imposing army had been so easily defeated. Some imagined that Hull had been bribed by the British to give up Detroit. Brock saw morale in Upper Canada improved; for example, he wrote that the militia had been "inspired" and "the disaffected are silenced."[59] There began an important change of attitude toward the government. Michael Smith observed, "After this event, the people of Canada became fearful of disobeying the government; some that had fled to the wilderness returned home; and the friends of the United States were discouraged, and those of the King encouraged ... The people now saw that it was as much as their property and lives were worth to disobey the orders, and now what they had been compelled to do, after a while they did from choice."[60] An unnamed writer informed General Van Rensselaer that public sentiment in Upper Canada had changed, partly because of the behaviour of Hull's troops after the invasion but, more importantly, "The success of General Brock established the change of sentiment. He has since made the most of it, has become personally highly popular and, in short, has taken every measure that a judicious officer could take in his circumstances for the securing of this Province. A determination now prevails among the people to defend their country."[61] Out of self-interest appeared a tiny spark of national feeling.

There were even longer-term effects that strengthened the hands of the provincial government. Several residents of the London and Western Districts who had joined Hull were captured at Detroit and four of them were indicted for treason at Sandwich in September. Elsewhere in the province, open treason had been much less common (in most cases people fled to the United States) though a good deal of pro-American sentiment and talk was reported. The government began to enforce more rigorously the oath of allegiance on the militia. Brock's Militia General Order of August 26 required militiamen "to take and subscribe the oath of allegiance, as directed in the last Militia Act." Any refusing or neglecting to swear the oath without a legal excuse could face prosecution as provided by that act. By mid-October there would be nearly 300 prisoners charged with sedition and treasonable practices in the jail and a blockhouse at Niagara.[62] The numbers may not so much have represented widespread disloyalty as the vigour of the government in acting against those it considered dangerous.

When General Brock reached Kingston on September 4th, he arrived in a town that was rapidly changing. Lieutenant David Wingfield, an officer who arrived eight months later, wrote in his journal:

> Kingston is situated on the border of Lake Ontario, just at the head of River St. Lawrence, and previous to the war, was a place of no great importance. But a large naval establishment being formed, and York having lost its former advantages [owing to its vulnerability to American attacks] ... all the trade followed to this place.... Consequently, building became the rage, and at the conclusion of the war Kingston had risen into a large town.... In Kingston bay are a few wharfs for the convenience of loading and unloading

small vessels…. The harbour for the men of war, called Navy Bay, is about a quarter of a mile from the town, and is formed by a long point of land, called Navy Point, and two small islands, making good shelter, and forming a breakwater to prevent the ice from injuring the ships, when it breaks up in the spring. On Navy Point is our dockyard, none [having been] established previous to our arrival in the country….

The whole is commanded by a high ground, little more than a musquet shot off, upon which is built, since the commencement of the war, a large and strong fort, for that part of the world. It likewise commands the town, and all the outworks, and could, if required, level the whole with the ground.[63]

When the *Royal George* arrived carrying Brock, he was "saluted by a discharge of nineteen guns by the Militia Artillery … In the afternoon he reviewed the Militia," and expressed his pleasure at their appearance and their drill. "In the evening he was waited upon by the Magistrates, Clergymen, Officers of the Militia, and others in a body, who presented him an Address," that rhapsodized on his "extraordinary" victory at Detroit. He displayed typical astuteness by giving the credit to others: "Nothing but the confidence which the admirable conduct of the York and Lincoln regiments of Militia excited, could have induced me to undertake … [the] expedition …" against Detroit.[64] He concluded by speaking highly of his confidence in the bravery of the Kingston district militia.

That same day, Prevost's letter arrived, announcing the end of the ceasefire and that hostilities would resume that very day. Brock sailed from Kingston for Fort George that night to take over personal command of the Niagara frontier from Sheaffe. Brock reached Fort George on September 6th and learned from Sheaffe of growing American strength across the river. The next day he wrote to Prevost, "I expect an attack almost immediately."[65] The Americans were far from ready.

CHAPTER EIGHT

# Brock's Last Battle

Early in September, Major-General Van Rensselaer and Major-General Sheaffe exchanged letters agreeing that the armistice on the Niagara frontier would end at noon on Tuesday, September 8th.[1] Now both sides were facing the questions of who would attack, where, and when. The geography of this river frontier would have to be the first consideration for any strategy.

Despite its waterfall and rapids, the Niagara River had long been a crossing place for native peoples and later European arrivals. The first twenty miles downstream from Lake Erie were passable in a few minutes and the banks were low, rising ten to twenty feet above the water on the American side and about ten feet on the Canadian side. An American engineer reported the river was about 600 yards across and the current about five miles per hour. He saw several good crossing points on this upper part of the river.[2] The next nine miles to Queenston varied from very difficult to cross to impossible because of the falls and rapids in the gorge. From there the river flows at about four miles per hour in a channel a little over 200 yards wide. It could be crossed in about ten minutes by rowing, but the banks on either side rise almost perpendicular to a height above the river of some 350 feet on the east side and around 253 feet on the west. This height marks the escarpment that stretches inland and provides a ridge that commands communications across the Niagara Peninsula. Downstream, the river winds and broadens, its surface disturbed by eddies reflecting the currents underneath, until it reaches Lake Ontario, six miles away. Below the escarpment, the banks on the Canadian side vary in height above the water, from about fifty feet at Queenston to approximately forty feet at Vrooman's Point to about thirty feet at Fort George. On the east side, the bank's height is lower, ranging from thirty to forty feet between Lewiston and Fort Niagara. On both sides only a few gullies slash through to banks to give easy access from the water to the undulating plain above.

The plain was the bottom of Lake Iroquois some 15,000 to 8,000 years ago. At the foot of the escarpment, the land raises to a plateau, which was the shoreline of that lake. In effect, at Queenston and at Lewiston opposite there is the river shoreline, then a steep bank rising to the plain, next the plateau, and, finally, the escarpment (also referred to as the Heights or the mountain). The village of Queenston was located on the plain, at least fifty feet above the river, while a further seventy feet up a redan — a V-shaped fieldwork — had been constructed. In it an 18-pounder long gun commanded the river and the landings.[3] In the woods and fields around the present site of Brock's Monument the final battle would take place.

Queenston had about 300 inhabitants residing in some twenty to forty scattered dwellings surrounded by gardens and orchards. In 1791, the Queen's Rangers had constructed a wharf, blockhouse, stone guardhouse, and a row of huts for barracks along the riverbank. The bank was pierced by several gullies that provided easy access to the plain above and one of those was chosen by Robert Hamilton as a place to land cargoes from ships or to load goods onto them. Higher up the slope, he built a magnificent two-storey stone house. From this site ran the route for portaging goods around the obstacle of the Heights and the falls, which gave it the name of the portage road. Its terminus was Chippawa, a village of about twelve houses at the mouth of the Chippawa Creek or Welland River. At Chippawa, cargoes were loaded on to boats and taken to Fort Erie where they were transferred to lake vessels.

From Queenston another road ran inland to the village of St. Davids, with a branch that ascended the ridge about a mile westward and finally united with the portage road above. Queenston was also connected to Fort George by a wagon road, known as the river road. It also ran to nearby Niagara (now Niagara-on-the-Lake) with its "five hundred inhabitants, six taverns and twenty dry-goods shops where 'every item could be purchased on the same terms as in Montreal.'" It was the most significant settlement in the peninsula.[4] The heaviest populated area was along the Niagara River, particularly north of Chippawa, and the Lake Ontario shore.

Across from Queenston was the settlement of Lewiston, named after an earlier governor, Morgan Lewis. Peter B. Porter and associates ran a portage business from a landing there but the village grew slowly. A road along the riverside connected it with Youngstown, a village of perhaps eight houses, and nearby Fort Niagara.[5] At Five Miles Meadows the bank dropped to about ten feet, which provided an easy ascent to the river where the current was reported to be about three miles per hour. Across from it was Field's Point and further inland Field's brick house. Fort Niagara commanded the mouth of the Niagara River and both Niagara and Fort George were within range of its guns. Fort Niagara had a wooden stockade enclosing barracks and the two-storey stone building known as the French Castle, but General Van Rensselaer believed it could not be defended without strengthening the works and adding considerably more ordnance. Lieutenant-Colonel John Fenwick, commander of a Regiment of Light Artillery, arrived in early September and was put in charge of the work. He removed the roof of the "old stone mess-house" and installed a battery of two 12-pounders and a howitzer. He strengthened its walls and about a mile upriver, opposite to Fort George, erected a battery of three 18-pounders.[6] Above Lewiston, in a breastwork designated Fort Gray, the Americans placed two 18-pounders and two six-pounders.[7] Further south, on the river was Fort Schlosser, was a small blockhouse.

The command structure on the United States side affected the coming campaign and, therefore, deserves a brief explanation. The Republican governor of New York state, Daniel Tompkins, appointed as commander on the Niagara frontier Stephen Van Rensselaer, a wealthy landowner and prominent Federalist. He belonged to the party that opposed the war and although a militia major-general, he had no military experience. It may be that Tompkins appointed him hoping to influence other Federalists to support the war. Van Rensselaer was put into a politically awkward position, for if he refused the command he would appear disloyal to his country, and if he took command he would have to prosecute a war he opposed. In short, it was an appointment made for political reasons. Van Rensselaer himself felt honour bound to carry out his duty but, recognizing his limitations, he insisted on appointing his cousin, Lieutenant-Colonel Solomon Van Rensselaer, as his aide-de-camp; Solomon possessed military skill and experience. The regular forces on the frontier came under command of Brigadier-General Alexander Smyth, a political appointee who had no practical military experience.[8] Even worse, "vain and pompous, he refused to place himself under Van Rensselaer's command despite

*Fort Niagara, 1812, late fall or early spring, with a bateau in foreground.*

Painting by Peter Rindlisbacher

explicit orders from the War Department to do so."[9] Brigadier-General William Wadsworth, the elderly commander of the New York militia, also lacked military experience and tried to get out of his command.[10] Canada's defenders were fortunate to be faced by such reluctant leaders leading virtually untrained, inadequately supplied, and poorly disciplined forces.

Major-General Van Rensselaer, appointed on July 13, took formal command of his troops at Niagara on August 13. He assured the officers and soldiers that he would "require prompt obedience to orders and strict discipline," and in return his men could "expect his unremitting exertions to render their situation at all times as eligible as possible." He ordered inspection of the troops at Lewiston for 10:00 a.m. the following day. He expected commanding officers to make out returns that would "account for their men, arms, and accoutrements" and that would "note the deficiencies of arms or accoutrements" so that he could seek to alleviate such deficiencies.[11] It looked like the American force could look forward to decisive and concerned command. According to the general's secretary, John Lovett, this was still their outlook early in September, when he wrote that the troops "are patient, patriotic, and exceedingly attached to their General ... this confidence is all that saves us from every sort of disgrace."[12] Both the commander and his men were to be disappointed in each other.

At Lewiston, on September 1st, General Van Rensselaer reported he had only 691 militiamen fit for duty (with over one hundred on the sick list), but "many of the men are without shoes and all clamorous for pay." He continued with many complaints: lack of reinforcements, insufficient tents, ordnance, and ammunition, "nor have we lead to make cartridges." They were deficient in medicine and hospital stores and had no bandage cloth or surgical instruments. The only regular troops he referred to were a small company of artillerymen at Fort Niagara under Lieutenant-Colonel John Fenwick.[13] Two weeks later, his militia force had increased to "about sixteen hundred" but there were still shortages of shoes, clothing suitable for cold weather, and the men were still "extremely clamorous for their pay." He feared if money was not

*A young Solomon Van Rensselaer, watercolor on ivory, attributed to Robert Field.*

provided very soon, men would begin to desert. Another indication of discontent was the increasing number of courts martial dealing with "deserters, drunks and dissent." Even the horses may have suffered, for grain could not be obtained to feed them.[14]

At this time, Brock was aware of the problems among the forces opposite. He wrote to Prevost, "The troops on the opposite shore ... [were] anxious for an opportunity of deserting a service in which they are not only badly fed, but remain without pay.... Great sickness prevails along the whole line." His officers had observed at Black Rock "during the last week one, and often two, Military burials of a day." He told the story of seven deserters from the U.S. Sixth Regiment, six of whom drowned as they attempted to cross the river. Only one succeeded in reaching the Canadian shore. The regulars felt the militia were "better fed and otherwise better treated, which occasion great jealousy."[15] The militia, Brock believed, were anxious to attack. While Brock was able to collect information, Van Rensselaer found he could not get accurate information about defensive preparations across the river or what Brock might be planning. Reinforcements and supplies had arrived safely by water from Oswego during the period of the armistice (arranged by Deaborn and Prevost). After it ended on September 8th, Van Rensselaer believed it would be "very hazardous" to proceed the same way from Oswego in the face "of our active enemy, having command of the water."[16] The Provincial Marine, whatever its shortcomings, was a valuable ally for Brock.

Van Rensselaer instituted routine and training but as the hot and humid summer turned into a windy, rainy autumn, conditions for the troops seemed not to have improved much. Dearborn ordered reinforcements of both militia and regulars to march to the Niagara frontier as well as bateaux to be sent to Fort Niagara. General Smyth, after arriving on September 29th, set up a training camp near Black Rock and decided that the place to attack Upper Canada was between Chippawa and Fort Erie. He demonstrated discourtesy in his correspondence with General Van Rensselaer, as well as insubordination.[17] His attitude foreshadowed trouble for the American campaign and Van Rensselaer lacked the experience of military command to nip it in the bud.

A bewildering mix of reinforcements, both regular and militia, continued to arrive. In his correspondence, Dearborn, who remained at Albany or across the Hudson River at the military camp at Greenbush and made no move against Lower Canada, stepped up the pressure. In the middle of September, he ordered more regiments to the Niagara front and informed Van Rensselaer that their arrival should give him a force of at least 6,000 men, which should provide "a force sufficient *to enable you to act with effect, although late.*" Nine days later, Dearborn wrote rather obscure instructions: *"By putting on the best face that your situation admits, the enemy may be induced to delay an attack until you will be able to meet him and carry the war in Canada. At all events, we must calculate on possessing Upper Canada before winter sets in."*[18] He also expressed his assurance that General Harrison would invade from Detroit with a force of six to seven thousand men, but where that assurance or numbers came from are a mystery. John Armstrong neatly expressed Dearborn's situation, writing that his army "continued to slumber on its arms" during this whole period.[19]

General Van Rensselaer frequently expressed concern about the ability of his "little army" to defend itself if Brock attacked. He took comfort from "the belief, that we have not yet suffered any disgrace." At least until the end of September, Van Rensselaer was more worried about being surprised or defeated than about launching an invasion of Upper Canada.[20] As late as September 27th, he felt consoled "to learn that I shall soon be partially relieved from that severe suspense and solitude which have for some weeks past been inseparably connected with my situation." He may have been encouraged by the arrival of more regular officers and troops, but he still emphasized acting on the defensive "with better prospects."[21]

His confidence and morale may also have been weakened by increasingly open dissent among his officers. His ADC, Colonel Solomon Van Rensselaer, alleged that Peter Porter and others were plotting for "party purposes against the commander." (Porter was a Republican while the two Van Rensselaers were Federalists.)[22] They were spreading rumours that the general planned to surrender his army when he crossed the river, an intended comparison with Hull's surrender at Detroit. Solomon thought that the general's ability to command had been so undermined that he suggested to former Brigadier-General Morgan Lewis, "It would be well if General Dearborn could with propriety remove him to New York or some other place where his position may be equal to his sacrifices in private life."[23] Some officers even absented themselves from conferences held by General Van Rensselaer in which plans for invasion were discussed. The lack of co-operation would decrease the number of regulars available for the eventual invasion from Lewiston, but there is no certainty that their presence would have changed the outcome of the battle on October 13th. Perhaps more serious, the lack of co-operation would mean that simultaneous attacks from Lewiston and across the river above Chippawa could not be undertaken. If those had been attempted on October 13th, the prospects of successful defence by Brock and his forces would have been very much reduced.[24]

In light of the small size of his force on the Niagara frontier and Prevost's insistence on defensive strategy, Brock could only wait for his opponents to move. During the period of the armistice, the Americans opposite had received "vast supplies" of food, as well as reinforcements and artillery. Now, in early September, they were building batteries opposite Fort George. Brock expected to be attacked "almost immediately" and he needed more "officers, men and heavy ordnance." He asked Prevost for another 1,000 regulars, which he would put in a central location ready "to act as exigencies might require," because his present force was stretched along the Niagara River. Prevost's reply showed the governor's excessive caution, for he suggested that Brock evacuate Detroit and the Michigan territory. Then he could reinforce his front with the troops taken from Amherstburg rather than taking them from the forces at Kingston.[25] Prevost's proposal reflected the traditional strategy of concentrating forces rather than trying to hold onto the interior and, from his point of view at Quebec, it was not necessarily the wrong advice. But to follow it would have meant reversing the victory at Detroit and the capture of Fort Michilimackinac. It would have delivered a message to native allies and Upper Canadians that they were being abandoned by their mother country in spite of Brock's promises in his opening speech to the Legislature in February. Then he had stated, "The acknowledged importance of this Colony to the Parent State, will secure the continuance of her powerful protection." Brock had sought to "dispel any apprehension which you may have imbibed of the possibility of England forsaking you." Upper Canada had a "just claim ... to the protection of his Royal Highness [the Prince Regent]." On September 28th, Brock rejected this pessimistic course of action.

About the middle of September, Brock expressed both confidence and uncertainty in writing to his brother Savery, "I am really placed in a most awkward predicament," for he believed that if allowed to he could "sweep everything before me between Fort Niagara and Buffalo." Instead, he had to wait on events. He had information that the American force was to increase to 7,000 and when that happened they would invade. Although he feared he would not be able to stop them, at the same time he discounted their militia because of its lack of discipline and widespread sickness. In contrast, among his own troops Brock noted that since the war began he had not lost a single man on the Niagara frontier by death or desertion. His situation was also improved by the arrival of flank companies of the Royal Newfoundland Regiment and a few of the 10th Royal Veterans (whom he proposed to send to Michilimackinac). He expressed confidence in the 41st ("An uncommonly fine regiment, but wretchedly officered,") and the 49th ("Although the regiment has been ten years in this country, drinking rum without bounds, it is still respectable, and ... ardent for an opportunity to acquire distinction").[26] Rum, indeed, was shipped to the upper province in large quantities; for example, in August, 3,000 gallons were sent — along with other supplies — from Montreal with another 2,000 gallons to follow shortly.[27]

Brock also did what he could to strengthen physical defences at the fort and along the river. As early as July, American officers had observed gun batteries being prepared on the Canadian shore from Fort George to Lake Ontario and two between the fort and Queenston.[28] Later in the summer, at Fort George, a curtain wall was built between bastions facing the river and "the two Curtains on the Right and Left of the East Gate" were strengthened.[29] A 12-pounder and 18-pounder were mounted on "a bastion on the river side" and a 24-pounder, from Detroit, was placed on the North or Cavalier Bastion. (A Cavalier Bastion was built much higher than a regular bastion so that its guns could fire over the wall, *en barbette*, rather than through a narrow slot. The guns were usually designed to traverse, or move, thereby widening their field of fire.) Brock also referred to this bastion as the York Bastion because York militiamen did some of the labour on it. At the mouth of the river, directly across from Fort Niagara, a 24-pounder and a mortar were placed.[30]

From Fort George to Queenston, batteries were placed at points where they commanded the river as well as the American shore opposite.[31] The most important for the coming battle were the 24-pounder at Vrooman's Point (about one mile north of Queenston) and the 18-pounder in the redan above Queenston.[32] Brock sent sixty men of the 41st Regiment to Chippawa, twenty of whom were to be added to the detachment "stationed at the head of Navy Island," which lies just south of the mouth of Chippawa Creek. Captain Selby's company of York militia was to march to Brown's Point.[33] A system of beacons was established from Lake Erie to Queenston and thence inland to Pelham Heights. Messages could be sent during daytime by means of coloured balls or flags, or at nighttime by burning wood in a basket hung on a pole. An American officer wrote to General Van Rensselaer about "the Combustible telegraph" on the Canadian side of the Niagara River.[34] As well, Brock ordered Major Merritt to have a militia dragoon ready at Fort George by noon daily for the purpose of carrying messages to and from posts along the Niagara River as well as mail to Fort Erie.[35] Muskets and equipment captured at Detroit were distributed among the militia. Money came from General Hull's military chest and from Lower Canada, but Brock still needed more.

No further reinforcements came from Lower Canada after mid-September but ninety of the 41st returned from Detroit. These troops paraded ostentatiously in view of the Americans. In the first week of October, Brock showed greater concern about the American threat to invade by having a garrison order issued requiring the regulars and militia to be under arms "at first break of day" and to remain so until daylight had arrived. One-third of the men were to be clothed "and accoutred during the night with their arms at hand in readiness...."[36] In the first week of September, 500 to 600 warriors from the Grand River under the leadership of John Norton camped near Niagara. Benn identifies them as, "Grand River Iroquois, their Mississauga neighbours, and ... Delawares and Ojibways...." They patrolled the riverbanks keeping an eye on enemy movements. The problem was maintaining them so far from their homes. As Norton explained, "After a few weeks the want of supplies and the approach of the season for hunting cause my party to diminish in number."[37] By October 9, only about 300 warriors remained.

At the fort, Brock had another infantry unit available, the Coloured Corps. The Niagara District probably had the largest number of free blacks of any district and this specialized corps of what was called coloured men was formed late in the summer from the Lincoln sedentary militia and put under command of Captain Robert Runchey of the 1st Lincoln militia. Early in October this body was increased by the transfer of fourteen men from the 3rd York militia, for a total of thirty-eight men. Runchey proved to be a troublesome commander and Lieutenant James Cooper of the 2nd Lincoln militia took over and would lead Runchey's Corps (or Company) in the battle of Queenston Heights.[38] The Corps seems to have continued with that name until March 1813, when it would become the Provincial Corps of Artificers under Lieutenant Robertson (or Robinson). It fought in defence of Fort George in May and took part in several other actions in 1813 and 1814. The corps would be disbanded in March 1815.

Only a few days before launching his invasion of Upper Canada, Van Rensselaer wrote at great length to Dearborn about his "innumerable difficulties and embarrassments" since he had taken command three months before. He had no doubt "that the Niagara River must be the scene of our decisive operations," but from the tone and content of this letter, he was not ready to launch an invasion. He stated he had passed a "crisis" but feared "a new crisis is opening," the outcome of which would have consequences for both of them. What he meant was not only the failure of the

United States to make any gains in a war it had declared, but also the disgrace it was suffering owing to the British victories in the north and west. Public support for the war would decrease unless he could bring the present campaign to "brilliant close." Time was short: "The blow must be struck soon or all the toil and expense of the campaign will go for nothing, and ... will be tinged with dishonor." Van Rensselaer was having trouble being decisive, for while he believed, "With my present force it would be rash to attempt offensive operations," he was "adopting decisive measures for closing the fall campaign." His measures would not have been called decisive by Brock.

Van Rensselaer intended to call a meeting with the regular and militia commanders where he would explain his intentions. Then he would inform Dearborn and ask for his approval as well as for "the arrival of a competent force to execute it." Why, after three months of preparation, was his force not competent? He reported he had "only 1700 effective men of the militia on the whole line," which seems to have been a very low estimate and he gave no figure for his regulars. And the troops had problems, "Our best troops are raw, many of them dejected by the distress their families suffer by their absence, and many have not necessary clothing." The weather was against them, for it was cold and "the season is far advanced and unusually inclement; we are half the time deluged by rain." There was disagreement among his officers. Some wanted to invade between Fort Erie and Chippawa, but Van Rensselaer objected. He proposed a two-pronged attack, the regulars against the rear of Fort George to "take it by storm" while he would lead the militia from Lewiston against Queenston. His goals were many: to break the British line of communication, gain control of the river, remove any rallying point for opposition, demonstrate American power to Canadians, "save our own land, wipe away part of the score of our past disgrace, get excellent barracks and winter quarters," and be ready early in the new year to launch a further campaign.[39]

A more aggressive spirit was shown by American naval officers. Isaac Chauncey, who was commandant of the New York Navy Yard, upon learning of his appointment to command Lakes Ontario and Erie, began to arrange for ordnance, munitions, supplies, and skilled workmen as well as seamen to proceed to Sackets Harbor. He also sent Lieutenant Jesse Elliott, U.S. Navy, to consult with Major-General Van Rensselaer about locations for naval bases and shipbuilding. Elliott reported from Buffalo on September 14th that the general knew nothing of the resources or suitable locations for shipbuilding, whereas General Peter Porter was well acquainted with the lakes. He had already built boats "intended for the Troops when invading Canada," and Elliott had contracted him to build more as well as "2 Ships of 300 Tons." Elliott had also examined "situations on Lake Erie" and found none suitable for a naval base but recommended a site at Black Rock, about three miles north of Buffalo and behind an island in the river. Chauncey arrived at Sackets on October 6th, and he pushed his men so feverishly that by the middle of November his little fleet of seven vessels would gain control of Lake Ontario. Provincial Marine ships took shelter at Kingston and York where they spent the winter.[40] Chauncey's achievements on Lake Ontario, rather than affecting Brock's campaign, had their impact on his successors. It was the energetic Elliott who influenced the campaign on the Niagara.

Growing tension along the border was turned up a notch by a minor clash on October 9. Early on that morning, Elliott captured two brigs anchored off Fort Erie. He managed to bring one of them, the North-West Company's *Caledonia*, to Black Rock, but a fierce artillery barrage from Fort Erie prevented him from towing the other, the *Detroit*, to shore, so that he had it run aground on Squaw Island about a mile downstream. The British forces were unable to do any-thing except fire on the enemy, who returned the compliment. Just after sunset, up rode General Brock from Fort George and imme-diately he prepared to recover the *Detroit*. Before he completed the arrangements, Elliott seeing what was afoot, sent out a party that succeeded in burning the vessel. The *Caledonia* contained a valuable cargo of furs belonging to the North-West Company while the other brig had cannon taken at Detroit. Brock was most upset by these losses.[41] Nevertheless, he continued to keep an eye on the larger scene, including Procter's needs at Amherstburg. He had intended to send him the flank companies of the Royal Newfoundland Regiment along with supplies of pork and flour, but the loss of the two brigs prevented him from sending the food.[42] Brock's swift movement to Fort Erie, as well as the departure of the two companies, gave his opponents the impression that he had taken a large proportion of his forces to Detroit, thereby weakening the Canadian frontier's defences. This impression contributed to the American decision to attack, which led to the battle at Queenston.[43]

It seems Van Rensselaer never carried out his intention to present his plan of campaign to a council of his officers. After the battle on the 13th, in his explanation to the secretary of war, he would refer to a much more limited plan. It was simply to gain a foothold in Upper Canada at Queenston and winter his troops there so that they would be ready early in the new year to continue the campaign. General Smyth did not agree with an attack across the Niagara against Queenston and simply refused to co-operate. Despite the lack of Smyth's regulars, Van Rensselaer intended to proceed and fixed early morning of the eleventh for the invasion. Troops were marched to Lewiston and boats collected there. But an officer who was to pilot this flotilla apparently deserted, causing the loss of most of the oars needed for the other boats.[44] The attack had to be postponed.

The American commander came under increasing pressure from his own officers and men to attack. As he later wrote, "On the morning of the 12th, such was the pressure upon me from all quarters, that I became satisfied that my refusal to act might involve me in suspicion, & the service in disgrace."[45] His force was increased by the arrival of nearly 400 regulars under Lieutenant-Colonel John Chrystie, Thirteenth U.S. Infantry, who also brought thirty-nine boats from Oswego, capable of carrying thirty men each. An attempt could no longer be delayed and it was arranged for the early hours of October 13. In troop strength the Americans were superior. A return of troops dated October 12 shows that at Lewiston, General Van Rensselaer had 2,270 militia and 900 regulars; at Black Rock and Buffalo (villages about thirty miles to the south) he had 386 militia and 1,650 regulars.[46] The most recent study of the battle gives the "effective" strength of Van Rensselaer's army as about 5,400 officers and men with some 4,600 of these available for the attack at Queenston.[47] Of course, all Brock could know was that he was being threatened by a large and growing enemy army and he could not be certain at what place or time it would attack.

Brock's army in October numbered about 2,340 officers and men made up of some 1,230 regulars, 810 militia, and 300 native allies.[48] He had fifteen companies of regular infantry, just over fifty men of the Royal Artillery with five field pieces, "a troop of militia drivers, a troop of Provincial Cavalry besides the flank companies of the five Lincoln and two York militia regiments." Regular artillerymen were so scarce that a volunteer corps of gunners had been formed from the regular infantry and from the Lincoln militia. The line between Fort Erie and Chippawa was guarded by over 250 men of the 49th Foot, 118 of the Royal Newfoundland Regiment, over 300 of the 41st, 200 Lincoln militiamen, and a small Royal Artillery detachment. In and around Queenston were approximately 420 men, made up of the 49th Grenadier Company (about ninety strong) in the village under Captain James Dennis and the Light Company (ninety strong) under Captain John Williams at the redan and in its vicinity. Also in the village were two flank companies of the 5th Lincoln militia under Captains Samuel Hatt and James Durand (about a hundred men) and two of the 2nd York militia under Captain John Chisholm and William Applegarth's company, about eighty men in total. Some of the 1st Lincoln Artillery Company, under Lieutenant John Ball, were present to assist the six members of the Royal Artillery, with Sergeant Thomas Edlerton, at the redan battery. There were even a few members of the 41st Foot. At Vrooman's Point, Lieutenant Archibald McLean commanded Duncan Cameron's flank company of the 3rd York militia. Part of the 3rd York militia, under Captains Duncan Cameron and Stephen Heward, was at Brown's Point, three miles north of Queenston, serving a 9-pounder. There was an under strength company of York militia at Field's Point, which appears to have been the same place as Brown's Point or else very close to it. The remaining companies of the 41st, 49th, Lincoln and York militia, and Royal Artillery under Captain William Holcroft were stationed at Fort George.[49]

What is more significant than sheer numbers is the fact that Brock combined regulars and militia in a remarkably successful partnership for defence of the province. Militia and regulars did not always mesh well together and not all regular commanders could achieve a harmonious combination, particularly on the American side. In part, the regulars and militia worked well together in this battle because they were defending their land and homes whereas the American militia were invading another country for reasons that probably most did not understand.

Brock could not concentrate any large number of troops at one place, nor could they be marched from one end of the line to the other in much less than two days. His deployment of the bulk between Fort Erie and Chippawa, where the river was fairly calm and easy to cross, and around Fort George indicates where he saw the greatest threat of invasion. (Lieutenant Governor Gore shared Brock's view that invasion was likely to come above Chippawa and not between Fort George and Queenston.)[50]

As if the increasing threat of attack was not enough, Brock was suddenly faced by a crisis among the troops at Queenston. On the evening of October 11, while at dinner, he handed Brigade-Major Thomas Evans a note from Captain Dennis, commander there of flank companies of the 49th.[51] It told of "the highly mutinous state of his detachment, his men having deliberately threatened to shoot their officers, etc." He must have found this news very disturbing, for less than a month earlier (September 18) Brock had expressed his confidence in the 49th Regiment and he was not one to treat mutineers lightly. He ordered Evans to proceed there the next morning and "march, as prisoners ... half-a-dozen of those most culpable," to Fort George. He also gave Evans the mission of crossing the river to negotiate an exchange of prisoners with Van Rensselaer or, at least, allowing British prisoners to return home on parole. Evans arrived early next morning and found the guardhouse gutted with many of the grenadiers confined. He was about to select the men to be marched away when "a scattered fire of musketry from the American shore took place" and one of those musket balls passed between him and Dennis. Evans's response to "such unusual insolence" was to insist on crossing the river with a white handkerchief (borrowed from Mrs. Dickson) as a flag of truce. It was not an easy trip. He and Thomas Dickson "launched our frail canoe amidst an unsparing shower of shot which fell all around us;" it continued as they fought the rivers' currents almost until they reached the other shore. His greeting there was far from cordial.

A sentry, with fixed bayonet, prevented them from landing, and when he asked to speak to Colonel Van Rensselaer "with whom [he] usually conferred" he was told the colonel was sick. After a delay, he did speak with a man claiming to be the general's secretary, who told him "that nothing could be done till the day after to-morrow" and, after some delay, reported that the prisoners had been marched away so that they could not be exchanged. By then Evans was anxious to get back to Brock. He had observed enough to convince him an attack was imminent. The American militia had increased with, in his words, "A horde of half-savage troops from Kentucky, Ohio and Tennessee," and many boats hidden along the riverbank. Rather than reduce the number of troops who could defend Queenston, Evans took the responsibility of releasing them "on the specious plea" that their misbehaviour had arisen from over-indulgence in liquor. He appealed to "their loyalty and courage," exhorted Dennis to keep a sharp eye for any movement by the enemy, and hurried off to Fort George. Along the way, he warned the posts to be ready for action. He rode "at full speed," reaching the fort past 6:00 p.m., but was too exhausted to give a report until he had eaten. Brock listened, hesitated, then told Evans to "follow him to the office" to give him full details. The general then returned "to the dining room" and immediately issued orders. Dispatches were written and sent off with riders of the Provincial Dragoons, "calling in the militia of the vicinity that same evening, those more distant to follow with all alacrity." Evans was told to prepare the fort for action, which took him until almost midnight.[52]

That same evening, Brock completed a letter to Prevost in which he expressed his conviction that an attack was imminent.[53] He did not expect it at Queenston, regarding the abortive attempt of the 11th as a feint. Instead, he thought it would come from the lakeside against Fort George. In line with this belief, a day or two prior to the battle, he wrote copious instructions for the officers commanding the posts along the river. The document begins without preamble and on the back is written, "1812 — Instructions sent to Officers commanding forts by Major-General Brock some days prior to the attack on Queenston."[54] Brock repeated his belief that the principal attack would be delivered north of Fort Erie, but warned his officers not to be lulled into a false sense of security, since he believed the enemy "more disposed to brave the impediments of nature ... in preference to the certainty of encountering British troops ready formed for his reception." A prophetic utterance, which if Brock had realized its implications might have led to a very different result at Queenston Heights.

Precautions elsewhere were not neglected. The forces on Navy Island, if they heard an alarm from the direction of Fort Erie, were not to move until they were certain that no attack was underway. The security of Chippawa was a prime consideration because of its location at the upper end of the portage and the mouth of Chippawa Creek, which was navigable for a considerable distance inland. Only such troops as could be safely spared were to march from this post to another part of the line. But Brock expressed no thought that the bank between Chippawa and Queenston, or the latter place itself, would be in any danger. His was a professional military appraisal but it was probably a widely held opinion.

Almost three years earlier, Lieutenant Governor Gore had given his appraisal of where an American invasion might come in the event of war. He put Amherstburg as the likeliest "first object of Attack." However, this would not be feasible if the British maintained control of the lakes. In that situation an invasion would probably be attempted between Chippawa and Fort Erie where the Niagara River was wide with low banks and islands that would mask American preparations. He judged, "It would probably not be attempted between Fort George and Queenston where the Banks are steep ... and the River so narrow no movement could escape observation."[55] Norton, however, thought that a crossing at Queenston was quite possible because "the River being there the most narrow, and the Eddies on both sides favouring the Traverse," which is not to say that an attack there was likely.[56] It should not be surprising that neither Brock nor Sheaffe (who had served on the Niagara frontier for at least four years in the 1790s and from 1802 to 1804) would imagine that the Americans would attempt to scale the cliff to the Heights above Queenston. Militia Captain James Crooks would later write, "Such implicit reliance was placed on its natural position that there was not even a look out."[57] There may have been a path winding up that steep ascent although only one participant, Major Evans who was at Fort George, mentions it and he believes it was deemed impracticable for soldiers to climb. In secondary accounts there is a story of a "fisherman's path" that would be taken by the Americans to reach the top. It may have existed, but proof is lacking.

There are numerous accounts from participants in the battle that took Brock's life on October 13, some written soon afterward and some years later. An American participant, Major David Campbell, wrote to his brother that a correct account would be almost impossible to provide because of the confusion of the battle. What follows is based primarily on eyewitness reports tempered with Campbell's caveat.[58]

The American preparations on the night of the 12th and early morning of the 13th were cloaked by darkness as well as the noises of the wind and river ripples. James Crooks, in his Niagara home, did not hear the gunfire from Queenston on October 13th because of a "gale off the Lake." John Norton, who was near Fort George, could hear the gunfire from Queenston "although [it was] hardly distinguishable from the high Wind blowing."[59] At Lewiston, the previous night between eleven and twelve boats, and about 4,000 troops, were assembled. According to General Van Rensselaer's "orders issued upon this occasion, the two columns were to pass over together as soon as the Heights should be carried Lieutenant-Colonel Fenwick's flying artillery was to pass over: then Major Mullany's detachment of regulars, and the other troops to follow in order." The two columns were to be 300 militia commanded by Colonel Solomon Van Rensselaer and the same number of regulars under Lieutenant-Colonel Chrystie. What the general meant by "the Heights" is not entirely clear, but the arrangements he laid out

LAC, C111307

*Major-General Sheaffe. Pen and ink drawing. Artist and date unknown.*

seemed workable.[60] General Van Rensselaer set the time for the first wave to cross at 4:00 a.m. — about two hours before sunrise — and it reached the Canadian shore within fifteen minutes under cover of darkness. (W.H. Merritt, who was in the vicinity of Fort George, states the American embarkation began about 3:00 a.m.)[61]

Chrystie's boat lost an oarlock and began to be swept downstream. He ordered the pilot, who was "panic struck," to make for the Canadian shore but he was "groaning with fear" and the guide for this crossing, Hopkins, "was useless." Chrystie took the oar in hand and returned to the American shore. Other boats were swept downstream while crossing to Upper Canada or during the return trip. Several landed at Hamilton's Cove, at the northern end of the village, where their occupants suffered many killed and wounded. The survivors were taken prisoner.[62] The only regular officers that appear to have landed were captains and lieutenants of the Thirteenth U.S. Infantry. Colonel Van Rensselaer thus became the senior officer of the invaders on the Upper Canadian shore. An American officer, Captain Armstrong, wrote that Colonel Van Rensselaer and about one hundred men first reached the opposite shore and while the officers crept up the bank to reconnoitre, the men in the boat began to talk and that alerted the sentries above. As the Americans struggled to ascend the bank and form a line, they were met with heavy musket fire that inflicted heavy casualties and wounded many of the officers, including Colonel Van Rensselaer (and Captain Armstrong) who received no less than four wounds — and a least two more later. To avoid further casualties, Van Rensselaer ordered the men "to fall below the bank" where they were sheltered from artillery fire and less exposed to musketry.[63]

Artillery on both sides came into action early in this engagement. The British 18-pounder at the redan, a 9-pounder near the stone guardhouse in the village, and two guns at Vrooman's Point fired at the boats and the embarkation place while the American battery in Fort Gray, above Lewiston, aimed their shot at Queenston.[64]

Chrystie returned to the New York side. He "found there a scene of confusion hardly to be described." Under fire from British guns, wounded men and others returned and left the boats where they landed, while others would take a boat across to the Canadian side and leave it on the shore or let it go adrift. Some boats were carried as far as Fort George according to Ensign John Smith, who saw boats drift past "with six or 7 Corpes in them who had been destroyed by the shot from our batteries."[65] No one had direction of the boats and boatmen, with the result that reinforcements trickled across and only some of the wounded made it back. No wonder many boatmen and militia were deterred from crossing.

The first light of morning sun began to burn off the fog shortly after 6:00 a.m. A few boats continued to push off from Lewiston, where Chrystie was trying to create some kind of order. He then observed the American troops ascending "the east side of the hill of Queenston ... [and] finding no work nor even a sentinel on the hill, they marched to the north side half-way down, which was a one-gun battery open in the rear." They were above the redan and approaching it. Meanwhile, the 49th light company had been ordered down from the redan to add their firepower to that of the defenders below, but who gave that order is not clear. Eyewitness accounts suggest that this move was made before Brock arrived at the south end of the village.[66] Captains Wool and Ogilvie of the Thirteenth U.S. Infantry appear to have led the first ascent. Later, there would be a brief controversy over which officer had proposed to attempt the climb and was the principal leader, apparently the result of a newspaper report of a conversation that gave Ogilvie the credit. Several officers, including Chrystie and Ogilvie, made it clear that Wool deserved the major share of credit.[67]

Once the invaders had used this route, they rapidly moved reinforcements up, putting them into position to attack the redan from the rear. After a brief skirmish, the Americans gained control of the redan and, with greater safety from British gunfire, they were able to send more men to the summit of the escarpment.

Brock had gone to bed around midnight after writing the orders for the militia. There are different versions about how Brock, and others in Fort George and Niagara, became aware of the American

Painting by Peter Rindlisbacher

*The American attack at Hamilton's Cove, 1812. This painting shows the difficulties the invaders faced early in the battle of Queenston Heights, and why at this cove, at the north end of the village, the Americans suffered heavy casualties in killed, wounded, and captured.*

attack. Tupper, who was not present, states that Brock had risen before he heard the firing from Queenston but it seems unlikely that he would be up about 3 to 4:00 a.m., even if he was normally an early riser. Sheaffe later wrote that he awakened Brock and Macdonell. Merritt claimed that a mounted Dragoon arrived at Fort George at 4:00 a.m. with the news of the American attack. Major Thomas Evans states that he was aroused by cannonade soon after 2:00 a.m. It did not awaken Colonel William Claus in his home near Fort George. Instead, he was awakened "about 6 o'clock a.m." by J.B. Rousseaux, an interpreter, knocking on the door. Informed that the enemy were crossing at Queenston, Claus "immediately got up and on my way down to my front gate I met Major-General Sheaffe, who ordered me to the garrison at Fort George, from whence I dispatched every Indian I could collect and a number of militia."[68] Militia Captain James Crooks, in bed in his house, looked out at the cold, stormy weather and, instead of rising to give orders to his men, decided to stay in bed and "have another snooze." Almost immediately one of his men knocked on his window to tell him that the Americans had crossed at Queenston, "But strange to say no messenger had reached us, nor did we hear the report of any guns … so strong was the gale off the lake." Crooks arose and went about his duties.[69] Ensign Smith, who was at Fort George, believed, "It was nigh 7 o'clock before we knew of the Enemy Landing," but he may have been mistaken about the time.[70]

What seems most likely is that after the American invasion had begun, Brock was aroused by a messenger. He may then have heard the thunder of distant artillery, which informed him that a serious fight was taking place at Queenston. There are no reports of blazing beacons sending a message. Brock hurriedly dressed then mounted his horse, but still thinking that the great American threat was to Niagara, he ordered only limited forces to move while the remainder of the garrison was to stand ready to act in any direction when the enemy's intentions became known. Captain Holcroft, with two guns, and Norton, with a party of warriors, were to follow him.[71] The general hastened toward Queenston, followed soon after by his

ADCs, Captain Glegg and Lieutenant-Colonel Macdonell. As he spurred his horse on, Brock could hear the booming of cannon from batteries on both sides of the river and the crack of musket fire. He did not know if the battle ahead was the main attack or a feint to draw him away from Fort George. He had to go and see; rest and food were not important.

As he dashed onward, he met the young George Jarvis, a gentleman volunteer in the 49th Regiment, galloping furiously in the opposite direction. Jarvis quickly reined in his horse, wheeled it about, and rode after Brock to tell him the Americans had landed at Queenston. Captain Duncan Cameron had begun to lead his flank company of the 3rd York militia from Brown's Point toward the noise of battle when Brock galloped by, "Unaccompanied by his aide-de-camp or a single attendant. He waved his hand to us, desired us to follow with expedition, and proceeded with all speed to the mountain. Lieutenant-Colonel Macdonell and Captain Glegg passed immediately after...."[72] Lieutenant McLean recalled (many years later) that Brock stopped briefly at Vrooman's Point to ask, "Why don't you fire that Gun?" McLean replied that the

Author's photo

*Cannon fire, showing large amounts of smoke produced.*

carronade's balls fell short. The general simply answered, "It can't be helped," and put spurs to his horse and galloped away for Queenston.[73]

A story about this ride that later appeared in secondary accounts had Brock stopping to receive a cup of coffee from the hands of his financée, Sophia Shaw.[74] She was supposedly visiting her sister, the wife of John Powell, at her home on the River Road. He stayed in his saddle while hurriedly drinking the cup and with a wave he rode off to war. Susan was the daughter of militia Major-General Aeneas Shaw, adjutant general of the militia and a prominent politician. There is no documentary evidence of this relationship, no mention at all in any surviving correspondence to, from, or about Brock, and even evidence to discredit the story of his engagement.[75]

Whether refreshed or not, the commander rode into the village probably between 6:30 and 7:00 a.m. No man present stated that he went to the redan or ordered down its guard. Crooks, years afterwards, claimed that Brock was at the redan when the Americans began firing at it from above, but the militiaman was not present then.[76] (Crooks arrived later for the battle on the Heights.) Brock may have hurried to the south end of the village and uphill to survey the attacking and defending forces.[77] American forces continued to cross the river while shot crashed into the houses and orchards behind Brock. The Americans appeared to be stymied at their initial landing site. Unknown to all the defenders, the enemy were already above the redan and Brock's survey of the situation was rudely interrupted by their charging down upon the rear of the battery. The artillerymen fled, perhaps first spiking the gun to make it inoperable.[78] (Spiking meant driving a nail into the gun's touch-hole so that a powder charge could not be ignited.)

It was now clear that the principal attack was underway against Queenston, although Brock could not be sure that no other attacks were occurring. Acting on what he did know, he dispatched orders to Sheaffe at Fort George to send the companies of the 41st and of militia, which were prepared to move and to turn all the fort's guns on the American batteries opposite. Brock hurried to the north end of Queenston, where he collected the light company of the 49th and perhaps some of the grenadier company. According to fifteen-year-old George Jarvis, who was present, Brock on horseback led his men southward, telling them just before they reached the foot of the Heights, "Take breath boys — you will need it in a few moments."[79]

The crest of the Heights was thickly wooded. Lower down there were more open spaces and at the base were rail-fences and a few low stone walls. The Americans had excellent cover on the hillside and reinforcements were continuing to arrive. Most of the 49th grenadier company and some militia remained in the village to keep the Americans by the riverside in check. One participant mentions that Captain Williams remained at the redan.[80] If so, and if Captain Dennis was occupied commanding the grenadiers, that may explain why Brock, instead of one of his captains, led the charge. (In a letter of September 18 to his brother Savery, Brock had mentioned that the 49th was "bare of experienced officers.") After exchanging a few shots, the Americans fell back, perhaps a retreat or a move to draw the British on. In any case, after dismounting, Brock led his men uphill toward the battery, waving his sword. His tall figure in an officer's uniform and wearing a "Round" hat[81] made him an obvious target. An eyewitness described the general's last moments,

> [P]lacing himself at the head of the light company of the 49th, he led the way up the mountain at double quick time in the very teeth of a sharp fire from the enemy's riflemen, and ere long he was singled out by one of them, who, coming forward, took deliberate aim and fired; several of the men noticed the action and fired — but too late — our gallant General fell on his left side, within a few feet of where I stood. Running up to him I enquired, "Are you much hurt, Sir?" He placed his hand on his breast and made no reply, and slowly sunk down. The 49th now raised a shout, "Revenge the General!"

SURGITE

*Brock on horseback. An artist's dramatic depiction.*

Courtesy of Special Collections, James A. Gibson Library, Brock University

It is not known when Jarvis wrote his narrative but the exactness of some details, such as Brock falling on his left side after being shot, suggest that his recollections were clear.[82]

There are other versions of Brock's last moments that have him delivering encouragement. Lieutenant Archibald McLean of the 3rd York militia wrote, "Immediately before he received his death-wound, he cried out to some person near him to push on the York Volunteers, which were the last words he uttered." He had not been shot when he spoke those words. Whereas Major Glegg reported that after being hit, Brock "uttered in a feeble voice: 'My fall must not be noticed or impede my brave companions from advancing to victory.'"[83] Lieutenant George Ridout of the 3rd York militia wrote on October 14th that after he was shot, Brock exclaimed, "Push on the Brave York Volunteers."[84] Merritt wrote that Brock's "last words were, 'Push On, my brave fellows.'"[85] These four men were nearby but not on the hillside with Brock when he was killed. Charles Askin wrote his father that Brock received his wound early in the day and "I believe never spoke a word after." Askin, writing the day after the battle, was not present at it but was nearby and may have heard from participants.[86] (When the attack began he was lying ill in the Hamilton house, owned by George Hamilton, son of the late Robert, but Askin moved out as the fighting progressed. The house was damaged during this battle.) The general's last words, according to Ensign Smith, were, "Never mind me my Boys push on."[87] However, Smith was even farther distant at Fort George and wrote his letter five days afterward, so there is no doubt he was relying on what he was told. What became important was what people read in the newspapers and what they wanted to believe would have been a hero's last words.

Other participants in the battle were not with Brock's troop but were close by. Lieutenant John Beverley Robinson wrote that after Brock was hit by "a ball in his breast.... Several of the 49th assembled around him. One poor fellow was severely wounded by a cannon ball and fell across the General."[88] Robinson's company from the 3rd York militia was approaching Queenston and saw evidence showing how fierce the fighting was. As they advanced they "met troops of Americans on their way to Fort George under guard, and the road was lined with miserable wretches, suffering under wounds of all descriptions and crawling to our houses for protection and comfort." Despite their shock at seeing such human misery, they "hurried to the mountain," believing that the battle was almost ended. It had only begun.

Robinson's corps sheltered behind Hamilton's stone house at the north end of the village. In a few minutes they "were directed to advance on the mountain.... We scrambled to the top at the right

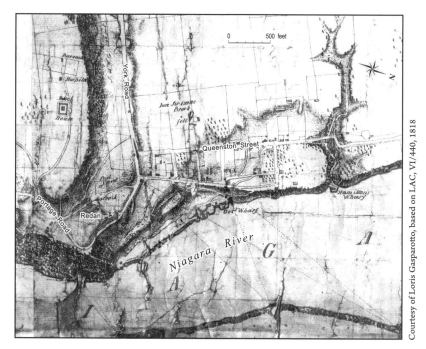

*Queenston — the spot where Brock fell.*

Courtesy of Loris Gasparotto, based on LAC, VI/440, 1818

of the battery which they [Americans] had gained.... There we stood and gathered the men as they advanced and formed them in a line." They had to act quickly because they were under incessant fire of muskets and artillery. Only about fifty men had collected, some thirty from the York militia and the remainder from the 49th Light Company. "Lieutenant-Colonel Macdonell was there, mounted and animating the men to charge. He was seconded with great spirit and valor by Captain Williams ... But the attempt was unsuccessful." It was, in fact, a rout. Macdonell's horse was shot and, as it turned, Macdonnell was also hit and fell; Williams was wounded in the head ("Partially scalped by a rifle ball," according to Evans) and Lieutenant McLean in the thigh. Several men were taken prisoner, including volunteer Jarvis. Captain Cameron managed to carry off the badly wounded Macdonell and Williams recovered in time to join the retreat. "Our forces rallied about a mile below."[89] The Americans suffered few casualties in these clashes.

Brock's "lifeless corpse was immediately conveyed to a house at Queenston" and left there until the battle ended when it could be removed to Fort George. Macdonell, according to Glegg, was carried to the rear for medical assistance while Colonel Clark wrote that both "bodies ... were at once removed to a dwelling nearby."[90] Major Glegg believed that the Americans had not discovered Brock's corpse during their brief control of the village but it is possible that some of them did see it without recognizing who it was. (Guy St-Denis has undertaken a thorough search for the house in Queenston where Brock's body lay and concludes that it was a stone house standing on the lot now numbered 20 Queenston Street.)[91] Macdonell was taken to Government House where, Glegg wrote, "He received every aid and attention. I never quit his bed for more than a few minutes." But he had to end his letter of October 14 with obvious sadness: "Half-past one o'clock. My poor friend Macdonnell has just expired."[92] Preparations were soon underway for the funeral of two heroes.

Macdonell was a young lawyer from a prominent family in Glengarry County who was moving ahead rapidly in his legal career. When the province's attorney general departed for England, Gore appointed the twenty-six-year-old to the post. He had the support of the very influential Chief Justice William Dummer Powell, the most prominent legal and political leader in Upper Canada, who was pleased at this appointment of the first "native-trained barrister" to such a high position.[93] In April 1812, Brock named Macdonell as one of his provincial aides-de-camp and a lieutenant-colonel in the Glengarry militia. Brock's choice, although possibly influenced by Powell, was not made at random. Macdonell had influence in the eastern part of the province (an area Brock did not know well), he was an elected member of the assembly, and a Roman Catholic.[94] Macdonell's appointment was confirmed the following year and in requesting it Brock praised Macdonell's services, "Both in his Civil and Military Capacity," going on to state, "His Conduct since the Commencement of the War, particularly at a time when the Invasion of the Province by the Enemy, seemed to have intimidated a large portion of the population, was beyond all praise." He died gallantly, but his biographers suggest that his charge was "foolhardy."[95]

The Death of Brock at Queenston Heights, *watercolour on paper, by C.W. Jeffreys. Artistic licence was used here, since the uniform is that of a major-general but Brock wore the uniform of brigadier-general in this battle.*

## CHAPTER NINE

# Sheaffe's Day

With Brock's death, Major-General Roger Sheaffe immediately succeeded as commander, but he did not mention in his report at what time he learned of the news or when he started for Queenston. General Sheaffe would lead his troops in the defeat of the American forces on Queenston Heights and would take the surrender from their commanding general, William Wadsworth. His leadership would be methodical and careful. His victory would be made possible by the abilities and mistakes of others. Let us turn to those.

At Fort George, about 8:00 a.m., Claus received Brock's orders from Glegg "not to cease firing until every stone was down in the American garrison."[1] In other words, the guns of the fort and nearby batteries were to be turned on Fort Niagara. In spite of having "not sufficient men left in this Garrison to work the Guns," they did a lot of damage. According to Ensign Smith, "We played on the Opposite Garrison to the best of our Judgment having no Artillery Officers to Direct us," with the result that, "We drove them from their Fort by our Shott & Battered it completely."[2] Evans agreed that they crippled the Americans guns "but not before he had burnt to the ground many buildings." The town of Niagara would indeed suffer cruelly from "a very well directed Fire of Red hot Shott from a 6, 12 & 18 Pounders," which burned the courthouse, jail, and "a Dwelling House & Tan yard belonging to Mr. Greer very early in the day."

These critical events would occur after Sheaffe had departed, leaving Major Evans in command at Fort George. What he then saw around him was "awfully discouraging" as "the gaol and court house were suddenly wrapped in flames," but, luckily, a group of militiamen arrived and he put them to work with water-buckets borrowed from townspeople. Smith describes how a shot "entered our Regimental Store & very luckily it lodged between 2 Bales of Grey greatcoats … otherwise I think all Navy Hall would have burned to the ground." He also mentions defensive action at the other end of the line when the detachment at Fort Erie "blew up the Enemies Magazine & part of their Barrack at Black Rock," which would certainly distract American forces there. [3]

Later in the day, after most of the militia and regulars had been sent off to Queenston, an even greater danger threatened Fort George. Just as Evans was heading toward the battle, the American guns opened up with hot shot on the fort and town. He decided he had "no alternative but to gallop back and ascertain the enemy's power for further mischief. Well it was I did so, for on reaching the gate of Fort George, I met a crowd of the militia with consternation in their countenances, exclaiming the magazine was on fire." This building of heavy stone construction with a wooden roof contained 800 barrels of gunpowder that, if ignited, would have levelled the fort and caused serious damage to the town. There was no time to waste. Whether ordered by Evans or not, Captain Vigoreux of the Engineers and a small group of volunteers got on to the roof, ripped off the tin to expose at the burning wood beneath, and extinguished the flames.[4]

Outside Fort George, Norton reported that on his way to his warriors' camp, Evans rode up, told him the Americans were in possession of Queenston, and urged him to "hasten there." Norton "ran immediately to the Camp, & delayed no longer than was necessary to see the whole completely equipped with ammunition." His warriors' "shouts re-echoed from one to another [as] all ran towards Queenstown." About 160 Grand River men led by Norton, William Kerr, and John Brant (son of Joseph Brant) hurried away while regulars and militia marched along the river road. General Sheaffe rode past. Within less than three miles to Queenston, they heard that Brock had been killed and the enemy was advancing through the woods against their right flank. Although he thought the rumour to be false, Norton led his men off the road to the right where they divided into five or six columns. They met a few militiamen fleeing from Queenstown because, they said, 6,000 Americans had gained possession of the Heights. This news increased the determination of some warriors to push on, but many began to depart out of concern for the safety of their families back at Niagara. Norton estimated he had only eighty warriors left when they emerged from the woods and saw the enemy on the Heights. Determined to attack the invaders, he addressed his men, urging them to "ascend yon Path, by which unperceived, we may gain their rear; your Bullets shall soon spread Havock and dismay among those Ranks...." That was exactly what happened after they reached the Heights and began a series of skirmishes that, lasting several hours, would stalemate the American force.[5]

The Americans who had originally landed below Queenston displayed bravery, determination, and resourcefulness. Michael Smith expressed a degree of admiration for his countrymen when he wrote that in the face of brisk musket and cannon fire "the brave Americans effected a landing, drove the British back & took possession of their batteries & cannon, which however were spiked."[6] The invaders gained control of both the Heights and the village, which a few took as an opportunity to slip into it to indulge in looting. Conditions were safer for reinforcements to come across, including Captain James Gibson of the Light Artillery, who brought over a 6-pounder gun, which his men hauled to the top of the escarpment. Joseph Lovett, observing from Lewiston, saw a pause in the fighting "about ten o'clock, the enemy's fire ... was silenced. Victory seemed complete." Colonel Van Rensselaer "bleeding at six holes" still exercised command. General Van Rensselaer crossed to Queenston and "had a bite of bread and cheese in John Bull's barracks (for he had eaten no breakfast)," but instead of taking control of the battle, he returned to the opposite shore to secure more reinforcements.[7]

Colonel Van Rensselaer, bleeding profusely from his wounds, was taken back to Lewiston. Lieutenant-Colonel Chrystie crossed back and, finding a few of his troops had slipped into Queenston to indulge in looting, he issued orders "checking the disorders, to which some of the troops seemed inclined, and arranging the fragments of the different detachments of regulars in their proper order." He found the gun in the redan spiked "by one of our own artillerists," but does not mention if they were able to remove the spike.[8] Brigadier-General Wadsworth, of the New York militia, arrived and took command. They agreed that Chrystie should return to the New York shore both to meet General Van Rensselaer and to encourage more militia to cross. What he and other officers soon discovered was that New York militiamen, while waiting for hours to embark, had begun to conclude that their duty was to defend the state not to invade a foreign country. This decision did not mean these men were cowards, for many had shown great courage in the initial crossing and fighting. It was late in the morning (about 11:00 a.m.) and "at least half the boats we had in the morning were lost or damaged; not half the troops had crossed," wrote Chrystie. The men around him could see the lack of clear leadership at the departure site, the confusion about embarking, and the spirited resistance being encountered on the other side.[9] Lovett was beside himself when wrote about the refusal of troops to embark: "[General Van Rensselaer] mounted a borrowed horse and I rode with him, everywhere urging on the troops.... But the name of Indian, or the sight of the wounded, or the devil, or *something else* petrified them. Not a regiment, not a company, scarcely a man would go."[10] It is hard to criticize a man who, standing on that riverbank, calculated that his chances of surviving death or injury if he crossed were not good.

At Fort George, the militia who had been ordered there earlier in the day stacked their arms and stood waiting for orders. These soon came from Queenston. Faced with a request for a reinforcement of 130 militia, James Crooks wanted to lead them but had to dissuade his older brother from taking on the responsibility. He could only gather about one-third the manpower of five companies (one-third had left that morning to guard the lakeshore and those of the day before had not yet returned), consisting of his own company of the 1st Lincoln and "Captain McEwan of 1st Regiment of Lincoln, Captain Abraham Miles, under Lieutenant Butler from Grimsby, Captain Selby from Young Street [*sic*] under Lieutenant Vanderburgh and Captain Burns from Newcastle District." When they reached McFarland's house, about a mile from Fort George, they learned that Brock had been killed. "This I endeavoured to keep from the men, fearing it might damp their spirits, but soon found they all knew it, although it seemed to make no impression on them."[11]

As he proceeded toward the village, Crooks was warned by officers at Brown's Point that if he continued on his way his men would all be taken prisoners, because the Americans had routed the defenders and some 400 of the enemy were marching on their flank through the woods toward Niagara. Crooks was rightly skeptical of this information and, in any case, he had been "ordered to go to Queenston and would do so if I could, ordering my men at the same time to load with ball cartridge." If he did meet an enemy force he intended to be prepared. His next stop was at Durham's, two and a half miles north of Queenston, where he "found the house filled with wounded men, both of our own and of the enemy, and ... my worthy friend the gallant Lieut.-Colonel McDonell ... lying mortally wounded." Again they awaited orders. Then his men began to complain of hunger, for they had not had breakfast before their departure. He ordered them to dig up potatoes growing nearby and boil them. "This was soon done and every pot and kettle in the house was soon walloping on the fire in the kitchen," but before the men had a chance to enjoy a hot meal, General Sheaffe arrived. He brought the remainder of the 41st and Captain Holcroft with artillerymen and a 6-pounder. One militia officer put his time of arrival there at just after 10:00 a.m.[12] Although Sheaffe was not given to hasty action, he wasted little time gathering his forces, which numbered close to 700 from Fort George and an unknown number from Queenston.[13] He began his march probably before noon because just over two hours later, after waiting for reinforcements from Chippawa, he began the attack on the American line. From the Heights, American Lieutenant-Colonel Chrystie saw Sheaffe's advance at about eleven o'clock.[14]

Whatever the timing, those potatoes were taking a long time to cook. Crooks wrote that the men were ordered to fall in "and the poor hungry fellows were obliged to leave their potatoes behind them."[15] Considering that these were not professional soldiers but militiamen with little or no experience of battle, they showed impressive discipline and determination when it came to preparing for battle.

From Durham's they marched inland toward St. David's. About two miles west of Queenston they followed "an old road ascending the mountain," as the writer refers to the escarpment.[16] At the top they formed in a ploughed field and marched to occupy a position on the road leading from Queenston to Chippawa. Before reaching the Heights, Crooks was ordered to detach twenty-five men to help cover Captain Holcroft who had come from Fort George with two 6-pounders and a howitzer. Supported by the light company of the 41st Regiment, he moved his guns into the village. Despite cannon fire from Fort Gray and from two 6-pounders on the opposite bank, as well as from a gun on Queenston Heights, Holcroft, in Crooks's words, "with the shelter of an old milk house on the bank of the river … maintained his ground and prevented any boat from crossing till the action ceased." Norton's men on the Heights heard Holcroft firing shrapnel (probably case or canister shot) shells that annoyed "the Enemy with the greatest Skill and Gallantry." Indeed, this artillery fire encouraged his warriors "to push with more forwardness than our small number should otherwise have authorized," but, owing to their nimbleness and the shelter of the trees, they avoided casualties. With Grand River warriors attacking their rear, the Americans were unable to launch a strike against Holcroft and the 41st light company.[17] Norton met a mounted militia officer and "entreated him to go with speed to meet the Troops & Militia from Chippawa, to hurry them to our support, and to tell them that we would amuse the Enemy in the meantime." That mounted officer may have been a dragoon sent by Sheaffe to order up reinforcements from Chippawa.

Meanwhile, Chrystie returned to Queenston accompanied by Lieutenant-Colonel Winfield Scott, who had apparently crossed without orders. Chrystie, Scott, and others "ascended the hill, seeing the regulars engaged three or four hundred yards from the river, near a wood, I hastened to that point, and urging my way directly to the front found there Lieut.-Colonel Scott, with a gallantry I cannot too much extol, leading and animating the troops." He had checked his troops' disorder and stopped a charge by Norton's warriors. It was probably in this skirmish that Norton's force lost two chiefs and a warrior, with many others being wounded. By now, with Wadsworth's agreement, Scott had taken command on the Heights and he realized that his men's musketry was doing little damage to their enemies, who took every advantage of being among the trees. He moved his men back across a cleared field to the shelter of a fence leaving a few regulars and volunteer riflemen in "a bush cantonment on our right.... These served to keep the Indians in check, though they still maintained a galling fire on the right flank." To reach the enemy, Norton's warriors would have to charge across an open space and while skirmishing continued some of his men fell back further into the woods. The Iroquois "now awaited with impatience the arrival of the Troops to fill the Space on our right, that we might then push the Enemy to the precipice, without being enveloped." Around this time, the Americans saw, "the first detachments of the British army" from Fort George approaching in the distance and they realized their "numbers instead of increasing were diminishing."[18] There should be no wonder at that with renewed artillery fire against the departure site and boats on the river and on the Heights, native warriors uttering their war cries.

Crooks and his men waited above the village for reinforcements of the 41st and militia that had been ordered from Chippawa. The 18-pounder at Fort Gray fired at them but the men lay down and the shot flew over them. Nevertheless, these inexperienced troops had time to worry about their fate under that gunfire and in view of American troops behind a "worm fence ... bayonets glistening in the sun." They were impressed "to see Norton, young Brant and Kerr, with about fifty Indians, driving in the outposts of the enemy on the edge of the Heights above us. They being reinforced, obliged the Indians to retire. This happened several times...."[19]

Norton "concentrated [his] men in a ravine and desisted from assaulting the enemy until the troops could form on [their] right, at the same time sending notice to Sir R.H. Sheaffe of [their] position."[20] The general inquired about the strength of the enemy as well as Norton's situation. Norton replied that his men were ready to attack the enemy's left flank as part of a general assault. Sheaffe had had time to ascend the Heights without any interference from the Americans because the Iroquois provided a screen, as Benn notes, equivalent to "effective light troops in battle. They had knocked out Scott's light infantry, thereby eliminating the American line's protective screen...." The Americans could not move inland to consolidate their hold nor prevent reinforcements from Chippawa arriving unhindered to combine with Sheaffe's troops. Benn also points out that the Six Nations warriors "had pushed Scott into what would become a perilous topographical position once Sheaffe advanced.... And finally, the Grand River men had upset the American line's equilibrium and weakened the invaders' capacity to take on the unharassed British line."[21]

Sheaffe formed his regulars and militia facing the Americans and awaited the arrival of reinforcements from Chippawa. Captain Richard Bullock brought about 140 men of the 41st Regiment and some hundred men of the 2nd Lincoln militia. Sheaffe then sent one hundred light infantrymen along with Runchey's Coloured Corps to act on his left. Closer to the edge of the Heights were the Iroquois, who were now increased by "a number of Caygwa Warriors" and also joined by volunteers Ralfe Clench and Joseph Willcocks.[22] With his army numbering about 900 strong, Sheaffe was ready to begin the attack.

When they saw Sheaffe's main force begin their advance, Norton's warriors "rushed forward, the Enemy fired, we closed & they ran." What Crooks saw was the light company of the 49th

> leading till fairly in front of the Yankees, when an
> order came for the Regular troops to front and attack,

but no orders for the Militia to do so ... [however] as they were marching in file, the distance was constantly increasing between the Militia and Regulars, seeing a Company in front fall into confusion upon hearing the booming of two 3 pounders we had with us under Lieut. John C. Ball of the Provincial Artillery ... I no longer hesitated to face to the front, and at double quick we soon encountered the enemy.

He mentions his men finding a 6-pounder abandoned by the Americans, which Colonel Clark put back into action against the foe. William Woodruff, of the 1st Lincoln flank company, could not hear orders because of the noise made by musket fire, "but as others moved we all followed." They came across the abandoned American gun, but they could not see much of the battle because of the smoke blowing "in our faces." Crooks gives a lively description of his experience of battle:

The battle, although not of long continuance, was a very warm and close one. I have been in many hail storms, but never in one when the stones flew so thick as the bullets on this occasion. The lines were very near each other, and every foot of the ground the enemy gave way gave us an advantage, as on their side it descended. After about half an hour's close engagement they disappeared in smoke, throwing down their arms, and ran down the Heights to the water's edge in the vain hope of reaching their own side, but Holcroft took good care that no boat could cross.[23]

For the Grand River warriors, as soon as that began they "rushed upon them and broke the flank, pursuing them with considerable slaughter till we raised the shout in the rear of the centre, which ... [threw] the whole into confusion ... [and] in less than half an hour, we had them down the precipice to the river."

Smith's colourful account — based upon what he had heard from others — gives great credit to Holcroft using his guns "to meet the Enemy coming down from the hill & to prevent their getting to their Boats which he executed in a Masterly Stile and great was the Distruction he made amongst them while retreating down the hill before the Infantry & while they were striving to get to their Boats or over the River."[24]

According to Chrystie, shortly after two o'clock "the British troops paraded in front of us, we being forced on the edge of the hill — the village in our rear, the river on our left and a bush cantonment on our right." He believed the British force numbered from 400 to 500 regulars with four guns, 500 to 600 militia, and 300 native warriors. "Our whole force," he wrote, "was less than three hundred, with but one piece of artillery and not a dozen rounds for it," yet they had no intention of surrendering.[25] At this time a note from General Van Rensselaer arrived for General Wadsworth "informing him that not a regiment or company would move to reinforce us." Van Rensselaer implied that the situation facing Wadsworth was hopeless but if he decided to retreat, Van Rensselaer would try to provide boats for the purpose. (That was an unlikely possibility as probably most of the officers realized.) After considerable consultation among the senior officers, and seeing the careful manoeuvres of the enemy, they decided to attempt a retreat. That required they change their position, and so they tried "to throw our right on the road leading from the hill to the village, and form with the river in our rear. To do this it was necessary to march by the left, which brought the militia in front of the column. They soon broke on the commencement of the enemy's fire and a perfect rout ensued."[26] Unable to get back across the river, the Americans faced the choice of death, wounds, or surrender.

Sheaffe began the attack sometime after 2:00 p.m. and reported that it ended about 3:00 p.m.; other first-hand accounts place it later, from 3:15 to 5:00 p.m.[27] The battle was short, bloody, and decisive. Robinson described the American retreat as a horrible spectacle of men in panic "driven by a furious and avenging enemy, from whom they had little mercy to expect, to the brink of the mountain which over-hangs the river." Many fell into the river while others "leaped down the side of the mountain ... and were dashed in pieces by the fall." McLean saw "some attempting to swim across the river, who were drowned or killed by our shot. A white flag was immediately hoisted by the Americans, and they surrendered prisoners of war." Some men — the "inconsiderate" in Norton's words — "continued to fire at them, until checked by repeated commands of 'Stop fire.'" Robinson saw two American officers "coming up the hill with a white flag, and with some difficulty the slaughter was suspended."[28] Captain Holcroft witnessed an officer hold up "his pocket handkerchief. We received him just in time to save him from the Indians." He was Colonel Winfield Scott.[29]

There may have been confusion in the British ranks as they manoeuvred before the final battle (according to Ensign Smith) as well as during the battle when the field was obscured by smoke (Crooks).[30] While Sheaffe demonstrated shortcomings as a battlefield general — this could also be said of the American commanders — he had accomplished what was needed to defeat enemy invaders holding a strong position. He had brought together a powerful force of many different units, well-officered and strongly motivated. He was not a battle-experienced veteran. The last time he had commanded men in combat was in October 1799 when he had led four companies of the 49th Regiment in the coastal dunes of Holland (See Chapter One). Thirteen years later, for his first time leading a large brigade in combat, he gained a clear victory.[31] He had reached the height of his career and received a well-deserved baronetcy from the British government.[32]

After the shooting stopped, the American officers asked Sheaffe for a cessation of hostilities. Crooks led his men down the hill where he met General Sheaffe, who ordered him to assist Captain Derenzy to escort the prisoners to Fort George. While this was being organized, the "American Militia General" William Wadsworth was brought in. In the traditional manner of one commander surrendering to another, he drew his sword and presented its handle to Sheaffe, who said, "I understand, General, your people have surrendered." Wadsworth's wordless reply was to nod his head.[33] He did not surrender a territory or an undefeated army, as had Hull, but American losses were large. The defenders estimated over 900 prisoners, including sixty officers, were taken. They were not far off, for Evans's official report put the number at 436 regulars and 489 militia, a total of 925. He estimated the total American force at 1,600 with killed and wounded (many of whom were taken back to the U.S. side) at 500. General Van Rensselaer reported to Dearborn that he could not give a precise account of casualties and his estimates were sixty killed, 170 wounded, and 764 taken prisoner.[34] The defenders also captured "One six-pounder with tumbrel and harness complete," the colours of a New York militia unit, an ammunition wagon, and officially 380 bayonets and 435 muskets, although perhaps many hundreds more were collected privately.[35]

American accounts agree that the prisoners were well treated. Chrystie reported, "We were taken to the village of Queenston and treated with the greatest delicacy and humanity by General Sheaffe. The wounded were attended to here, the prisoners ... were collected and marched to Newark, and after about an hour ... we marched with a guard, which was necessary to protect us from the Indians, to Fort George. We arrived there just at dark." While noting they were treated "with tenderness and respect," Captain Ogilvie complained that their captors "imposed no restraint upon their Indian allies from stripping and scalping the dying and slain that remained on the field of battle."[36] Major Mullany was so frightened that rather than surrender with the rest "he hid himself in the rocks for a day," until he and six privates were found by a search party of British and American officers "and a strong guard to prevent the Indians from scalping those that were scattered." While John Norton reported that the Americans "had not reason to complain of cruelty this day," there seem to have been some warriors who got out of control.[37]

The defenders' losses were much lighter: fourteen killed, fifteen wounded who later died, and perhaps another fifty-four wounded, as well as five Iroquois killed and nine wounded.[38] But as Norton put it, "The grief caused by the Loss of General Brock threw a gloom over the sensations which this brilliant Success might have raised." This sentiment was widespread.[39]

That same day, Sheaffe reported to Prevost the results of the battle. He was very thorough in praising the men for their service, mentioning not only the regular and militia officers but also three volunteers with the 49th and Norton's warriors. He singled out the contributions of Holcroft and Norton with his warriors for keeping the invaders occupied while Sheaffe moved his troops into position and joined up with reinforcements from Chippawa. While pointing out that losses were small, they included Brock "one of the most gallant and zealous officers in His Majesty's Service whose loss cannot be too much deplored, and Lieutenant-Colonel McDonnell ... whose gallantry and merit rendered him worthy of his Chief." Sheaffe was thorough, for in a later report to Prevost he apologized for not giving credit to Captain Chisholm, who commanded a flank company of York militia, and Lieutenant Ball, commanding a militia artillery corps.[40]

Sheaffe and General Van Rensselaer were also busy corresponding with each other. Sheaffe may have proposed a cessation of fighting of some sort, which Van Rensselaer took to mean a ceasefire for three days. Sheaffe claimed that was not his intention, but he accepted Van Rensselaer's agreement for that short-term armistice. Van Rensselaer also asked permission to send "some surgeons to attend the [wounded] officers and men." Sheaffe's reply proposed that wounded prisoners able to be moved "should be sent over to you, on condition of not serving again, until regularly exchanged."[41] Sheaffe's action was reasonable for it gave time to attend to casualties and the exchange of prisoners. He also needed a pause to learn about his new responsibilities and to take stock of the military situation. Suddenly, he was elevated to Brock's roles as commander of the forces and civil administrator. The transfer of command from a well-known, much-admired, and even beloved commander to an untried, much less experienced one could not have been easy. His inability to replace the energetic and dynamic Brock was soon evident.

On October 16, Sheaffe wrote to Van Rensselaer proposing a prolongation of the ceasefire until 4:00 p.m. on the 19th. He believed more time was needed to exchange prisoners and to send wounded

Americans across the river. American militia were sent home on parole, which aroused some resentment among the defenders. For example, a report in the *Upper Canada Gazette* of October 24 complained that the Americans did not deserve paroles because, while in possession of Queenston, "they plundered the houses of everything they could conveniently carry away." It was alleged they were promised houses and farms, "A specimen of what we have to expect should we allow them to get possession here."[42] The regulars were sent to Montreal and, eventually, to Boston.[43]

The report added, "Part of this day is to be devoted to paying the last offices of humanity to the remains of my departed friend and General," meaning Brock's funeral. Van Rensselaer agreed to extend the armistice and added that he would order a salute for Brock's funeral. This exchange, written in most courteous language, concluded with Sheaffe's expressing regret "that Colonel Van Rensselaer is badly wounded," and wishing for the return of peace between their two countries.[44] Again, it may have been reasonable to add only three more days of truce to finish dealing with the consequences of a major battle. However, Sheaffe agreed to a request from Van Rensselaer's successor, General Alexander Smyth, to extend the ceasefire into November. This longer armistice he thought necessary "both as corresponding with the system of forbearance ... and as permitting my coming to this place [York] to revive the supreme civil authority, the prolonged extension of which might have proved highly detrimental to the public service."[45] He came to York to meet the executive council and take the oaths of office "as President to administer the Civil Government of this Province."

Agreeing to a prolonged ceasefire suggested to some that Sheaffe was reluctant to fight the Americans. He opened himself to serious criticism. It came from local officers, but more important, Governor Prevost disagreed with Sheaffe's actions of paroling the American militiamen and extending the armistice without seeking the governor's approval.[46] He even suggested that Sheaffe could have vigorously pursued the Americans and, perhaps, have captured Fort Niagara. To some extent Prevost contradicted his opinion and the orders for the defence of the Canadas, which were to stay on the defensive. On October 19, Prevost wrote to Brock, unaware that had been killed, and cautioned, "In the present state of the war, I still would have you refrain from unnecessary hostility, calculated to weaken our force, to widen the breach existing between the two countries, and unproductive of real advantage."[47] Although Sheaffe continued to strengthen defences along the Niagara frontier and the adjacent shores of Lakes Erie and Ontario, and General Smyth's two invasion attempts (November 28 and December 1) were repulsed, the major-general did his reputation no good when he suggested that if Fort Erie came under attack by an overwhelming American force, its commander should consider retreat. The commander, Lieutenant-Colonel Cecil Bisshop, and his officers responded with outrage.[48]

In the days after the Battle of Queenston Heights, these problems lay in the future. Sheaffe was occupied with many tasks, including arrangements for Brock's funeral. Brock and Macdonell lay in state in Government House for public viewing while Glegg's "choice of a cavalier bastion in Fort George" was made ready for the interment of the general and his aide-de-camp. Only four days earlier, Brock had supervised the improvements made to that bastion (and named it the York Bastion) and the mounting on it of a 24-pounder gun taken from Detroit. "Little did poor General Brock think," wrote Ensign Smith, "it was to be his place of Burial on the 16th."[49]

According to Major Glegg, aide-de-camp and long-time friend, Brock had an aversion to ostentatious display, but "this last tribute of affection [should be performed] in a manner corresponding with the elevated virtues of my departed patron." In other words, the funeral would be a military ceremony honouring the military commander of the province who also had been its civil head and who had died heroically. A District General Order specified,

> The officers will wear crape on their left arms and on their sword knots, and all officers will, throughout the province, wear crape on their left arm for the space of one month.

Captain Holcroft will be pleased to direct that minute guns be fired from the period of the bodies leaving government house until their arrival at the place of interment; and also, after the funeral service shall have been performed, three rounds of seven guns from the artillery.[50]

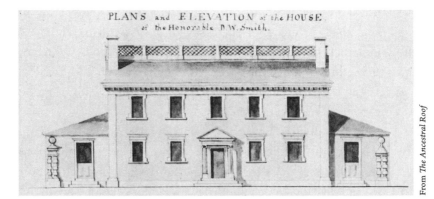

Government House. Residence in Niagara of the Honorable D.W. Smith, surveyor-general of Upper Canada. The house faced King Street and was located near the site of the present courthouse. After Smith moved to York, the capital, the provincial government bought the house for official use. It was destroyed when the town was burned in 1813.

The procession from Government House to Fort George began at 10:00 a.m. on October 16 and Lieutenant Ridout did not exaggerate when he wrote, "The burial was the grandest and most solemn I ever witnessed or that has been seen in Upper Canada." Between a cordon of regulars, militia (Crooks estimated there were about 5,000 men), and Iroquois, first Macdonell's casket and then Brock's were carried on ammunition wagons to the fort. They were preceded by sixty men of the 41st Regiment, sixty of the militia, two 6-pounders firing minute guns, the band of the 41st, drums muffled in black cloth, and Brock's horse "fully caparisoned, led by four grooms." The Reverend Robert Addison read the funeral service.[51] Guns fired a salute as the caskets were interred. General Van

Rensselaer showed his respect for Brock by ordering a salute to be fired at Lewiston and at Fort Niagara and this was done at sunset.[52] It was an amazing and generous tribute from the enemy.

Upon Brock's coffin was fastened "a small oval Silver Plate" with the inscription:

> Here lie the Earthly Remains of a Brave and Virtuous Hero, MAJOR-GENERAL BROCK, Commanding the British Forces, and President, Administering the Civil Government of Upper Canada, who fell when gloriously engaging the Enemies of his Country at the head of the Flank Companies of the 49th Regiment, in the town of Queenston, on the Morning of the 13th October, 1812. Aged 42 years.[53]

In a letter to William Brock, Major Glegg mentioned commissioning the silver plate and asked for "a neat white marble slab" to be sent to be placed on the bastion in Fort George. The white marble slab never appeared (and probably was never sent) and it is odd that Glegg seemed to have disregarded the fact that Brock had achieved his forty-third birthday on October 6th.

How ironic and tragic that ten days earlier, on October 6th, the *London Gazette Extraordinary* proclaimed the news of Brock's victory at Detroit and as the word spread in the city guns were fired and bells were rung. On the 10th, the Prince Regent appointed Brock "an extra knight of the most honorable Order of the Bath."[54] He was never to know of the honour bestowed on him nor what other benefits would flow from his success. In 1814, the government would award a gold medal to officers who had participated in this campaign (as well as two others) and one was designated for Brock.[55] During the 1840s a General Service Medal would be distributed to veterans — militia, regulars, and native warriors — of the capture of Detroit.

Early in November, another great tribute honoured Brock's memory. At the Council House at Fort George, members of the Six Nations — Hurons, Chippawas, and Potawatamies — held "a

General Council of Condolence." Koseaneyonti, "Little Cayouga Chief Speaker," spoke about "your much lamented Commander General Brock his Aid de Camp Colonel McDonell and several Warriors" who had fallen at Queenston. He offered eight strings of White Wampum to "wipe away your Tears" and a "Belt of Wampum" to place on Brock's grave so that it "shall receive no injury." (The placement was symbolic, not actual. The belt may have been given to Sheaffe because of his position.) He then addressed Sheaffe, asking for his confidence and assuring him "of our readiness to support him to the last."[56]

## CHAPTER TEN

# The War Continues

Despite Sheaffe's success on October 13th, there were critics of his conduct of the battle. Crooks wondered why Sheaffe, upon learning that the invasion was at Queenston, did not call in "his piquets and guards" who were along the lakeshore and other places but "within call" and take them to the village.[1] He went to question the tactics Sheaffe used on the Heights:

> Who ever heard of an army defiling in front of an enemy occupying a strong field position? It is true that the Regular troops ... when they had nearly gained the front of the enemy's position, ordered to attack in line, but no such order was given to the Militia ... and had it not been that the right or last company (the attack being from the left) without orders dashed upon the enemy, it is hard to say what would have been the fate of the day, more particularly ... as one Company had fallen into disorder. The General must have seen all this, following the attack as he did with a stick in his hand, and a reserve Militia under Captain James Hall.

The last part of his criticism may reflect Sheaffe's unpopularity. The militia around Fort George, Crooks thought, wanted to cross the river on a schooner lying at Navy Hall and take over Fort Niagara, which he claimed was abandoned. He went on to criticize the armistice made by Sheaffe and Van Rensselaer, claiming that it prevented an opportunity to capture Fort Niagara without a shot but, more realistically he concluded, "… [O]ur force was very much exhausted."

On the American side, Jared Wilson, writing to a friend in November 1812 about his experience at the battle, was happy to be permanently out of the military.[2] A lieutenant in the Battalion of Riflemen, he had crossed and was on the Heights where he fled for his life when attacked by "a party of indian Devils — about two hundred …. greedy for plunder and thirsting for blood … firing and yelling in the most frightful manner." Here he reflected the fear widespread among American troops of the so-called savagery of native warriors. Nevertheless, he claimed he had fought bravely until forced to yield to overwhelming numbers because 2,000 militiamen refused to cross. He blamed General Van Rensselaer for the lack of support from the militia and the absence of General Smyth's regulars. Van Rensselaer failed to have sufficient boats and scows to bring over artillery pieces. Above all, he castigated Colonel Solomon Van Rensselaer, claiming he was "allured by the prospects of acquiring unfaded Laurels," by invading "Canada with a few regulars and a few milita." The ambition of Solomon and the folly of Stephen "brought disgrace upon our country." However severely he criticized the leaders, Wilson was not against the war. He was prisoner of war in Upper Canada for only six days before being sent home on parole. Some of General Van Rensselaer's political opponents even suggested he had warned the British of the coming attack.[3]

While the armistice continued, Sheaffe strove to encourage the militia's morale in the face of "privations … imposed on them." He told them that supplies would soon arrive from Lower Canada and, in the meantime, he had confidence they would defeat any invasion attempt once the armistice ended. He insisted that officers make sure there were no irregularities in the distribution of provisions. Two days later, he informed Prevost that many of the militia were "in a very destitute state with respect to clothing and … bedding and barrack comforts in general," which had caused some to desert. One positive development, however, was the arrival of a paymaster for the district; Sheaffe had appointed two more because one was not enough to catch up to the arrears.[4]

Shortly afterwards, Nichol arrived with clothing and other supplies for the militia. They were to receive red coats, great coats, and blankets free of charge, but would have to pay for shoes, shirts, and "trowsers etc." Lieutenant-Colonel Cecil Bisshopp had also arrived, inspected the militia, and then "promised to get every thing he possibly can to make the men comfortable." Askin, the letter writer, expressed confidence in the flank companies compared to the ill-disciplined American troops and the unsteady militia. They knew of conditions across the river from deserters and another source who spoke to Major Evans. According to John Burkholder, an American-born resident of Upper Canada, "people [were] much divided and discontented" about the war. The American militia suffered from inadequate and "badly prepared" provisions and lack of vegetables, with the result that many fell sick. Nevertheless, he expected them to attack soon, probably across the upper Niagara River.[5]

Sheaffe had the same expectation because he knew the Americans were moving troops and boats to the river above the falls. He, therefore, "strengthened the right of our line" (the upper river) and had work done on Fort George to better protect its interior including making the magazine "secure from the effects of hot shot."[6] With the destruction caused by American guns on October 13th still evident, this was a sensible precaution, but the real threat came from General Smyth on the upper river. Colonel Winder, at Fort Niagara, was aware of Smyth's intentions. To assist him, he planned to collect his militia to "make some indications of crossing," in order to "draw them [Sheaffe's troops] toward this end of the line."[7] It was Sheaffe who acted to divert American attention by authorizing a bombardment of Fort Niagara on November 21st. The guns of the two forts kept up a fire (the Americans using hot shot) all day. An American participant reported seeing a schooner sunk and buildings in Niagara and Fort George in flames. Out of this event emerged an American heroine, Betsy (sometimes called Fanny) Doyle. In the absence of her husband, a private in the artillery, she provided hot shot to a six pounder.[8]

Meanwhile, General Smyth "for a month … did little but march his troops and issue bombastic proclamations about the impending conquest of Canada." He was gathering troops and when he ended the truce (November 20th) his force amounted to about 5,000 men. He sent two detachments across on the morning of November 28, and at some spots there was fierce fighting. The Americans, however, failed to gain control of a beachhead and by late afternoon Smyth decided to recall the troops. He planned a night attack for November 30th, but by the time some 1,500 soldiers had climbed into boats it was daylight. Even Smyth could appreciate the risk of an attack under those conditions and, after consulting his officers, he cancelled it. Upon their return to camp "mutinous soldiers threatened his physical safety, the militia was disbanded and the army retired to winter quarters."[9] Smyth departed to his family home and Congress passed legislation that removed him from the army.

It was not until November 20th that Dearborn, leading 6,000 regulars and militia, finally attempted an invasion of Lower Canada. The defenders had plenty of warning and put up a strong resistance. Some of the invaders became confused and began firing at each other while Vermont and New York militia refused to cross the border. Dearborn recalled the troops and withdrew to Plattsburgh, ending the campaigning for the year.

The only promising development for the Americans in 1812 occurred on Lake Ontario. Commodore Isaac Chauncey of the U.S. Navy arrived at Sackets Harbor on October 6 to take command of naval efforts on Lakes Ontario and Erie. He had previously sent men and *matériel* to Sackets and, shortly after his arrival, he bought merchant schooners to be converted to warships. By November 8, he was ready to take his six schooners led by the brig *Oneida* onto Lake Ontario to challenge the Provincial Marine. He chased the *Royal George* into Kingston Harbour but could not pursue farther because of guns on shore. His squadron captured three vessels, one being the sloop *Elizabeth*, which had Captain James Brock on board, paymaster of the 49th Regiment, and "a part of the Baggage" of his cousin, the late general. Vincent, in command at Kingston, asked that Captain Brock be allowed to return on parole and Chauncey agreed. Presumably, Captain Brock brought with him the deceased general's possessions.[10] From this time until winter closed navigation, the Provincial Marine ships remained in harbour, leaving Chauncey in control of the lake.

*Henry Dearborn.*

Lossing, 249

One of Sheaffe's chief concerns was American naval strength. He urged the fitting out of additional warships at Kingston, York, and Amherstburg. Prevost had requested the Royal Navy to take over the naval forces on the lakes and in May 1813, Commodore Sir James Yeo arrived at Quebec with more than 450 seamen and officers. Some would serve on the upper St. Lawrence River, Lake Erie, or Lake Champlain, but the majority bolstered the naval forces on Lake Ontario.[11]

Sheaffe met the assembly in February and gained its support for measures to strengthen the province's defences. The members passed a bill to recognize army bills as legal tender, authorized the prohibition of the export or distillation of grain, and also sought to improve the militia by replacing the flank companies with incorporated militia. It would be made up of volunteers who would enlist for the duration of the war, thus providing a more stable, long-term force. To attract volunteers, a cash bounty was authorized. Sheaffe considered the initial amount of eight dollars per man too low, and on his own he raised it to eighteen dollars as well as offering land grants to all ranks at the end of their service. Recruitment was slow to start but by the end of the year the Volunteer Incorporated militia numbered about 300 rank and file, and it would prove its military worth during 1814.[12]

There could be no question that the Americans would increase their war efforts in 1813. In January, Matthew Clay, representative from Virginia, boasted,

We have the Canadas as much under our command as she [Britain] has the ocean; and the way to conquer her on the ocean is to drive her from the land ... I would take the whole continent from them, and ask them no favors. Her fleets cannot then rendezvous at Halifax as now, and having no place of resort in the North, cannot infest our coasts as they lately have done ... if we get the continent, she must allow us the freedom of the sea.[13]

The Americans made the first strike in 1813. The year would see them gain victories on land and water yet fail to conquer either Upper or Lower Canada. The campaign opened with an American attack on York on April 27. Besides the prestige of capturing the provincial capital, the invaders intended to take the vessels in the harbour and destroy a ship under construction. The town was weakly garrisoned and its small fort offered little deterrent when Chauncey's fleet of fourteen ships carrying 1,700 regulars arrived. The 600 to 700 regulars and militia along with fifty to sixty native warriors were no match for the American troops and their warships' guns. Sheaffe's leadership did not inspire the defenders and, realizing he could not hold York, he advised the militia officers to surrender and ordered the unfinished ship, naval storehouse, and the magazine to be destroyed. To save the regulars he led them eastward out of York. His departure left the people "standing in the street like a parcel of sheep," complained York's sheriff, John Beike.[14]

Sheaffe saved his regulars to fight another day, a sensible decision because there was nothing to gain by remaining to fight, suffering many more casualties and probably ending up in captivity. They arrived at Kingston and Sheaffe remained there until June. It was the end of his fighting career. Major-General John Vincent took command in the Niagara Peninsula, where serious fighting occurred in May and June. In May, the Americans captured Fort George and Vincent retreated to Burlington. It appeared that a successful conquest of Upper Canada could not be long delayed. However, by the end of June the Americans had suffered defeats at Stoney Creek and Beaver Dams. Their response was to abandon Fort Erie and Queenston, discard supplies, weapons, and provisions, and withdraw into Fort George and the town of Niagara.

Prevost removed Sheaffe from command of Upper Canada and put him in charge of troops in the Montreal District. Since no fighting was occurring in this area, Sheaffe could neither win glory nor do any harm. In September, Prevost removed Sheaffe from the Montreal command and gave him responsibility for the reserve. In fact, the governor was seeking Sheaffe's recall to England and, after being ordered home, he sailed from Quebec in November. His remaining years were spent in Britain, where he achieved the rank of general through seniority. He died in 1851, in Edinburgh.[15]

Sir George appointed Francis Baron de Rottenburg as major-general, a post he retained until December 1813. He had been born in Danzig, Poland (at that time under Russian rule), and had experienced combat in Europe and the West Indies as well as diplomacy and military command. Perhaps more relevant to his appointment was the fact that he was the senior general officer (aside from Sheaffe) and the rules of the service required he be considered first for a detached command. Prevost believed he could trust Rottenburg with the "important duty" of commanding Upper Canada.[16]

Rottenburg had no familiarity with the colony and left political affairs to officials in York. He did not meet the Legislature — as did all the other officers who commanded in Upper Canada — and worked through a few advisers, the most influential of whom was Chief Justice William D. Powell.[17] Rottenburg's main concern in Upper Canada was to preserve the army rather than protect the residents or maintain the alliance with native peoples. In one of his first communications as commander, he wrote to Procter of a plan to retreat if Yeo's fleet was destroyed. Rottenburg would withdraw his troops to Kingston and have Procter retreat northward and travel via the Ottawa River to Montreal. In short, he was willing to abandon the province west of Kingston.[18] This plan was never needed; instead, Rottenburg carried out a series of attacks against the Americans entrenched around Fort George and raids across the Niagara River. An instance when he may have been too cautious was his refusal to send reinforcements of the 41st to Procter, which he needed to carry out a raid on Presque Isle (Erie), Pennsylvania.

That was the site of a naval base established by Chauncey in January 1813. Master Commandant Oliver H. Perry was having ships constructed there to challenge British control of Lake Erie. The British naval commander on that lake, Robert H. Barclay, and Procter planned a combined assault on the American base, but Procter believed a stronger force was needed. For this purpose, he expected to receive more regulars. Presque Isle was not raided and Perry managed to get his fleet out onto Lake Erie.

He defeated Captain Barclay and his Lake Erie fleet on September 10, thereby severing Procter's lifeline for supplies or reinforcements by water. Furthermore, a large and well-organized American Army, led by Major-General Harrison, was approaching Detroit. Procter knew Harrison was no Hull and would not hesitate to attack his much depleted and exhausted troops. The needs of the troops, civilians, and native allies could not be supplied by overland routes, which left Procter no choice but to retreat. His native allies were vehemently opposed and Tecumseh made an impassioned speech against retreat: "Listen, Father! The Americans have not yet defeated us by land; neither are we sure that they have done so by water; we therefore wish to remain here, and fight our enemy…. Our lives are in the hands of the Great Spirit. We are determined to defend our lands, and if it is his will, we wish to leave our bones upon them."[19] Nevertheless, on September 27 Procter began a slow withdrawal but was forced to turn and fight Harrison on the banks of the Thames River, near Moraviantown, on October 5th. Procter was decisively defeated and Tecumseh, fighting to the end, was killed. Harrison established civil administration for the Michigan territory and western Upper Canada, but the Americans never took firm control of the area. Harrison did not advance against the British position at Burlington Heights. Harrison placed garrisons in Detroit, Amherstburg, and Sandwich (commanded by Governor Lewis Cass of Michigan Territory) and in 1814 the Americans carried out hit-and-run raids in the Western Districts that drained its resources for war. Although the British continued to have native allies in Upper Canada — "in July, 1814, 582 braves marched to the lines" — they ceased to have any significant impact on the warfare.[20]

On the Niagara front there was a stalemate. The Americans could not break out from Fort George while Rottenburg could not recapture it. At the end of September he observed large numbers of American troops departing by water toward Sackets Harbor. In October, he sent troops to Kingston and soon followed, leaving Vincent in command. Later, Rottenburg would instruct Vincent to hold on to Burlington Heights and to establish a base at Long Point on Lake Erie. From the middle of October, Rottenburg commanded from Kingston and his final military decision, as commander of Upper Canada, was to send Lieutenant-Colonel Joseph W. Morrison in pursuit of Major-General James Wilkinson's army advancing down

Author's photo

*Tecumseh monuments, near site of Battle of Moraviantown.*

the St. Lawrence River. He knew by then that Prevost intended to replace him in charge of Upper Canada.[21]

Lieutenant-General Gordon Drummond arrived at Quebec on November 3rd as second-in-command to Prevost and on December 13 took both civil and military command of Upper Canada. He was the youngest of the general officers to hold those positions and had had more combat experience than either Brock or Sheaffe. He soon showed what kind of commander he would be. He discussed with Rottenburg about the conditions of Upper Canada and began to make decisions about the disposition of forces there, which indicated he intended to advance against the Americans. While he was at York, the Americans evacuated Fort George and burned the town of Niagara. Drummond wasted no time in transferring his headquarters to St. David's and having boats brought in secrecy overland to the Niagara River above Fort Niagara. On the night of December 18, British forces crossed the river and quickly captured the fort. What followed were the attacks against Lewiston, where guns threatened Queenston, Black Rock, and Buffalo. Towns were burned, four vessels of the American Lake Erie fleet destroyed, and many guns and stores captured. His initial dynamic and successful leadership compares well with Brock's record.[22]

Drummond, like Brock, initially encountered weak opponents on the Niagara frontier, but his situation would change in 1814. The United States government increased the size and improved the training of its army, as well as appointing better commanders, particularly on the Niagara front. The Americans continued to dominate Lakes Erie and Huron until September, and Ontario from mid-June until October. Drummond did not have the convenience and security of naval superiority that Brock had enjoyed. American control of Detroit and their freedom to raid throughout the Western district maintained a threat as far east as Burlington Heights. Native pressure against the Americans in the Detroit and Ohio areas had been eliminated and the British had lost important aboriginal allies. The province's war-sustaining resources had decreased. Food ran short in the contested regions of the west as well as in the Niagara Peninsula; the refusal of farmers elsewhere to sell foodstuffs to the government suggests shortages there too. The strains on the population increased through demands for more fighting men (and from increased casualties caused more by disease than by fighting), more money, and the reduction of civil liberties. The possibility of American conquest in 1814 remained high and peace was no more than a dream.

The only bright spot was the defeat of Napoleon in Europe and his exile to Elba. This change meant more troops became available for the defence of the Canadas. By July, fourteen regiments had been sent from Europe. It also helped to convince the United States government to enter negotiations with Britain to end the war. Those negotiations at Ghent dragged on for most of the year. Thus, 1814 would see hard fighting on both large and small scales, increased destruction of property, and heavier casualties than in previous years. Drummond could expect his military strength to grow (and it did, from 6,600 men in June to 11,600 in September) but the burden on his troops — and on Yeo's seamen and on the militia — became heavier rather than lighter.[23]

Drummond continued with the initiative by a raid in May on Oswego that achieved only limited success. The major fighting of the year was begun by the Americans on July 3rd when Major-General Jacob Brown crossed the Niagara River and quickly seized Fort Erie. He advanced northward along the river, and on the 5th defeated Major-General Phineas Riall at Chippawa and moved on to occupy Queenston. Drummond received the news in Kingston and hurried to York and then Niagara. He met Brown at Lundy's Lane on July 25 and they fought the bloodiest land battle of the war. American casualties were almost 900 and over 800 British were killed, wounded, and missing. Drummond demonstrated determination to accept whatever losses were necessary in order to defeat a well-led and larger army. Although the Americans captured the British guns posted on a hill that was the key position, they did not take the artillery with them when about midnight they withdrew to Chippawa. Drummond's forces remained on the battlefield and held it the next day, which gave him reason to claim a victory. The Americans fell back to Fort Erie and

Drummond, who was wounded in the neck and also suffering from a "severe cold and sore throat," waited several days before pursuing.[24]

He began an investment of Fort Erie that lasted until September 21. Drummond's bombardment of the fort caused heavy American casualties but an assault on August 15 failed with severe losses to the British. An American sortie caught the besiegers by surprise and with increasing sickness among the troops, Drummond decided to end the siege. By mid-October he had withdrawn across the Chippawa River and the last fighting in the Niagara Peninsula featured a brief skirmish at Cook's Mills.

Although faults can be found in Drummond's conduct of the siege of Fort Erie, what was important was that he tied down large numbers of American troops so that they were not available to serve elsewhere. In fact, the Americans shifted troops to Niagara from the eastern front facing Prevost, thus perpetuating their major strategic error of the war. When Major-General George Izard brought some 4,000 reinforcements and faced Drummond (who had about 1,800 men) across the Chippawa, Izard hesitated to undertake a large-scale attack against a tough, stubborn opponent. All that the invaders held was a small area of the peninsula of no strategic value and they suffered heavy losses for their effort. Drummond maintained the investment of Fort Erie under conditions that were difficult and getting worse. He began this holding action at a time when Chauncey controlled Lake Ontario, which created difficulties in getting supplies to Drummond's army. He did manage to maintain his position until Yeo gained naval supremacy in early October and could bring him reinforcements as well as take away wounded troops.[25]

Brown and Izard withdrew from Fort Erie and, on November 5, blew it up. Drummond then returned to Kingston, and his troops to winter quarters. Both sides expected fighting to resume in 1815, and Drummond made plans for naval bases on Lakes Erie and Huron.

The Treaty of Ghent, signed on December 24, 1814, ended the war and obliged each side to return any territory it had conquered. Nothing was said about impressment, blockade, or neutral rights — the ostensible causes of the war. A British demand for a permanent native barrier state south and west of Lake Erie was flatly refused by the Americans. Article 9 of the Treaty of Ghent guaranteed the restoration of "all the possessions, rights, and privileges ... [that native] tribes or nations ... [had] enjoyed or been entitled to" in 1811, before the outbreak of war, but the treaty provided no means of enforcing this term or of preventing continuing American westward expansion.[26] It might appear to be an unimportant treaty that ended a futile war, yet its consequences remain with us still. Both the United States and Britain gradually recognized a new relationship, one in which they would settle their disagreements by negotiation rather than by war. Later, after Canada became independent, it would negotiate for itself with the United States. Never again has the United States made war on Canada (or Britain). The Treaty of Ghent deserves recognition as a landmark treaty in international diplomacy.

The news of peace reached Upper Canada in February 1815. Prevost was recalled to England and departed in April. Drummond took over as administrator and commander of the forces and held those positions until May 1816. He returned to England to receive honours and promotions. When he died in 1846, he was the senior general in the British Army.

The preponderance of fighting on Upper Canada's lakes and land and the attendant destruction and suffering occurred after Brock's death. Yet, it was Brock who became commemorated as the saviour of Upper Canada, a status given to no other officer or warrior of that war. Let us see how that came about and, perhaps, understand the why.

## CHAPTER ELEVEN

# The Making of a Hero: Reflections on Brock

Almost immediately after the battle of Queenston Heights, Brock's behaviour was seen as heroic and idealization of his leadership began to flourish. It seemed that more than anyone else, Brock saved Upper Canada from conquest and occupation, for he was seen as the victor at Detroit and even at Queenston. Under subsequent commanding generals the province experienced military defeats, severe losses among the troops and militia, widespread destruction, shortages, and enemy occupation. Generals such as Sheaffe, Procter, Rottenburg, and Drummond could be held responsible for failures, but not Brock. His record was perceived as unblemished. This view can be seen in tributes from two militia officers who had participated in the fighting on October 13th. Captain James Crooks wrote, "To say that General Brock's loss was irreparable was but too truly proven by the subsequent events of the war," for although later commanders were brave and capable "none possessed the confidence of the inhabitants to the extent that he did." Lieutenant Ridout said much the same in his letter to his brother five days after Brock's funeral: "In losing our man, not only the President of the Province but our ablest General, is an irreparable loss under the existing circumstances, when his moderation and impartiality had united all parties in pronouncing him the only man worthy of being at the head of affairs."[1] (These comments also contain a hint of criticism of General Sheaffe.) William Hamilton Merritt expressed similar sentiments in the part of his narrative dealing with the battle of Queenston Heights. Approaching the village, he and his men learned of Brock's death: "A circumstance that damped our minds most was the loss of our gallant and much lamented Brock. In him we lost a host. All ranks and descriptions of people placed such implicit reliance on his skill, bravery and good judgment, that led by him, they were confident of success."[2]

A young British officer, Lieutenant-Colonel Cecil Bisshopp, heard about the victory at Queenston less than a week after he arrived at Quebec from England. On October 22nd he wrote to his sister, "M.G. Brock is universaley lamented, as he as an excellent officer…."[3] He made no mention of Sheaffe in connection with the battle.

The Crooks and Ridout view among militiamen might not have held if Brock had lived. Stanley points out that Brock's victory at Detroit greatly boosted the morale of the militia and afterward "it was … possible to give a large number of militiamen on the Detroit front leave to return home without incurring the stigma of desertion." After October 13th the militiamen were "still short of necessaries and were fed up with carrying out their military duties while lacking suitable clothing and shelter," and the result was increased desertion "even among those corps which had hitherto been noted for their reliability."[4]

In early November, Sheaffe himself reported to Prevost that shortages of clothing, bedding, and "barrack comforts in general" for the militia were causing increased discontent and desertion. He complained of the delay in forwarding supplies from Lower Canada. By mid-November the flank companies had received clothing consisting of a pair of "pantaloons each, 1 pr. shoes or two pr. Shoe packs and 1 Jacket, Shirts & Stockings," as well as flannel and thread.[5] But for some militiamen, conditions had not improved. According to Charles Askin, writing from Queenston, as winter tightened its grip "desertions and sickness has [sic] been very common of late among the militia," and despite clothing arriving for the flank companies, it was still lacking for other militiamen.[6]

Shortages of clothing during winter certainly created hardship and the militia's difficulties were still not solved — at least, not to Prevost's satisfaction — as late as March 1813. He offered advice to Sheaffe (probably not needed) when he called out the militia: "They should be regularly paid, properly fed and comfortably clothed. In my late visit to Upper Canada those essentials appeared to me not sufficiently attended to, and to be the cause of serious complaint."[7] Brock had tried to provide for the needs of the militia, but was he to blame for the shortages so evident later?

An officer who worked closely with Brock later criticized his administration. Major Thomas Evans wrote to Chief Justice Powell that the militia, barrack, and commissariat departments were seriously inefficient. He believed that the ultimate responsibility lay with Brock, not on the heads of those departments. Evans and Lieutenant-Colonel Myers, deputy quartermaster-general, had informed Brock of the sorry state of those departments, but "it is a melancholy truth that everything that had for its object arrangement and method was obliged to be done by stealth. Poor General Brock's high spirit would never descend to particulars, trifles I may say in the abstract, but ultimately essentials."[8]

The letter, written in January 1813, is the only instance in the documents of such a criticism, but given Evan's position and experience, it cannot be ignored. Evans did admit that he wrote the letter in defence of Sheaffe, who was under fire from prominent civilians and losing confidence of a number of regular officers. Perhaps there was some validity to Evans's complaint, but there is no evidence of similar criticism from other officers or from civilians, including militiamen. Moreover, there is no doubt that Brock had the reputation, going back at least to 1806, of an active concern with order, honesty, and efficiency. For example, he would not accept the misuse of government funds in the Commissary Department, he strove to correct inefficiencies in the Marine Department in Upper Canada, and it was Governor Craig who wanted him in the upper province "that a scrutinizing eye may correct the errors and neglect that have crept in, and put all in order again."[9] A final judgment on the validity of Evans's criticism may have to wait for the appearance of further evidence if it exists. In the meantime, let us accept that Brock was not perfect — as few human beings are.

Newspapers made major contributions to the image of an unequaled hero. The *York Gazette*, in its report of Brock's funeral, referred to "the last words of the dying Hero," and printed a lengthy poem, its title all in upper case: "To GENERAL BROCK, A GARLAND."[10] The *Quebec Mercury* reprinted this poem along with a report of the battle and included the misleading statement that Brock "gloriously fell when preparing for victory."[11] In its report on the battle of Queenston Heights, the *Montreal Herald* referred to "the severe loss of Major-General Brock. That hero possessed the full confidence of every good man, and was the idol of Upper Canada."[12] In the *Kingston Gazette's* report of Sheaffe's assumption of office, it was Brock's heroism that received more emphasis. According to the paper, after Sheaffe took the oaths of office at York he was presented with two addresses. The one from the executive council first praised the general for the victory at Queenston, but in a much longer second paragraph lavished praise on Brock, and it concluded with a short third paragraph. The other address presented by "a deputation" representing the magistrates and inhabitants of York, combined some praise of Sheaffe with condolences: "[We] beg leave to condole with your Honor on the Death

Library and Archives Canada, Acc. No. 1990-317-1

*His Excellency Sir James Henry Craig, captain-general and governor-in-chief of Lower Canada and Upper Canada.*

of our most Gallant and beloved Commander General BROCK."[13] The *Quebec Mercury*, in both prose and poetry, combined flattery of Brock with exultation in Britain's age of glory because of heroes such as Nelson, Moore, Abercromby, and Wellesley (later Duke of Wellington).[14] Distinguished company indeed for Brock! These images found resonance in England, as the *Mercury* reported in June 1813, taking "From a Late London Paper" great praise for Brock's heroism. At the same time, the *Herald* praised Procter and Vincent by referring to them as "Surviving Brocks."[15] Less than a year after his death, Brock had become the standard for heroism.

Another form of remembrance was songs, two of which appear to date from the 1820s. The best known has various titles such as, "The Bold Canadians" or "Come All You Brave Canadians," which praises the York volunteers (militia) who accompanied Brock to Detroit. The piece is attributed to Private Flumerfeldt of the York Volunteers upon their return to York from Detroit. Janet Carnochan, in a talk delivered in 1906, quoted four verses out of eleven. They give the flavour of the "ditty" and highlight the one name that appears:

> Come all you brave Canadians,
> I'd have you lend an ear
> Unto a simple ditty
> that will your spirits cheer.
> At length our bold commander,
> Sir Isaac Brock by name,
> Took shipping at Niagara
> And unto York he came.
> He said: "My Valiant heroes,
> Will you go along with me
> To fight those Yankee boys
> In the west of Canada"
> Success unto the volunteers
> Who thus their rights maintain.
> Likewise their bold commander,
> Sir Isaac Brock by name.

The other is titled "The Battle of Queenston Heights." It consists of four verses, Brock is named in the first, second, and fourth but no one else is mentioned, least of all General Sheaffe. Indeed, sole credit is given to one group: "... ere the set of sun/ Canadians held the rugged steep, the victory was won," and none to aboriginal allies or British regulars. The ditty also reinforced the image of Brock's final utterance being directed at the York militia. Here is the last line: "His dying words will guide us still: 'Push on, brave Volunteers!'"[16] These songs seem to represent a popular — certainly not a critical — view of Brock's leadership.

Prevost made his own contribution to Brock's heroic image when he wrote, in April 1813, to the British colonial secretary about Brock's "eminent military talents," which he believed Sheaffe could not match.[17] An indication of the attitude of Montreal fur traders may be seen in a letter from John McGillivray to Simon McTavish in which the former complained bitterly that the fruits of Brock's victory over Hull had been thrown away by the government.[18] (McTavish, McGillivray and Company dominated the fur trade out of Montreal.) Another prominent fur trader who also had business interests that took him to Upper Canada was Isaac Todd. He wrote to William Brock, praising his brother for saving the province from conquest and expressed the hope that "his country" (Britain) would find a way to honour Isaac's memory and provide some reward for his family.[19] Given all these testimonials of how essential Brock had been to the survival of Upper Canada, it is not surprising that the assembly made its own contribution. In March 1813, the members petitioned the Prince Regent to grant land to "his family," and only three months later Bathurst instructed Sheaffe to proceed with a grant.[20] In 1817, his four surviving brothers were granted 12,000 acres of land in Upper Canada as well as a yearly pension of £200 each.[21]

The *London Gazette Extraordinary* of November 27 printed Prevost's report as well as Sheaffe's of the victory at Queenston. The following July, the British House of Commons voted £1,575 for a memorial to Brock to be erected. It was located in St. Paul's Cathedral, in London, not far from the resting places of other British heroes such as Nelson. It depicts Brock looking like a Roman warrior lying dead in the arms of a British soldier, watched over by a native warrior.[22]

The Upper Canadian assembly did not take long to follow this example. On March 14, 1814, it voted unanimously to contribute £500 toward a monument on Queenston Heights.[23] What a tribute that represented because with the war still raging there continued to be heavy demands on the province's diminishing resources. In March 1815, with the war over, the assembly passed an act for the erection of a monument and included a grant of £1,000 (in 1826 it would vote an additional £600).[24] The story of the monuments to Brock would unfold over the next forty-two years. Another memento of Brock was a "common penny" that circulated in post-war Upper Canada. On one side it read, "Success to commerce and peace to the world," while on the other side was the new catch-phrase, "Isaac Brock, the hero of UC."[25]

Americans knew of Brock before they met him in battle. In July 1812, a newspaper contained the comment, "He is stated to be an able and experienced officer with undoubted courage." After the battle on October 13, an American officer at Lewiston wrote to his brother about Brock and Macdonell, "They were the two best Offices in the British service in Canada." Quite a sweeping tribute![26] The Americans had shown respect for Brock at the time of his funeral. That attitude continued, according to Colonel Winfield Scott, who had been captured at Queenston Heights and who would participate as a leader in several major campaigns of the war. In the battle to capture Fort George in May 1813, he led the first wave ashore and, later, undertook to enlarge the fort. While doing that work, Scott wrote, "Great care was taken ... not to disturb the bastion in which the remains of General Brock lay interred."[27] More than fifty years after Brock's death, Winfield Scott wrote to a friend about the great respect Americans had had for Brock. He told the story of a raid near Dunkirk (a small settlement in Pennsylvania) by "a provincial commander of a small vessel of war on Lake Erie" who "robbed several farm families of ... table silver, their beds etc." Brock was indignant and "took the vessel from the buccanier [sic] commander & sent her back, under a flag of truce, with the plundered property, not destroyed & money for the remainder. Such conduct could not fail to win all noble hearts on both sides of the line."[28] The story sounds too good to be true. Whatever had happened, Scott's memory gave it all a rosy hue.

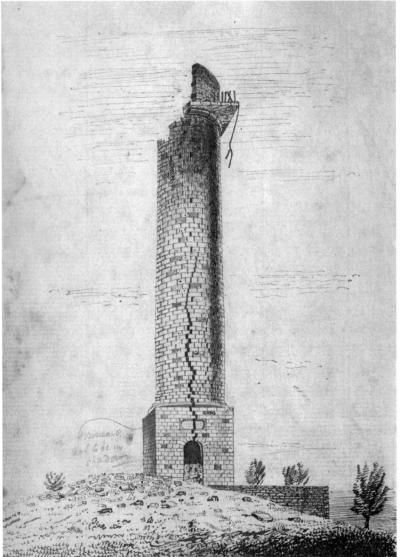

*First Brock monument, sketched by Major Thomas Glegg on May 9, 1841, shows the monument as it appeared after the 1840 explosion.*

OA, 4579 S-12404, Thomas Glegg Fonds

228

The bastion was disturbed in 1824, when the burial site was ready in the first monument on Queenston Heights still under construction. A funeral even grander than the first was planned for October 13th. This event required the removal of the two bodies. Here is the astonishing observation of one viewer, the Reverend John McEwan, who at the time was a young boy: "On 13th October, 1824, I was present when the remains of General Brock and his aid were taken from the ramparts of Fort George to the monument on Queenston Heights. When General Brock's coffin was opened, the flesh was still on his face, it continued thus however only for a moment or two after the air struck it." He described the procession, which had some unusual features: "The hearse was a large army wagon covered with a black cloth, it was drawn by four black horses, driven by a black driver, four black men walked by the head of the horses." This twelve or thirteen-year-old boy was so intrigued that he walked from Niagara to Queenston to see the full ceremony.[29]

The monument was completed in 1827, but the proposed statue for the top was deleted as an economic measure. The Tuscan-style column rose 135 feet with an interior staircase that opened onto an observation deck. The monument became an attraction for visitors. Its story came to a shattering end before dawn on April 17, 1840, when a charge at its base exploded. The lieutenant governor offered a £1,000 reward for the capture of those responsible but no one was ever apprehended. An investigation led to speculation that Irish-born Benjamin Lett had been responsible but it was never proved against him.[30] (His family had come to Lower Canada, then moved to Upper Canada, but were forced to flee the colony because they were terrorized by an armed band of local Orangemen following the Mackenzie uprising of 1837. To retaliate against the authorities, he joined the Patriots forces and "burned, killed, and destroyed for nearly four years" along the frontier. He may have attacked Brock's monument because he saw it as "a symbol of British power and domination," which the Patriots were trying to overthrow. He escaped capture in Canada and was never tried there.)[31]

Author's photo

*Hamilton family cemetery, Queenston.*

The structure was beyond repair and a competition was begun for a design of a new monument. The proposal of Thomas Young of Toronto was chosen but shortage of funds delayed construction. By 1852, Young's design, which contained no stair or lookout, had lost favour and, therefore, a second competition was launched. Out of seven entries the winner was a design by William Thomas of Toronto. (He was a prominent architect and among other buildings, designed the courthouse that still stands in Niagara-on-the-Lake.) It featured a column of "of the Roman Composite Order" surmounted by a statue of Brock, "his left hand on his sword and right arm outstretched," pointing northward over the province he died defending.[32]

When the rubble of the old monument was removed in the summer of 1853, the coffins of the fallen heroes were found to be badly damaged. Some eyewitnesses complained in the press that the bodies had been removed in a careless and disrespectful manner. The charge could not be left unanswered. Thomas, therefore, wrote in reply that each coffin had been carefully placed in a specially made "separate shell" and these were then buried eight feet deep in "the burial ground of the Hamilton Family at Queenston."[33]

A fourth burial was planned for October 13th, and again it was to be grand public ceremony. Thousands came on foot or by carriages, wagons, and steamships from across the lake. A newspaper reported that owing to a delay "in getting ready the Funeral Car, the Procession did not move forward until near 2 o'clock." As it moved from the town of Niagara toward Queenston, the procession was headed by the "Canadian Rifles, with arms reversed. Band, with muffled drums. Enrolled Pensioners." Then came the "Funeral Car with the Remains of the late lamented Maj. Gen. Sir Isaac Brock, and his Aide-de-Camp, Lieut. Col. McDonell" with six pallbearers on each side. Following was a column of distinguished guests including "the survivors of 1812, and Indian Chiefs, as Chief Mourners ... Grimsby Brass Band ... [and finally] Chippawa Fire Brigade."[34] The two coffins were placed in vaults to the accompaniment of artillery and rifle volleys. Prominent men then made the customary lengthy speeches and the ceremony ended with three cheers for Queen Victoria. Located 200 yards to the west of the first monument, the second one rose to 185 feet. At that date it was taller than any other column in the world except for Wren's Monument to the Great Fire in London. Brock's Monument was completed in 1857, but it was not until 1859, again on October 13th, that the official inauguration took place. It too featured a large public meeting and several prominent speakers. The inscription on the monument states that Brock "fell in action near these Heights on the 13th of October 1812, in the 43rd year of his age." But it was, in fact, the 44th year of his age because on October 6 Brock reached the age of 43.[35]

Two other monuments, one of Brock and one of his horse, Alfred, have been placed in Queenston. The first was intended to mark the spot where Brock fell when he was shot. William Thomas received the contract and set out to locate the place but soon found there was a good deal of uncertainty. Archibald McLean (a York militiaman who had participated in the battle of Queenston Heights) admitted he "could give no information as to the exact spot." Among the correspondence on this question is a diagram showing the intersection of the road to Niagara with the road to St. David's and beside them is written, "The spot about 4 yards in from Road & about a Rod south of the Corner of Mr. Hamilton's Fence as it then stood & by finding the corner of the fence the exact situation can be found."[36] Whether or not the location was correct, the monument was raised in time for the Prince of Wales (future King Edward VII) to dedicate it on September 19, 1860. It records with some caution, as well as some inaccuracy: "Near this spot Major-General Sir Isaac Brock KCB Provisional Lieutenant Governor of Upper Canada fell on 13 October 1812 while advancing to repel the invading enemy." In 1976, a bronze statue of "Alfred," the horse given to Brock by Governor Craig, was placed on its sandstone base near the 1860 cenotaph. In 1981, a plaque commemorating the native warriors' part in the battle of Queenston Heights was mounted on a granite boulder and placed nearby.[37]

Author's photo

Monument at spot where Brock fell: "This stone was placed by His Royal Highness Albert Edward Prince of Wales on 18 September 1860." The stone is incorrect, Brock was not the provisional lieutenant governor of Upper Canada, and his designation was K.B. not K.C.B.

In Guernsey, in his birthplace of St. Peter Port, there are plaques to Brock inside and outside the parish church as well as one on the building where he was born. It is appropriate that one of the memorials was placed by the Archeological and Historic Sites Board of the Province of Ontario.

The most recent bust of Brock is found in Ottawa in the new Valiants Memorial located near the National War Memorial. Unveiled in November 2006, the new memorial consists of nine busts and five statues as well as a large bronze wall. The Memorial honours fourteen individuals for their heroism from the seventeenth century to the twentieth as Canada developed from a colony to a nation.[38]

Brock has been commemorated more frequently and publicly in place names, monuments, speeches, and writings than any other British or Canadian leader of that war. He is even honoured in the name of the town of Brockton in Massachusetts. He has been depicted in much writing as a commander without equal in the defence of Upper Canada or, as an American historian puts it, "Conventional wisdom rates Major-General Isaac Brock as the best British general [in the war in British North America] and this assessment is undoubtedly correct...." [39]

Some authors, however, express reservations about Brock's leadership, for example, referring to him as "venturesome and carefree" and "a brave man who took chances," meaning that was not the role of the commander of the forces of Upper Canada.[40] Yet, Stacey (an army officer experienced at leading troops in war) writes in his biography of Brock, "Boldness was his way; but boldness almost always succeeds ... and it saved Upper Canada in 1812."[41] In the most recent work on the battle of Queenston Heights, Malcomson believes that Brock was "ready to take calculated risks," and did so in his orders to Captain Roberts to capture Fort Mackinac, his dismissal of the assembly, and his tactics at Detroit.[42] This comment may suggest an officer more careful than carefree, yet in his charge uphill at Queenston, Brock, acting in haste, took a great risk.

There are critics of his civil or political role and, certainly, Brock did not get the assembly's approval for some measures he considered important — in particular, suspension of habeas corpus. Requests by Sheaffe and Drummond had more success but it should be noted that Sheaffe did not ask for suspension of habeas corpus or for authority to declare martial law. In 1814, Drummond obtained approval for the suspension perhaps because assembly members were feeling especially embittered over the recent burning of Niagara.[43]

Brock was a commander willing to take risks with his life. He did so on the approach to Detroit, riding at the front of the column in the face of American artillery loaded and ready to be fired. If one artilleryman had disobeyed orders or carelessly touched his slow match to the vent of a gun, the resulting shot would have slaughtered many of the approaching troops and probably Brock as well. He had, however, a good deal of information about the depressed mood of the opposing commander and his unwillingness to act decisively. At Queenston, on October 13, conditions were very different.

Let me try a brief summary of factors that may have underlain Brock's fateful charge uphill. In wars as widespread as India, Egypt, and Europe, a frequent British tactic was attacking "with alacrity" often frontally and commanding officers were expected to lead rather depute the task to a subordinate.[44] Early that misty morning, Brock saw American forces above the redan, and must have believed he had no choice but to launch an immediate counterattack. American control of the Heights would outflank his entire defensive line along the Niagara River. He had no time to wait for reinforcements. Even if he had larger numbers, he still had the considerable disadvantage of being on the low ground. A careful wide-flanking movement, such as Sheaffe later used, was not feasible. Brock may also have assumed that the inadequacies of the American forces at Detroit would be found at Queenston. For weeks, he had been restrained by truces and orders from launching a spoiling attack. He wanted action and he expressed this mood less than a month previous to his brother, Savery: "You will hear of some decided action in the course of a fortnight ... I say decisive, because if I should be beaten the Province is inevitably gone, and should I be victorious, I do not imagine the gentry from the other side will be anxious to return to the charge .... I am quite anxious for this state of warfare to end."[45] He found himself in a situation that seemed to allow no time for reflection or consultation. (Who would he consult with? Sheaffe was not present, nor, it seems, were Brock's ADCs, Glegg and Macdonnell.) Moreover, he had had little sleep that night and little if anything to eat before galloping off to Queenston. A more rested commander, especially if his ADCs had been nearby, might have acted differently. Brock was a commander who had led troops in battle only twice: October 1799 and August 1812. He did not know the strength of the enemy forces above Queenston nor did he realize these troops could not be bluffed into retreat or surrender. Under Wool's command, they were determined and well placed in a stronger position than their attackers.[46]

The debate about Brock's actions — rash, heroic, unwise, necessary — is not finished yet. Another debate that may never end is whether or not Brock's actions made any difference to the outcome of the war. He deserves some credit for Captain Robert's decision to seize Fort Michilimackinac and that victory had consequences for warfare further south. Brock participated in two battles and won one, thereby stopping the first American invasion of Upper Canada. His gallant death at Queenston inspired the defenders but it was Sheaffe who really gained that victory.

Of the three years of warfare, arguably 1812 was the critical one since that year Britain was least able to provide aid to the Canadas. Thus, defence of the colony rested upon the forces and *matériel* actually present. It was the skilful use of these by British officers, aided vitally by native allies, that prevented American conquest. Yet, without Brock's leadership and given Procter's caution, it is unlikely that he and Tecumseh would have defeated Hull. If his invasion had succeeded he could have advanced deep into Upper Canada, outflanking both Michilimackinac in the north and the Niagara front. Van Rensselaer would have had a strong incentive to invade earlier than he did. There were no defences strong enough to repulse two American armies at Burlington Bay or at York. It is likely that Upper Canada west of Kingston would have fallen to the Americans. The loss of Upper Canada in 1812 would have made defence of

Lower Canada extremely difficult in 1813. American morale would have been greatly boosted — perhaps enough to overcome New England's reluctance to participate. The willingness of the Upper Canadian militia and of native allies to resist the Americans would have been greatly lessened. The Americans could have concentrated their efforts on the two key targets of Montreal and Quebec at a time when Britain was still deeply committed in Europe. It can be argued that what Brock, Sheaffe, and their native allies achieved affected the entire course of the war. Their determination to preserve Upper Canada demonstrated that British sovereignty there would continue. Whatever course the fighting in the Canadas took in subsequent years, regardless of whatever victories American invaders achieved, it would have been impossible for the British government to abandon Upper Canada — one of their bravest generals was buried there.[47]

Finally, let us look at Isaac Brock as a man as well as a soldier. We have seen that he was warm-hearted and cared for the welfare of his soldiers. There is the example of FitzGibbon (Chapter Three) and of Ellis. He was a ten-year-old boy, "the natural son of Captain Ellis formerly of the 49th who was drowned on his passage home from this country...."[48] Brock had no children and Glegg wrote that Ellis "had lived under the General's roof for two years previous to his [Brock's] death and would I believe have been provided for had he lived." Glegg had "put him to a good school and he wants for nothing." It would be interesting to know if the young man ever wrote down his impressions of General Brock. His friendly, warm personality is suggested in a story told by a daughter of Dr. Joseph West, who was a surgeon at Fort Niagara. Here is part of her reminiscences quoted in an 1849 publication,

> There was a constant interchange of civilities and kindnesses, between the officers of Fort Niagara and the British Fort George and the inhabitants of the little town of Niagara, until the War of 1812 severed many ties of friendship. I well remember the Sunday

previous to the receipt of the declaration of war; being at church at Niagara; on our return Gen. Brock accompanied us to the boat, and taking myself and sisters by turns in his arms, said: "I must bid good bye to my little rosy cheeked Yankees;" then extending his hand to my father, said: "Farewell, Doctor; the next time we meet it will be as enemies." [49]

There is plenty of evidence that Brock enjoyed dinners and dances and the company of his officers as well as civilians. Richardson wrote of him, "In manner he was exceedingly affable and gentlemanly, of a cheerful and social habit, partial to dancing, and although never married, extremely devoted to female society." [50] What Brock left behind included wine decanters, bottles and casks of wine, tea, coffee, and many kinds of foodstuffs along with dishes, cutlery, glasses, and napkins. Carnochan mentions an inventory of Brock's possessions recently found and among other items it lists pickled mushrooms, champagne, claret, port, and "even a cow and pigs." His possessions also included a library of many volumes of a great variety of books, several of them in French. [51] (A full listing is in Appendix E.)

What is missing from these lists is clothing. A letter from Glegg to William Brock suggests what happened to some of those possessions. Glegg wrote on December 30, 1813, that he had sent some of the late general's personal effects by his servant, Thomas Porter, to the family in Guernsey: "I trust and hope, Porter's arrival has put you in possession of a few interesting articles of our lamented friend ... I allude to the Uniform and military appointments — which the Hero wore on that fatal day." He regretted that some articles had fallen into American hands when they captured York in April 1813, but, "The sword sent home, your Gallant Brother wore on the fatal day, and is the one he accepted from me when I joined him ... in 1807 at Quebec, the other I took the liberty of taking as a valuable remembrance of my esteem and veneration....." [52] The articles sent to Guernsey included a coatee that most likely Brock wore when he was killed (a plain or undress coatee), a *ceinture fléchée* (a non-military sash), and a cravat as well as the sword. After remaining with the family for almost a century, Isaac Brock's grandnieces, Henrietta and Emilia Tupper, decided to donate their artifacts to Canadian institutions. In 1909, the Dominion

*Sir Isaac Brock, portrait by J.W.L. Forster, 1900. The depiction of the uniform and sword may have been based on the actual relic.*

OA, MGS692993

238

Archivist received the plain coatee, the *ceinture fleche*, and the cravat, while David R. McCord received a dress coatee, presumably owned by the general. (It is preserved in the McCord Museum in Montreal.) The cravat seems subsequently to have disappeared. The authenticity of the remaining items has been a subject of considerable scholarly investigation ever since.

Isaac had never forgotten how his career had been advanced by loans from his brother William. After the funeral, Glegg wrote to William that he and "two particular friends" had searched for a will, "which is not to be found nor do I think he ever made one. Of late when speaking upon the Subject He used to say in his usual cheerful way, 'I have no occasion for a will, for all and much more than I have belongs to my brother William.'"[53] Besides the sums gained from the sale of Brock's possessions, there was the possibility that the major-general's heir(s) would receive £1,500, half a year's salary as civil administrator, and a share of the property captured at Detroit.[54]

In descriptions of Brock's appearance, about the only consistency is that he was a tall, imposing man. Part of the reason for uncertainty about his exact appearance was stated by Glegg: "I never possessed a good likeness of your Brother, nor did he ever sit for it being taken in this country."[55] Nevertheless, there are portraits mostly based upon a pastel portrait attributed to William Berczy, circa 1808–09, who probably made a copy.[56] (Berczy was promoter of settlement in Upper Canada, a writer, architect, and a respected painter of portraits.)[57] This original was the basis for the portrait painted in the 1890s by J.W.L. Forster, who was producing a series of portraits of historical persons (Major-General James Wolfe, Major-General Aeneas Shaw, Colonel John Graves Simcoe) to decorate the Legislative Buildings in Toronto. Forster's portrait, unlike the Berczy one, portrays the full figure of the man, thereby giving a more accurate idea of his appearance.

We have the impression of Andrew Kemp who, as a boy of age thirteen, saw Brock at Amherstburg and later wrote, "He was a fine jolly looking, middle aged man." On Aug 16, 1812, at Detroit, two American officers described Brock:

Colonel William Stanley Hatch spoke of him as an "officer of distinction," and they elaborated on his appearance in these terms: "His personal appearance is commanding; he must have been six feet three or four inches in height; very massive and large boned, though not fleshy, and apparently of immense muscular power." Later, General George Sanderson ... [included] an element of personal aversion ... in his description of Brock as "a heavily built man, about six feet three inches in height, broad shoulders, large hips and lame, walking with a cane. One of his eyes, the left one I think, was closed, and he was withal the ugliest officer I ever saw." [58]

Richardson, who was also at Detroit, provided much more detail: "In person he was tall, stout and inclining to corpulency: he was of fair and florid complexion, had a large forehead, full face, but not prominent features, rather small, grayish-blue eyes, with a very slight cast in one of them — small mouth, with a pleasing smile, and good teeth." [59] Brock's nephew, Ferdinand Brock Tupper, may have had available some first-hand information for his description: "In stature he was tall, erect, and well proportioned, although in his later years his figure was perhaps too portly.... His fine and benevolent countenance was a perfect index of his mind, and his manners were courteous, frank and engaging." [60]

Brock was a large man of great character. It is not often that in failing a person gains both a victory and immortality.

# Timeline of Brock's Life

**1769**    October 6, born in St. Peter-Port, Guernsey.

**1779**    Age ten, boarding school in Southampton, England.

**1783**    Age fourteen, studies under a French pastor in Rotterdam in the Netherlands.

**1784**    Age fifteen, obtains a commission ensign in the 8th Regiment of Foot (King's Regiment). On garrison duty in England.

**1790**    Purchases lieutenant's commission; gains rank as captain by raising an independent company. Moves to Guernsey and Jersey.

**1791**    Exchanges into 49th Regiment of Foot and goes to Barbados. Falls ill and returns to England on sick leave.

**1795**    Purchases majority.

**1797**    Purchases lieutenant-colonelcy and becomes senior lieutenant-colonel of 49th.

**1799**    August to November, expedition to Holland, battle at Egmont-op-Zee.

**1801**   March to April, expedition to Copenhagen, Denmark.

**1802**   August 20, arrives Quebec City with 49th Regiment, September in Montreal.

**1803**   Takes 49th to Upper Canada in August, desertion from 49th at Fort George. Later, Brock forestalls mutiny and desertion.

**1804**   Commanding officer of Quebec City garrison.

**1805–06**   On leave in England.

**1806**   September, becomes brevet colonel and senior officer in the Canadas, and therefore, commanding officer of the forces, resides Quebec City.

**1807**   October, Sir James Craig arrives and replaces Brock. He supports proposal to raise a Highland Fencible regiment (later, Glengarry Light Infantry Fencibles).

**1808**   March, moves to Montreal as nominal brigadier-general, this rank confirmed July 3.

September, in Quebec City.

**1810**   September, sent to Upper Canada, commander of the forces.

**1811**   June, moves to Montreal.

June 4, becomes major-general. June to September, commander of Montreal garrison (Drummond commander of the forces).

September, moves to Upper Canada, on 30th takes oaths of office as commander of forces and administrator of Upper Canada. His term begins October 8.

**1812**   January, gets permission to go to England but decides not to go.

February 3, Brock opens fourth session of Fifth Parliament of Upper Canada.

February, Brock gives a ball.

March 6, Brock closes meeting of Legislature.

April, Brock attends a council meeting on Grand River.

June 18, President Madison signs declaration of war.

June 26, Brock at York learns of declaration of war.

July 12, General Hull invades Upper Canada.

July 17, Captain Roberts captures Fort Michilimackinac.

July 27, Brock opens first session of Sixth Parliament of Upper Canada.

August 5, Brock closes meeting of Legislature.

August 6, Brock departs York for Amherstburg.

August 8, departs Port Dover, Lake Erie.

August 13, arrives Amherstburg.

August 13–14, meets Tecumseh.

August 16, captures Detroit and issues a proclamation to inhabitants of Michigan. During summer and autumn, he learns of bankruptcy of William Brock's firm and consequent family financial difficulties.

September 4, at Kingston.

September 6, at Fort George.

October 9, rides to Fort Erie upon hearing of American attack on two brigs.

October 10, appointed "an extra knight of the most honorable Order of the Bath."

October 11–12, writes what is believed to be his last letter.

October 13, killed at Battle of Queenston Heights.

October 16, funeral for Brock and Macdonell, who are buried in a bastion of Fort George.

APPENDIX B

# Brock's Speeches to the Legislature

Speeches at the opening and closing of the Legislature were the means by which the head of government tried to influence the members to approve the measures he was proposing. These speeches were printed in full in newspapers, which was the only means to reach the public generally and, thereby, persuade them of the rightness of government policy. In Brock's case, his speeches were also designed to show his superior, Governor Prevost, that he was working strenuously to prepare Upper Canada's defences against American attack.

An informative introduction for this Appendix and Appendix C is *The War of 1812*, Arthur Bowler, ed. (Toronto: 1973).

On February 3, 1812, Major-General Brock, accompanied by a numerous suite, opened the session of the Legislature at York with the following speech to the legislative council and the house of assembly:

> Honorable Gentlemen of the Legislative Council, and Gentlemen of the House of Assembly.
> I should derive the utmost satisfaction, the first time of my addressing you, were it permitted me to direct your attention solely to such objects as

tended to promote the peace and prosperity of this Province.

The glorious contest in which the British Empire is engaged, and the vast sacrifice which Great Britain nobly offers to secure the independence of other nations, might be expected to stifle every feeling of envy and jealousy, and at the same time to excite the interest and command the admiration of a free people; but, regardless of such generous impressions, the American government evinces a disposition calculated to impede and divide her efforts.

England is not only interdicted the harbours of the United States, while they afford a shelter to the cruisers of her inveterate enemy, but she is likewise required to resign those maritime rights which she has so long exercised and enjoyed. Insulting threats are offered, and hostile preparations actually commenced; and though not without hope that cool reflection and the dictates of justice may yet avert the calamities of war, I cannot, under every view of the relative situation of the province, be too urgent in recommending to your early attention the adoption of such measures as will best secure the internal peace of the country, and defeat every hostile aggression.

Principally composed of the sons of a loyal and brave band of veterans, the militia, I am confident, stand in need of nothing but the necessary legislative provisions, to direct their ardour in the acquirement of military instruction, to form a most efficient force.

The growing prosperity of these provinces, it is manifest, begins to awaken a spirit of envy and ambition. The acknowledged importance of this colony to the parent state will secure the continuance of her powerful protection. Her fostering care has been the first cause, under Providence, of the uninterrupted happiness you have so long enjoyed. Your industry has been liberally rewarded, and you have in consequence risen to opulence.

These interesting truths are not uttered to animate your patriotism, but to dispel any apprehension which you may have imbibed of the possibility of England forsaking you; for you must be sensible that if once bereft of her support, if once deprived of the advantages which her commerce and the supply of her most essential wants give you, this Colony, from its geographical position, must inevitably sink into comparative poverty and insignificance.

But Heaven will look favourably on the manly exertions which the loyal and virtuous inhabitants of this happy land are prepared to make, to avert such a dire calamity.

Our gracious Prince, who so gloriously upholds the dignity of the empire, already appreciates your merit; and it will be your first care to establish, by the course of your actions, the just claim of the country to the protection of his Royal Highness.

I cannot deny myself the satisfaction of announcing to you from this place, the munificent intention of his Royal Highness the Prince Regent, who has been graciously pleased to signify that a grant of £100 per annum will be proposed in the annual estimates, for every future missionary of the Gospel sent from England, who may have faithfully discharged, for the term of ten years, the duties of his station in this province.

Gentlemen of the House of Assembly.

I have no doubt but that, with me, you are convinced of the necessity of a regular system of military instruction to the militia of this province — on this salutary precaution, in the event of a war, our future safety will greatly depend, and I doubt not but that you will cheerfully lend your aid, to enable me to defray the expense of carrying into effect a measure so conducive to our security and defence.

I have ordered the public accounts to be laid before you, and have no doubt but that you will consider them with that attention which the nature of the subject may require.

Honorable Gentlemen of the Legislative Council and Gentlemen of the House of Assembly.

I have, without reserve, communicated to you what has occurred to me on the existing circumstances of this province. We wish and hope for peace, but it is nevertheless our duty to be prepared for war.

The task imposed upon you, on the present occasion, is arduous; this task, however, I hope and trust, laying aside every consideration but that of the public good, you will perform with that firmness, discretion, and promptitude, which a regard to yourselves, your families, your country, and your king, calls for at your hands.

As for myself, it shall be my utmost endeavour to co-operate with you in promoting such measures as may best contribute to the security and to the prosperity of this province.

The addresses of the provincial parliament in reply were highly satisfactory, and in answer Major-General Brock observed:

The congratulations offered upon my appointment to the honorable station I hold in this province, and the confidence you so early repose in me, are, be assured, received with pride and heartfelt satisfaction. Impressed with the assurance of your support,

I feel a most perfect reliance that the exertions of this province will be found equal to meet every emergency of this important crisis.

*Journals of the Legislative Assembly of Upper Canada*, 1812, 1–97. Brock's opening address is on 4–5. Tupper, *Life and Correspondence*, 144–46.

March 6, 1812

Honorable Gentlemen of the Legislative Council, and Gentlemen of the House of Assembly.

I embrace the earliest moment to prorogue this session of the Legislature that the Country may derive at this critical juncture the full benefit of your personal influence and example. The exigency of the times can alone authorize me to give my assent to the amended Militia Bill, for under circumstances of less urgency its very limited duration would oblige me to reject it. Your liberality in affording me the means to enable me to carry its otherwise salutary provisions into effect demands my warmest acknowledgements. Whilst the true interests of the Country are consulted, every possible regard will be paid to the comfort and convenience of the individuals whom the Militia Law may call into action.

The other Bills which you have passed this Session, I trust, will effectually promote the beneficial purposes for which they are intended.

I place full reliance in the exertions of your best endeavors to cherish and maintain that spirit of loyalty and attachment to the true principles of the Constitution, which happily at this time pervades every class of the community. Any attempt to disseminate dissatisfaction among us will be repelled with indignation, and you will not fail in your respective stations to point out and bring to justice all such persons as by their conduct may endanger the public tranquility.

Having communicated everything that occurs to me on this occasion, Gentlemen, I now dismiss you, with a confident hope that you will not cease individually to give full efficacy and support to those laws which can alone preserve the peace and promote the prosperity of this Province.

After which, the Honorable the Speaker of the Legislative Council said:

It is His Honor, the President's will and pleasure that this Provincial Parliament be prorogued until Friday, the tenth day of April next, to be then here held, and the Provincial Parliament is accordingly prorogued until Friday, the Tenth day of April next.

Certified by Donald McLean, Clerk of the Commons House of Assembly

*Journals of the Legislative Assembly of Upper Canada*, 1812, 97.

On July 27, 1812, Major-General Brock returned to York from Fort George, on which day, accompanied by a numerous suite, he opened the extra session of the legislature, and delivered the following speeches:

Honorable Gentlemen of the Legislative Council, and Gentlemen of the House of Assembly.

The urgency of the present crisis is the only consideration which could have induced me to call you together at a time when public, as well as private, duties elsewhere, demand your care and attention. But, gentlemen, when invaded by an enemy whose avowed object is the entire conquest of the province, the voice of loyalty, as well as of interest, calls aloud to every person in the sphere in which he is placed to defend his country.

Our militia have heard that voice, and have obeyed it; they have evinced, by the promptitude and loyalty of their conduct, that they are worthy of the king whom they serve, and of the constitution which they enjoy; and it affords me particular satisfaction, that while I address you as legislators, I speak to men who, in the day of danger, will be ready to assist, not only with their counsel, but with their arms.

We look, gentlemen, to our militia, as well as to the regular forces, for our protection; but I should be wanting to that important trust committed to my care, if I attempted to conceal (what experience, the great instructor of mankind, and especially of legislators, has discovered,) that amendment is necessary in our militia laws to render them efficient.

It is for you to consider what further improvements they still may require.

Honorable Gentlemen of the Legislative Council and Gentlemen of the House of Assembly.

From the history and experience of our mother country, we learn that in times of actual invasion or internal commotion, the ordinary course of criminal law has been found inadequate to secure his majesty's government from private treachery as well as from open disaffection; and that at such times its Legislature has found it expedient to enact laws restraining, for a limited period, the liberty of individuals, in many cases where it would be dangerous to expose the particulars of the charge; and although the actual invasion of the province might justify me in the exercise of the full powers reposed in me on such an emergency, yet it will be more agreeable to me to receive the sanction of the two houses.

A few traitors have already joined the enemy, have been suffered to come into the country with impunity, and have been harboured and concealed in the interior; yet the general spirit of loyally which appears to pervade the inhabitants of this province, is such as to authorize a just expectation that their efforts to mislead and deceive will be unavailing. The disaffected, I am convinced, are few — to protect and defend the loyal inhabitants from their machinations, is an object worthy of your most serious deliberation.

Gentlemen of the House of Assembly.

I have directed the public accounts of the province to be laid before you, in as complete a state as this unusual period will admit ; they will afford you the means of ascertaining to what extent you can aid in providing for the extraordinary demands occasioned by the employment of the militia, and I doubt not but to that extent you will cheerfully contribute.

Honorable Gentlemen of the Legislative Council, and Gentlemen of the House of Assembly.

We are engaged in an awful and eventful contest. By unanimity and dispatch in our councils, and by vigour in our operations, we may teach the enemy this lesson, that a country defended by free men, enthusiastically devoted to the cause of their king and constitution, can never be conquered!

*SBD*, I, 389–91; *DHC*, 3, 147–48; Tupper, *Life and Correspondence*, 220–22.

August 5, 1812. York. His Honor the President gave Royal Assent to five bills passed by the Legislature. His speech to both houses:

Upon the eve of a necessary absence, I learned that you had got through such Bills as were thought expedient to submit to me for his Majesty's assent.

That you not unnecessarily be detained from your homes, I hastened at a moment's preparation to meet you, to declare his Majesty's assent to the Bills you might present, and close the present Session of the General Assembly.

Gentlemen of the House of Assembly.

I thank you in his Majesty's name, for the liberal grant of all the monies at your disposal and assure you that they shall be faithfully applied, to the best of my judgment, in the defence of the Province against its enemies.

*Kingston Gazette*, September 5, 1812.

# Proclamations

## Hull's Proclamation, dated July 13th, 1812

"Inhabitants of Canada!

After thirty years of peace and prosperity, the United States have been driven to arms. The injuries and aggressions, the insults and indignities of Great Britain, have once more left them no alternative but manly resistance or unconditional submission. The army under my command has *invaded your country* and the standard of Union now waves over the territory of Canada. To the peaceful, unoffending inhabitant, it brings neither danger nor difficulty. I come to find enemies, not to make them. I come to protect, not to injure you.

Separated by an immense ocean, and an extensive wilderness from Great Britain, you have no participation in her councils, no interest in her conduct — you have felt her tyranny, you have seen her injustice; but I do not ask you to avenge the one, or redress the other. The United States are sufficiently powerful to afford you every security consistent with their rights and your expectations. I tender you the invaluable blessings of civil, political and religious liberty, and their necessary result, individual and general prosperity. That liberty which gave decision to our councils and energy to our conduct, in a struggle for independence, and which conducted us safely and triumphantly through the stormy period of the revolution.

That liberty which has raised us to an elevated rank among the nations of the world, and which has afforded us a greater measure of peace, and security, of wealth and improvement, than ever fell to the lot of any people.

In the name of my Country, and by the authority of the Government I promise you protection to your persons, property and rights. Remain at your homes; pursue your peaceful and customary avocations, raise not your hands against your brethren. Many of your fathers fought for the freedom and independence we now enjoy. Being children, therefore, of the same family with us, and heirs to the same heritage, the arrival of an army of Friends must be hailed by you with a cordial welcome. You will be emancipated from Tyranny and oppression, and restored to the dignified station of freemen. Had I any doubt of eventual success, I might ask your assistance, but I do not. I come prepared for every contingency — I have a force which will look down all opposition, and that force is but a vanguard of a much greater. If contrary to your own interests and the just expectations of my country, you should take part in the approaching contest, you will be considered and treated as enemies, and the horrors and calamities of war will Stalk before you.

If the barbarous and Savage policy of Great Britain be pursued, and the savages let loose to murder our citizens, and butcher our women and children, this war will be a war of extermination.

The first stroke of the Tomahawk, the first attempt with a Scalping Knife, will be the signal of one indiscriminate scene of desolation! *No white man found fighting by the side of an Indian will be taken prisoner; instant destruction will be his lot.* If the dictates of reason, duty, justice and humanity cannot prevent the employment of a force which respects no right, and knows no wrong, it will be prevented by a severe and relentless system of retaliation.

I doubt not your courage and firmness — I will (not) doubt your attachment to liberty. If you tender your services voluntarily, they will be accepted readily.

The United States offer you Peace, Liberty, and Security — your choice lies between these, and war, slavery and destruction. Choose then, but choose wisely; and may He, who knows the justice of our cause, and who holds in His hand the fate of nations, guide you to a result the most compatible with your rights and interest, your peace and happiness.

H.Q. Sandwich
July 13th, 1812
By the General,
A.F. Hull
Captain of 13th U.S. Regt. of Infantry & Aid-de-Camp

Cruikshank, *Documents Relating to the Invasion of Canada and the Surrender of Detroit*, 58–60; Casselman, *Richardson's War of 1812*, 14–16 [LAC, C676, 168].

# Brock's Proclamation, dated July 22, 1812

The unprovoked declaration of War by the United
States of America against the United Kingdom of Great
Britain and Ireland and its dependencies has been
followed by the actual invasion of this Province, in a
remote frontier of the Western district, by a detachment
of the armed force of the United States. The Officer
Commanding that detachment has thought proper to
invite His Majesty's subjects, not only to a quiet and
unresisting submission but insults them with a call to
seek voluntarily the protection of his Government.
Without condescending to repeat the illiberal epithets
bestowed in this appeal of the American Commander
to the people of Upper Canada, on the administration of His Majesty, every inhabitant of the Province
is desired to seek the refutation of such indecent slan-
der, in the review of his own particular circumstances.
Where is the Canadian subject who can truly affirm
himself that he has been injured by the Government
in his person, his liberty, or his property? Where is to
be found in any part of the world, a growth so rapid in
wealth and prosperity, as this colony exhibits — settled
not thirty years by a band of veterans, exiled from their
former possessions on account of their loyalty. Not a
descendant of these brave people is to be found, who,
under the fostering liberality of their Sovereign, has
not acquired a property and means of enjoyment superior to what were possessed by their ancestors. This
unequalled prosperity could not have been attained
by the utmost liberality of the Government or the per-
severing industry of the people, had not the maritime
power of the mother country secured to its colonists a
safe access to every market where the produce of their
labor was in demand.

The unavoidable and immediate consequence of a separation from Great Britain must be the loss of this inestimable advantage. And what is offered you in exchange? To become a territory of the United States, and share with them that exclusion from the ocean which the policy of their present government enforces. You are not even flattered with a participation of their boasted independence, and it is but too obvious that once exchanged from the powerful protection of the United Kingdom, you must be re-annexed to the dominion of France, from which the Provinces of Canada were wrested by the arms of Great Britain, at a vast expense of blood and treasure, from no other motive than to *relieve* her ungrateful children from the oppression of a cruel neighbour; this restitution of Canada to the Empire of France was the stipulated reward for the aid afforded to the revolted colonies, now the United States; the debt is still due, and there can be no doubt the pledge has been renewed as a consideration for commercial advantages, or rather for an expected relaxation in the tyranny of France over the commercial world. Are you prepared, Inhabitants of Upper Canada, to become willing subjects, or rather slaves, to the Despot who rules the Nations of Europe with a rod of iron? If not, arise in a body, exert your energies, co-operate cordially with the King's regular forces, to repel the invader, and do not give cause to your children, when groaning under the oppression of a foreign master to reproach you with having too easily parted with the richest inheritance on Earth — a participation in the name, character and freedom of Britons.

The same spirit of justice, which will make allowance for the unsuccessful efforts of zeal and loyalty will not fail to punish the defalcation of principle. Every

Canadian freeholder is by deliberate choice bound by the most solemn oaths to defend the monarchy as well as his own property; to shrink from that engagement is a treason not to be forgiven. Let no man suppose that if in this unexpected struggle, His Majesty's arms should be compelled to yield to an overwhelming force, that the Province will be abandoned. The endeared relation of its first settlers, the intrinsic value of its commerce, and the pretensions of its powerful rival to repossess the Canadas are pledges that no peace will be established between the United States and Great Britain of which the restoration of these Provinces does not make the most prominent condition.

Be not dismayed at the unjustifiable threat of the commander of the enemy's forces if an Indian appear in the ranks. The brave bands of natives which inhabit this colony were, like His Majesty's subjects, punished for their zeal and fidelity, by the loss of their possessions in the late colonies, and rewarded by His Majesty with lands of superior value in this Province. The faith of the British government has never yet been violated; they feel that the soil they inherit is to them and their posterity protected from the base arts so frequently devised to overreach their simplicity. By what new principle are they to be prevented from defending their property? If their warfare, from being different from that of the white people, is more terrific to the enemy, let him retrace his steps, they seek him not and cannot expect to find women and children in an invading army; but they are men, and have equal rights with other men to defend themselves and their property when invaded, more especially when they find in the enemy's camp a ferocious and mortal foe, using the warfare which the American commander affects to reprobate.

The inconsistent and unjustifiable threat of refusing quarter for such a cause as being found in arms with a brother sufferer in defence of invaded rights, must be exercised with the certain assurance of retaliation, not only in the limited operations of war in this part of the King's Dominions, but in every quarter of the globe, for the national character of Britain is not less distinguished for humanity than strict retributive justice, which will consider the execution of this inhuman threat as deliberate murder, for which every subject of the offending power must make expiation.

God Save the King.
Isaac Brock, Maj. Gen. and President
Head Quarters, Fort George, 22nd July 1812
By order of his Honor the President J.B. Glegg,
Capt. A.D.C.
*DHC*, 3, 135–38; *Quebec Mercury*, August 11, 1812, 253

For an informative discussion of these two proclamations see R.A. Bowler, "Propaganda in Upper Canada in the War of 1812," in *War Along the Niagara: Essays on the War of 1812 and Its Legacy*, A. Bowler, ed. (Youngstown, NY: 1991), 77-92. Compare Hitsman, *Incredible War*, 68, and Stanley, *War of 1812*, 104-5.

## Brock's Proclamation to the Inhabitants of Michigan, August 16, 1812

Whereas the territory of Michigan was this day by Capitulation ceded to the arms of His Britannick Majesty without any other condition than the protection of private property, and wishing to give an early proof of the moderation and justice of His Majesty's Government, I do hereby announce to all the Inhabitants of the said Territory, that the Laws heretofore in existence shall continue in force until His Majesty's pleasure be known, or so long as the peace and safety of the said territory will admit thereof. And I do hereby also declare & make known to the said Inhabitants that they shall be protected in the full exercise & enjoyment of their Religion — Of which all persons both Civil and Military will take notice, and govern themselves accordingly.

All persons having in their possession, or having any knowledge of any public property, shall forthwith deliver in the same, or give notice thereof to the Officer Commanding, or Lt. Colonel Nicholl, who are duly authorized to receive and give proper receipts for the same.

Officers of Militia will be held responsible, that all arms in possession of Militia Men be immediately delivered up, and all individuals whatever who have in their possession arms of any kind, will deliver them up without delay.

Given under my hand at Detroit, this sixteenth day of August 1812, & in the fifty-second year of His Majesty's reign. Isaac Brock, Maj. Gen.

*SBD*, I, 473.

# Biographies of Significant Individuals

**CLAUS, William** (1765–1826). Born September 8, 1765, at Williamsburg (near present-day Amsterdam, NY). Married Catherine Jordan and they had three sons and two daughters who survived to adulthood. He died November 11, 1826, in Niagara. He was born into a wealthy and prominent family. His maternal grandfather, Sir William Johnson, had large estates in the Mohawk Valley and was superintendent of northern Indians. William's father, Colonel Daniel Claus, also held important positions in the Indian Department. The outbreak of the American Revolution forced the family to flee to Quebec in 1775. William enlisted in the King's Royal Regiment of New York (commanded by his uncle, Sir John Johnson) and took part in several battles. He gained his lieutenancy and in 1787 obtained the same rank in a regular British regiment, the 60th Foot; in February 1795 he was promoted to captain.

His uncle, Sir John, the superintendent general of Indian affairs, tried repeatedly to obtain a position for William in the Indian Department and finally succeeded in having him named deputy superintendent of the Six Nations at Fort George. He reached his post in October 1796, and immediately became involved in the controversy over Joseph Brant's claim that the Six Nations of the Grand River had the right to sell of portions of their land. Claus supported the government's refusal to recognize that claim. Allen summarizes his argument, first, that the Six Nations Confederacy of Iroquois were not indigenous inhabitants of Upper Canada and, secondly, "They had put themselves under the protection of the crown ... [and] by accepting the protection of the crown, their status had changed from faithful allies to loyal subjects who owed allegiance to the crown" (Allen, 94) (See Norton biography). On September 30, 1800, Claus became deputy superintendent general of Indian Affairs for Upper Canada and helped to frustrate Norton's mission to London on behalf of Brant. The Claus-Norton rivalry that developed undermined Brock's efforts to gain unequivocal support for his military goals from the people on the Grand. (See Chapters Five and Six.)

Claus was appointed lieutenant of the county of Oxford in 1802, which gave him authority to recommend militia officers. He was appointed colonel of the 1st Lincoln Militia in June 1812 and in July was put in command of the regulars and militia at Fort George and Queenston. On October 13, 1812, Sheaffe ordered him to take charge at Fort George and he "dispatched every Indian [he] could collect and a number of militia" to Queenston ("An Account"). He was also ordered to maintain the bombardment of Fort Niagara. In May 1813, again in command at Fort George, he wrote, "It became my duty to be in the garrison of Fort George every morning an hour before day with the militia" ("An Account"). He fought in defence of the fort against the American invasion of May 1813, and may well have been the last officer to leave the place before the invaders marched in (See Allen). He joined the retreat to Burlington Heights and was part of the British force at Stoney Creek, although it appears he did not fight in the battle. (He complains in his "Account" that Norton received credit which he did not deserve for leading warriors in pursuit of the retreating Americans. See also *Journal of Major John Norton*, cxix–cxx.) In September, General de Rottenburg sought the help of Claus and his followers to stem an increase in desertions along the Niagara. There seem good grounds for Allen's assessment: "Throughout the conflict Claus performed his duties with efficiency and dignity" (*DCB*). By 1814, his rivalry with Norton was absorbing more and more of his attention.

Norton's military participation gained him both greater prestige and authority (e.g., in March he gained the power to dispense presents to the warriors fighting with him). It was only after the war ended and Norton became less active in the department that Claus could escape the bitter rivalry. British policy toward aboriginal people in Upper Canada changed dramatically in the post-war years. They were no longer needed as warriors; what the province required were farmers. Hence, Claus's role was to negotiate agreements with native groups to extinguish their land titles, settle on reserves, and accept Christianization. His biographer believes that he "genuinely ... cared about the native people," as they tried to adjust to a very different way of life. In his efforts to obtain adequate funding for their needs, he sometimes clashed with his superiors. Yet, in his new position as "trustee of the Grand River community's investments," Benn writes, "As he had done before the war, Claus continued to abuse his office for personal profit."

Claus had many other roles, such as justice of the peace (since 1803) and member of the Legislative Council from 1812. In 1816, he became an honorary member of the executive council (whose role was to advise the lieutenant governor) and in 1818 a full member. He was also a trustee for the Niagara public school and commissioner of customs for the Niagara District. He is described as "a proud family man, and home life was important to him. His vegetable and flower gardens were among the best in the region and his orchards were renowned." The records he kept so carefully "provide excellent information on horticulture in Upper Canada." After he died, he was buried in Butler's Burying Ground outside the town.

*DCB*, 6, 151–3. R.S. Allen. Colonel William Claus, "An Account of the Operations of the Indian Contingent with our Forces on the Niagara Frontier in 1812–13," in NHS, *Campaigns of 1812–14*, no. 9, 23–40. *Journal of Major John Norton*, Bibliographical Introduction, Historical Introduction. Benn, *Iroquois in the War*, 34–7, 141–3, 179–80, 185; Allen, *His Majesty's Indian Allies*, 94, 112–13, 116, 147, 174–78.

**CRAIG, Sir James H.** (1748–1812). Became an ensign at age fifteen in the 30th Foot, June 1, 1763. He was educated in military schools in Europe. He served as ADC to General Sir Robert Boyd, lieutenant-governor of Gibraltar. He became lieutenant on July 30, 1769, and captain in the 47th Foot in March 1771. He accompanied his regiment to America in 1774 and was severely wounded in the battle of Bunker's Hill. In 1776, he came to Canada and fought in several battles. Burgoyne sent him home with dispatches and so he was promoted major without purchase into the 82nd Foot and, later, became lieutenant-colonel of the 82nd. After the war he became lieutenant-colonel of the 16th Foot and, in 1790, its colonel. He spent time on the continent studying Prussian tactics and discipline. When war began with France, he commanded troops in Jersey until 1794 when he transferred to the army in the Netherlands and was made adjutant-general. He was promoted major-general in 1794. After the army withdrew from the Netherlands, he commanded a force to help capture Cape of Good Hope from the Dutch. Major-General Clarke arrived with troops from India, but departed leaving Craig in command of the Cape until 1797. He was invested with the order of the Bath. He was given command of a division in Bengal, returned to England in 1802, and was promoted lieutenant-general as of January 1, 1801. He commanded troops in the eastern district until 1805; then, despite very bad health, he was given command in the Mediterranean. Bad health forced him to return to England, and on August 29, 1807, was appointed captain-general and governor-general of Canada. He was described (with some inaccuracy) as an "able administrator, he avoided a collision with the United States, and made himself loved and respected by the Canadians." He resigned in October 1811, returned to England, and was promoted general on January 1, 1812; he died eleven days later. "In person he was very short, broad, and muscular, a pocket Hercules, but with sharp, neat features, as if chiseled in ivory. Not popular, for he was hot, peremptory, and pompous, yet extremely beloved by those whom he allowed to live in intimacy with him; clever, generous to

a fault, and a warm and unflinching friend to those whom he liked."
[Cited in *DNB* from Bunbury, *Narrative*, 182.]

*DNB*, 4, 1368–70, HMS; *DCB*, 5, 205–14.


**DEARBORN, Henry** (February 23, 1751–June 6, 1829). Born in
New Hampshire, studied medicine, and began practice. He married Mary Bartlett and had two daughters. He fought in the War of
Independence and rose to the rank of lieutenant-colonel. "Although
his military experience was extensive, Dearborn at no time commanded more than 300 men in action; he obtained no experience
in strategical or tactical planning; and his knowledge of logistics was limited" (*ANB*). He was discharged in 1783 and in 1787
was appointed a major-general of militia. He served in Congress
from 1792–97 as a Republican supporting Jefferson and Madison.
"Because of Dearborn's party loyalty, military experience, and
northern constituency, Jefferson appointed him secretary of war in
1801, a position he held throughout Jefferson's presidency" (*ANB*).
He supported Jefferson's reduction of the army and tried to make
it truly republican by drawing officers from all classes and making
it less hierarchical. He supported the policy of "civilization and
assimilation" of native peoples and the details of how to implement
it "were left to Dearborn and his agents, who used manipulation and
force when persuasion failed." After the *Chesapeake* affair, he tried to
reform the militia and improve its training but Congress would not
approve. As a political reward, he was appointed collector of customs of Boston.

In January 1812, President Madison appointed Dearborn senior
major-general of the U.S. Army, "a position he accepted with reluctance," (*ANB*) because of his age and lack of military knowledge.
He was put in charge of the northeastern sector from Niagara to the
New England coast. He established his headquarters at Greenbush,
across the Hudson River from Albany, but spent weeks away in
Boston strengthening coastal defences and trying to persuade New

England governors to allow their militia to be used in an invasion of Canada. He did not succeed, which meant there was "no major offensive in the East. Inaction in Dearborn's theater contributed to the loss of Detroit and general failure all along the border in 1812" (*ANB*). His leadership improved slightly in 1813, but instead of putting the main effort along the Lake Champlain route to attack Montreal or Quebec City, American forces were scattered to the west. Even the successes at York and Fort George produced no decisive results. He suffered repeatedly from illness. Dearborn was relieved of his command in July 1813. He sat on General Hull's court martial, "An improper assignment since Hull could and did maintain that Dearborn had contributed to the disaster at Detroit for which Hull was held responsible" (*ANB*).

Dearborn was honorably discharged from the army in 1815. He remained active in politics in Massachusetts. From 1822 to 1824 he served as minister to Portugal. He was most effective as a follower rather than as a leader. His biographer sums up that he was moderately successful: "The near total failure of his military command in the War of 1812 being the notable exception."

*American National Biography*, 6, 299–301, H. Cole.


**NORTON, John also known as Snipe, Teyoninhokarawen** (Born about 1760; died 1825?). His father was Cherokee and his mother, named Anderson, was a Scottish woman probably living near Dumfermline, Scotland. After schooling in Scotland, which gave him a good grounding in English, he arrived a soldier in the 65th Foot at Quebec in 1785. He apparently deserted from the regiment at Fort Niagara and in 1788 was discharged. He served as a schoolmaster in the Mohawk settlement at the Bay of Quinte on Lake Ontario until 1791. He next appears in Detroit as an employee of the fur trader, John Askin. Norton conducted business in the Miami River area from 1791 until 1795 but as American expansion into the region continued, he knew he would have to leave.

In 1796, Norton became an interpreter in the British Indian Department at Niagara. Captain Joseph Brant (Mohawk war chief and most prominent leader of the Six Nations on the Grand) adopted Norton as a "nephew," made him his deputy and successor, and employed him as an interpreter. Norton resigned from the Indian Department and moved to the Grand River. In 1799, he received appointment "as Teyoninhokarawen, a rank as a chieftain for diplomacy and leadership in war," which gave him a strong but non-hereditary leadership position.

The Grand River Iroquois were seriously divided over the issue of ownership of the Grand River lands and the right to dispose of them with Brant and Norton opposed by William Claus (See Claus biography), other officials of the Indian Department, and Lieutenant Governor Gore. To present his view to the British government, Brant sent Norton to London in 1804. Although he did not achieve what Brant wanted, Norton made valuable contacts among members of the evangelical missionary movement and the British and Foreign Bible Society published his translation into Mohawk of the Gospel of St. John. He arrived back in Upper Canada in 1806 and in 1809 set off on a journey to the land of the Cherokees in the United States, where he visited relatives and learned about his native heritage.

He returned in 1810, but the following year, with rumours of impending war with the United States, he planned "to retire to the South West." Before departing, he spoke to Brock and after several conversations: "Norton emerged as the spokesman for the loyal British party among the Grand River Indians, and as the leader of their warriors" (*Journal of Major John Norton*). Thus, he served in the war from its outset, beginning with the Detroit campaign. He reached the high point of his military career in the battle of Queenston Heights. As a result, Major-General Sheaffe appointed him "Captain of the confederate Indians" (*Journal of Major John Norton*). After the fall of Fort George and the British retreat to Stoney Creek, most Six Nation warriors became more concerned with protecting their families than with fighting the Americans. Norton, however, continued his efforts to lead warriors in the campaigns of 1813, with only limited success. His influence over the Grand River people declined during the latter part of the year — and that of Claus grew. A change came in 1814, when Norton, with Prevost's support, was given a free hand in dealings with the Grand River Iroquois. Norton's success and recognition increased the antagonism between him and Claus.

After the war ended, he was brevetted a major in the British Army and granted a pension of £200 per annum. He wrote about his travels, about Cherokees and other native nations, as well as about the War of 1812. His journal of the War of 1812, completed shortly after the war ended, was not published until 1970 by the Champlain Society and is a valuable source of information on the man, events of the war, and native participation. He departed for the United States in 1823 and died there but the date is unknown.

He was described in 1814 by Thomas Scott (brother of Sir Walter Scott): "Captain Norton ... is a man who makes you almost wish to be an Indian chief. What do you think of a man speaking the language of about twelve Indian nations, English, French, German and Spanish, all well, being in possession of all modern literature ... having written a history of the five nations, and a journal of his own travels, now in London ready for publication, and being at the same time an Indian Chief, living as they do and following all their fashions. For, brother, you ask doth he paint himself, scalp, etc. etc.? I answer, yea, he doth; and with the most polished manner of civilised life, he would not disdain to partake of the blood of his enemy..." (*Journal of Major John Norton*, xx).

*DCB*, 6, 550–53. *Journal of Major John Norton*, xxiv–cxxiv; Benn, *Iroquois in the War*, 29–35, 105–6, 109–14.

**PORTER, Peter B.** (August 4, 1773–March 20, 1844). Born in Connecticut, where he qualified as a lawyer in 1795. He changed from being a Federalist supporter to a Republican in 1801 and was elected to the State Legislature. He became a land speculator along the Niagara frontier, with his home in Black Rock. In 1808, he was elected to the

House of Representatives, where he became an "articulate spokesman for western concerns" and a vigorous promoter of canal development. He became chairman of the Committee on Foreign Relations and, although considered a member of the War Hawk group, he opposed war in the summer of 1812 because he saw that the United States was unprepared. He became quartermaster-general of New York state militia. In December 1812, he almost fought a duel with Brigadier-General Alexander Smyth.

In 1813, he led a successful defence of Buffalo. In 1814, as part of General Jacob Brown's army, "Porter was authorized to command a brigade of volunteer infantry and Six Nations Indians." He fought at Chippawa and Lundy's Lane and his "brigade subsequently distinguished themselves during the protracted siege of Fort Erie." One historian calls his sortie from Fort Erie "his finest hour" (Hickey). He was promoted to major-general, and "for his services, Porter obtained a sword from the state Legislature and a gold medal from Congress; he is the only militia officer from this war who was so honored." In 1814, he was elected to Congress and in 1815 appointed New York's secretary of state. The Treaty of Ghent provided for commissions to settle boundary issues between the United States and British North America, and Porter served on the commission that determined the boundary for the Great Lakes to Sault Ste. Marie (article 6) and from there to the Lake of the Woods (article 7). (For a full treatment see F.M. Carroll, *A Good and Wise Measure: The Search for the Canadian-American Boundary, 1783–1842*. Toronto: University of Toronto Press, 2001.) In 1828–29 he was secretary of war, "during which time he advocated removal of Native Americans to lands west of the Mississippi River."

His biographer sums up, "A review of Porter's career reveals an abiding commitment to public service and a modicum of political talent.... On a national level, Porters' greatest contribution was in leading state forces throughout the difficult 1814 Niagara campaign."

*American National Biography*, v.17, 707–9. Hickey, *Don't Give Up the Ship*, 147.

**TECUMSEH (Tech-kum-thai)** (1768?–1813). He was born about 1768 in the Ohio Valley. He died October 5, 1813, in the Battle of Moraviantown. His father was a Shawnee chief and his mother may have had some Creek blood. After the United States achieved independence, many Americans pushed westward into native lands and the result was broken treaties and aboriginal resistance. Some native leaders tried to unify the various western tribes to resist this expansion and this was a tradition that Tecumseh inherited. His father and a brother were been killed during long years of warfare between the Shawnee and American backwoodsmen.

He served as a scout for warriors who defeated the Americans at the Miamis Towns in 1791 and he led a group of warriors in the battle of Fallen Timbers in August 1794. In the resulting Treaty of Greenville (August 1795), the natives surrendered most of present-day Ohio, but still American expansion continued to pressure aboriginal groups to give up land. By 1795, one biographer writes that he was "an influential young war chief with a growing following among many of the younger, more anti-American warriors" (Edmunds, 43). He presented an impressive figure: "At five feet ten inches, he stood slightly taller than the average Shawnee warrior, and [from] contemporary accounts … he was a muscular man of great physical vigor." He was also a skilled hunter who provided not only for his own family but also assisted aged and poorer members of the community. As a warrior he was skillful and brave but went against Shawnee tradition in refusing to allow the killing of prisoners.

Tecumseh lived as a band chief in several different locations and, in 1805, he joined his brother, the Prophet (Tenskwatawa) in his settlement at Greenville. The Prophet was a religious leader who preached a need to return to traditional native ways as the only hope for aboriginals to survive. Tecumseh "transformed the Prophet's religion into a movement dedicated to retaining Indian land." The Americans feared this movement and Governor Harrison of Ohio saw it as a British plot. The authorities in the Canadas hoped to recruit native support in case of war with the United States. Tecumseh did not intend to become a British ally or pawn. His aim was to create a confederacy of tribes and nations and to maintain traditional native common ownership of land.

In 1809, he began to travel south of the Great Lakes, visiting different tribes and promoting unity against encroachment. His strongest support came from Potawatomis, Ojibwas, Shawnees, Ottawas, Winnebagos, and Kickapoos, with some also coming from Delawares, Wyandots, Menominees, Miamis, and Piankeshaws. He and the Prophet attempted to stop a large transfer of native land that Americans had purchased from individual tribes. This action increased tension on the frontier with the result that Tecumseh went to a meeting with Harrison but it solved nothing. Another meeting was held in July 1811, which likewise solved nothing, but Tecumseh told Harrison that he was going south to promote the cause of unification. Harrison used his absence to march an army to Tippecanoe, where he hoped to inflict a decisive defeat on the natives under the Prophet's leadership. The result was the battle of Tippecanoe in November, after which the natives withdrew and the Americans burned the village. This defeat was a setback but Tecumseh continued his work to build a confederacy. Although his aim remained "to preserve and defend the lands and cultural values of his people, yet in the years ahead he also became one of the most important and valuable Indian allies of the British crown in their defence of Canada" (Allen).

He sought the traditional supplies from the British at Fort Amherstburg and by July 1812 was in Upper Canada preparing to support the British in resisting American attacks. On August 5, at Brownstown, he took part in the ambush of a supply train headed for Detroit and on August 9, at Maguaga, fought in skirmish with an American force sent to protect a supply train. A few days later he met Brock, helped him plan to the attack on Detroit, and led a large contingent of warriors. (He was not the only native leader there and others were older and even more prominent.) He did not have control over his followers the way an army officer did, but Tecumseh was very skilful at marshalling support. One biographer states, "By the autumn of 1812 Tecumseh had about a thousand warriors with him" (*DCB*, 5). Andrew Kemp, as a boy of thirteen, saw Tecumseh at Amhertsburg and described him: "He was a handsome, noble looking fellow, very clean and neat about his person, and usually dressed in a white shirt, deer skin leggings and other usual Indian apparel, but sometimes in a red-coat, for he ranked as a Major-General" (NHS, 11, "Reminiscences of Niagara," 6–11).

He and the Wyandot chief, Roundhead, led raids into northern Ohio but saw no further action until 1813. In April, he and Roundhead led a force of warriors and supported Major-General Procter's siege of Fort Meigs. The fort resisted successfully but a relief force was attacked and prisoners taken. Some warriors began to kill prisoners until Tecumseh stopped them. His "humanity on this occasion was long remembered." He also led a force in the siege of that fort in July and in a later attack on Fort Stephenson. After Captain Barclay's defeat at the naval battle of Put-in-Bay (September 10), Procter proposed to retreat toward Lake Ontario. After hearing this proposal, "Tecumseh rose to deliver a reply that witnesses unanimously declared to have been remarkable" (Sugden). He denounced Procter's intention as cowardly and begged to be given arms to remain to fight the Americans. Here is Richardson's eyewitness description of Tecumseh when he made his stirring speech opposing Procter's retreat: "Habited in a close leather dress, his athletic proportions were admirably delineated, while a large plume of white ostrich feathers, by which he was generally distinguished, over shadowing his brow, and contrasting with the darkness of his complexion and the brilliancy of his black and piercing eye, gave a singularly wild and terrific expression to this features." (For other descriptions see Sugden.) Quotations from the speech can be found in the studies by Edmunds and Sugden.

However, Tecumseh and others eventually agreed to join Procter's withdrawal, intending to stop on the route to fight their pursuers. The battle took place on October 5th at Moraviantown. Tecumseh was mortally wounded. What was done with his remains is unknown. (See Sugden Appendix.) There are monuments on Walpole Island and in Fairfield, Ontario. Although his death discouraged the resistance of some native tribes, the British still retained allies in the upper lakes and Mississippi areas and smaller numbers in Upper Canada.

Tecumseh was married twice, the first marriage ending in separation. His second marriage to Mamate, a Shawnee, produced a son named Pachetha. Mamate died shortly after her son's birth and Tecumseh asked his sister to look after the boy, which she continued to do after Tecumseh's death.

*DCB*, 5, 795–801. Casselman, *Richardson's War*, 207. Allen, *His Majesty's Indian Allies*, 114. Edmunds, *Tecumseh and the Quest for Indian Leadership*, is one of the best sources on Tecumseh's life and leadership. Sugden, *Tecumseh's Last Stand*, 54, 63, 98, 122, contains several descriptions from 1813. This work is essential for an understanding of Procter's retreat, the battle of Moraviantown, and some of its consequences.

**TOMPKINS, Daniel D.** (Born in New York state June 21, 1774; died June 11, 1825). Became a lawyer 1797 and practiced in New York City. Entered politics and elected to state assembly 1803, served on the New York Supreme Court 1804–07. Was elected governor in 1807 and every three years until 1816. He supported President Jefferson and was the main New York supporter of James Madison for the presidency. He had no military experience, but "as the commander of the militia of a widely exposed state, Tompkins was deeply involved in the war's prosecution, a Herculean task worsened by pervasive gross inefficiency and a total lack of system." He served as vice-president 1817–25 when "he may well have set a non-attendance record," partly because of his and his wife's ill health and partly because he was preoccupied with financial problems (i.e., large debts). His main achievement seems to have been "his selfless efforts to prosecute the War of 1812."

*American National Biography*, v. 21, 738–39, D. Roper.

**VAN RENSSELAER, Solomon** (1774–1852). Born in Greenbush, Rensselaer County, N.Y., on August 6, 1774. He was the son of Jeremiah Van Rensselaer, a Revolutionary War general, and a member of a powerful Dutch patroon family. He grew up in Albany and at the family country seat across the river at Greenbush. In January 1797, he married his cousin, Harriet Van Rensselaer. They had five daughters and one son who survived to maturity. When he was away from home "he wrote that he could not be happy apart from her" (Mahon).

His father obtained a commission for Solomon as a cornet in the U.S. Light Dragoons. He served in Anthony Wayne's army and was wounded in the Battle of Fallen Timbers. His biographer writes, "Van Rensselaer considered the fight against the Indians a glorious cause and showed scant sympathy for the 'savage' foe" (Mahon). He was also a harsh disciplinarian toward his men although he took good care of their physical needs. In 1795, he was promoted to captain of a volunteer company and to major in January 1799. The following year, when President Jefferson reduced the army, Solomon received an honourable discharge.

He was adjutant general of the New York State militia from 1801–11 and 1813–21. A lieutenant-colonel of the New York Volunteers, he served his cousin, General Stephen Van Rensselaer, as aide-de-camp. During the initial stage of the Battle of Queenston Heights in October 1812, he led the first wave of militia across the river and was badly wounded. He was evacuated to the New York side and weeks later returned to Albany to a hero's welcome. That ended his military career but advanced his political career.

He was elected as a Federalist to the United States Congress and served from 1819 to 1822. He resigned to become postmaster of Albany from 1822 to 1839 and again from 1841 to 1843. He died April 23, 1852.

*American National Biography*, v. 22, 243–4. J.K. Mahon. *Biographical Dictionary of the United States Congress.*

**VAN RENSSELAER III, Stephen** (1764–1839). The first child of Stephen Van Rensselaer II and Catharina Livingston. He was born November 1, 1764, and grew up in Van Rensselaer manor in Upper Hudson River region. He graduated from Harvard College in 1782. He married Margarita, daughter of General Philip Schuyler, and they had three children. (Philip Schuyler, 1733–1804, had been a prominent major-general in the Continental Army and a member of the Continental Congress.) After Margarita's death in 1801, he married Cornelia Patterson, daughter of the governor of New Jersey. Together they would have ten children, born between 1803 and 1820. On reaching his twenty-first birthday, he took title to the family estate called Rensselaerswyck or "Van Rensselaer's Manor." This large estate had originally been granted to the Van Rensselaers in 1629 by the Dutch West India Company.

When he became the "patroon" of the manor, he was by far the wealthiest individual in the Albany area and his estate was served by fifteen slaves. In 1786, he gained a commission as major in the New York state militia and by 1801 rose to rank of major-general. New York's Governor Tompkins offered him command of the United States Army of the Centre for political reasons. His defeat at Queenston Heights ended his military career. In 1813 he ran unsuccessfully for governor of New York.

He had served in the New York State Assembly (1789–91) and Senate (1791–96), and as lieutenant governor of New York State (1795). After the war he served on the canal commission from 1816–39 and sat in the United States House of Representatives from 1822–29. He was regent of the University of the State of New York from 1819–39 and, with Amos Eaton, the founder of Renssselaer Polytechnic Institute. He died January 26, 1839, and was remembered in local lore as "The Last Patroon" or "The Good Patroon."

W.W. Spooner, "The Van Rensselaer Family," *American Historical Magazine*, 2 (January 1907), 129–33; *Biographical Dictionary of the United States Congress.*

# Inventory of Brock's Estate and Purchasers

The information below comes from several sources (listed at end). There are gaps, parts are unclear (indicated by ?), and there may be duplication.

Petition of James Brock, York, November 5, 1812. Isaac died without a will and James was his nearest of kin in the province, therefore, he petitioned Sheaffe to be allowed, along with Captain Glegg, ADC to Brock, to administer the goods and chattels. Details are given in the sources of who purchased what. The largest purchaser was Sheaffe, some £602.7.1/2, and other major purchasers were Reverend John Strachan, William Allan, George Crookshank, Captain Brock, and Captain Glegg. The total value of all the sales was £843.7.4

**FOR THE TABLE**

| | | |
|---|---|---|
| 1 Mustard Pot and Spoon (silver) | 11 Tea Spoons | 1 plated Cream Pot |
| 26 Silver Forks | 4 Decanters | Cut Glass |
| Tea Pot (silver) | ? Doz. – plated | 6 Large Decanters |
| Plated | Knives | 6 Small Decanters |
| Toast Rack | 2 Branch | 4 Blue Decanters |
| Cruet Stand | Candlesticks | and Stands |
| Fish Knife | 5 pr Plated | 4 Large Plain Quart |
| 10 Salt Spoons | Candlesticks | Decanters |
| | 2 pr Snuffer & Stands | |

3 Small Plain Pint
Decanters
4 5/12 Doz.
Tumblers
18 Salt Cellers
12 Custard Glasses
1 Butter Cooler
2 Butter Stands
40 Blue Finger
Glasses
21 Green Glasses
41 Double Flint
Glasses
21 Long Wine
Glasses
6 Plain Wine
Glasses
11 Plain Wine
Coolers
20 Wine Coolers
6 Doz. Large Green
handles Knives &
Forks
6 Carving Knives
4 Doz. And 2 Small
[Knives]
1 Steel [Knife]
5 Knives
Sugar Knife
Sugar Tongs
1 Butter Knife
Tin Dishes
A number of White
Dishes & Plates &
Crockery

6 Small White
Dishes
10 Large White
Dishes
Dish Drawer
6 Vegetable Dishes
1 Side Dish
1 Tureen
35 Water Plates
30 Plates
Salad Dish
[Dish] Drainer
18 Covers for
Dishes
China Cups
Coffee Cups
4 Mugs
? small waiters
1 spoon tray
Bread Basket
6 Dessert Spoons
18 Table Spoons
4 Butter Spoons
6 Tea Spoons
2 Gravy Spoons
1 Egg Stand not
complete
? large Nippers
1 Soup Ladle
Funnel & Cleaver
Tea Caddy (not
complete)
1 Tea Tray
2 Tea Kettles/Black
Tin & Iron

1 Coffee Pot
Coffee Mill
Plate Basket
1 Iron Boiler
Fish Kettle
(Complete)
Fish drawer/cleaner
11 Saucepans
? Small Iron Pots
Baking Oven
(Complete)
2 Jelly Moulds
Cake Dish
(including Pastry
Pans etc.)
Vegetable Mould
Dripping Pan
2 Gridirons
4 Iron Trivets
Ladles
Skimmer
Sieve
Pepper Mill
two Graters
Beam & Scales with
weights

## FURNISHINGS

3 Kitchen Table
Cloths
1 Doz. Good
napkins,
1 Doz. worn
3 Large Damask
Table Cloths
2 Small Damask
Table Cloths
4 Smaller Damask
Table Cloths
2 Large Table Cloths
2 Green Cloths for
Tables
1 Table Cloth
28 Napkins
? Doilies
1 Dining Room
Carpet
1 Drawing Room
Carpet (Brussels)
1 Bed Room Carpet
(next to the
Drawing Room)
with 3 Small
Carpets,
1 Carpet in the
Room off the
Library
1 Carpet in the
Library
Rugs
1 Mahogany
Dressing Glass

1 Looking Glass
2 Handbells,
1 Bedstead in the
Room next to the
Drawing Room
with Mattresses,
Pillows & Curtains
1 Hair Mattress
Pillow & Bolster
6 Prs Cotton Sheets
4 Linnen Pillow
Cases
2 Pillow Cases
4 Rose Blankets
1 Cotton
Counterpane
1 Bodette
Matress Bolster and
Pillow
1 Box Soap
2 Card Tables
1 Oval Mahogany
Table
1 Small Maple Table
Writing Desk
Chest Drawers
?? Marble Table,
13 Chairs (the
Remainder of the
Windsor Chairs
belong to Major
Hatton)
4 Coat Stands
3 Top Covers

Fenders-viz.-
Drawing Room
with Andirons etc.
Dining Room with
Fenders
Captain Gleggs
Room with
Fenders
Library & Bed Room
with Fenders
6 Dining Room
Lamps
1 Passage Lamp
Drawing Room
Lamps
? 1 Soup Ladle
Funnel & Cleaver
3 Spermaceti
Candles
3 Wax Candles
15 Sets Windsor
Curtains
1 Sofa
5 Chairs
Wash Hand Stand
Fire Screen
2 Barrels for Spirits
& 1 for Sugar &
Keg for Vinegar
Patent? Churn
Jars & Jugs
3 Large Jugs
Drudging Box

## FOOD & DRINK

2 Bottles of Brandy
1 Cask Spirits 36
  gallons, and
  1 cask of 34
  gallons
32 Doz. Port Wine,
1 Doz. Port Wine, 5
  2/12 Doz. Sent to
  Fort George
10 Bottles
  Champagne
15 Bottles Porter
24 Bottles Quebec
  Ale
12 Bottles Shrub
Bottles Claret
1 Bottle Lime S?
45 Bottles Sweet
  Wine
1 Keg Vinegar, 3
  gallons
5 Bottles of West
  India Preserves
5 Loaves Sugar
  weighing 39 lbs
11 Cask Muscovado
  Sugar
81/2 Hyson Tea
8 Green Coffee
1 Durham Mustard
1 Bottle Essence of
  Lemon
3 Bottles Anchovy
2 Bottles Ketchup

6 lbs Currants
1 Box Bloom
  Raisins &
  a Pound of
  Pudding Raisins
1 lbs Bitter
  Almonds 0/5/ ;
4 lbs Sweet
  Almonds
¼ lb Isinglass
2 Bottles Qu?
  Sauce?
2 Bottles Lemon S?
1 Large Square
  Bottle of
Anchovies
1 Bottle of French
  Olives
2 Quart Bottles
  Capilarie ?
2 Large Jars of
  Preserved
  Cranberries
  weighing,
  exclusive of
  theJars,29 lbs
1 Brown Jar of 3
  Blue Plumbs,
1 Brown Jar of
  Cranberries
1 White Jar Currant
  Jelly
1 Bottle Orange
  Flower Water

2 Tin Boxes Sago
  Powder
2 Jugs Raspberry
  3 lbs
1 Bottle Pickled
  Mushrooms
1 Jar Preserved
  Quinces
1 Jar Pickles 10 lbs

## MISCELLANEOUS

2 lbs Starch
3 Bottles Army?
  Powder
2 Papers Powder
3 horses
3 saddles
2 bridles
3 halters
1 cart and harness
1 sleigh

**Here is a complete list of books in Brock's estate:**

Bell's edition of Shakespeare (20 vols); *L'Erudition Militaire; Elegant Extracts* (2 vols); *Expedition to Holland* ; Francis' *Horace* (4 vols); *Grammar of the French Tongue;* Gregory's *Dictionary of Arts and Sciences* (2 quarto); Guibert's *Oeuvres Militaires* (5 vols) and his *Reglement de l'Infantries* (2 vols) ; *L'Erudition Universalle Militaire;* Hume's *Essays* (2 vols); Johnson's Dictionary (2 vols); Johnson's Works (12 vols.); *King's of Prussia's Tactics* (also called *King of Prussia's Instructions*); *Life of Condé; Les Aventures de Telemagne;* McArthur on Courts Martial (2 vols); Marshal's Travels; *Military Memoirs Ancient and Modern;* Plutarch's *Lives* (6 vols); Pope's Works (8 vols); Murray's Grammar and Exercises (3 vols); Court Calendar; Reeds edition of Shakespeare (12 vols); *Reflexions sur les Principes Militaires;* Rollin's *Ancient History* (12 vols); *Siècle de Louis XIV* (4 vols); Voltaire's *Henriad;* Volumes of Plays (5 vols); *Walcheren Expedition;* Wharton's *Virgil* (4 vols); Whitlock's *Trial;* Road map of England, Scotland, and France; eight European and other magazines.

**Sources**

OA, F775MU2143, Miscellaneous Collection 1812. Inventory of Furniture, etc. belonging to the Estate of the Late Major-General Brock purchased by Major-General Sheaffe. Inventory of Brock's possessions resulting from the Probate of his estate. An Account of Sale of Effects of the later Major-General Brock sold at Auction on the 4th of January 1813. Toronto Public Library, Wm Allan Papers, S123. Inventory of the Effects of Sir Isaac Brock sold at York, November 1812.

# Notes

## Preface

1. Fryer, *Bold, Brave*, 13–14. She describes her study of Brock as, "A military history of a military man."

2. See Harvey, *War of Wars*, 270, 631, "There are few things the British like so much as a fallen hero…."

3. Harvey, *War of Wars*, 4.

4. Benn, *Iroquois in the War*, viii–ix. See also, Bamford and Carroll, *Four Years on the Great Lakes*, 31–2.

5. Hickey, *Don't Give Up The Ship!*, xxvi–xxvii. See also, Malcomson, *Lords of the Lake*, xix–xx, 343–52.

## Introduction

1. Adkins, *War for all the Oceans*, 280–314; Harvey, *War of Wars*, 672–75.

2. Adkins, *War for all the Oceans*, 168, 171, 197; Markham, *Napoleon*, Chapter 8.

3 Harvey, *War of Wars*, 141–42, 502–04, 515–16.

4. Indigo dye used to colour the blue of French troops' uniforms was imported from India. Adkins, *War for all the Oceans*, 197, 205.

Hitsman, *Incredible War*, 15, 22; Harvey, *War of Wars*, 536–38 mentions many products imported by the French government that were smuggled from Britain.

5. Latimer, *1812: War with America*, 16; see page 6 for a favourable view of the treatment of sailors in the Royal Navy. Adkins, *War for all the Oceans*, 375.

6. Adkins, *War for all the Oceans*, 105–12, 206–09; Dudley, *Naval War*, 1, 61–2; Latimer, *1812: War with America*, 16–18.

7. Dudley, *Naval War*, I, 491–93, A. Allen Jr. to all Officers of his Majesty's Ships of War or of Privateers belong to Subjects or his Majesty, September 16, 1812; see also, 134, 527.

8. Allen, *His Majesty's Indian Allies*, 61–5; Benn, *Iroquois in the War*, 18–20. See also, the discussion in Zuehlke, *For Honour's Sake*, Chapter 4.

9. Allen, *His Majesty's Indian Allies*, 69–73.

10. Prucha, *Sword of the Republic*, 20–38, provides a clear treatment. See also, Edmunds, *Tecumseh*, Chapters 2 and 3.

11. Ferrell, *American Diplomacy*, 66–72. Hickey, *War of 1812*, 6–7.

12. Allen, *His Majesty's Indian Allies*, 107; see also, 82–5. For the role of the U.S. Army in securing control of the trans-Mississippi territories see Prucha, *Sword of the Republic*, Chapter 5. The U.S. government's "factory system" (i.e., government trade stores) provided an important means to acquire more native territory. See Barr, *The Boundaries Between Us*, 178–83.

13. *ANB*, vol. 10, 223–26.

14. Allen, *His Majesty's Indian Allies*, 108–09, 117, n. 59. The Prophet's biography is in *DCB*, 7, 847–50. Tecumseh's is in *DCB*, 5, 795–801, and Appendix D.

15. Allen *His Majesty's Indian Allies*, 13, 19.

16. Allen, *His Majesty's Indian Allies*, 91.

17. Tupper, *Life and Correspondence*, 1–4. Brock, *The Brocks of England*, is a very useful source.

**18.** Graves, *The War of 1812 Journal of Le Couteur*, 5–6. He refers to Jersey and Guernsey.

## Chapter One

1. Vice-admiral of the Blue, first Baron de Saumarez, 1757–1836. See Adkins, *The War for All the Oceans*, Chapters 1 and 2. *The Dictionary of National Biography*, edited by Sir L. Stephen and Sir S. Lee. Oxford: O U P, 1959–60, v. 17, 803–06, for his brothers, Thomas and Richard, see 806–08.

2. Tupper, Life and Correspondence, 4 for both quotations. Tupper's daughter, Henrietta, compiled *Who Was Isaac Brock? Short Summary of the Life of Major-General Sir Isaac Brock, K.B.* to inform "some of the younger folk" of Guernsey about him.

3. See Appendix E.

4. General Orders and Regulations for the Army, 1811. I want to thank Ron Dale for finding and explaining these figures. He estimates the present-day cost of an ensign's commission would be about $100,000. Sutherland, *His Majesty's Gentlemen*, 4, 13, n. 21, provides different and higher costs for commissions.

5. 1812 Army List. Again, I want to thank Ron Dale for providing these figures. Spier, *The Army and Society*, 14–15, gives the figure of £365 for a lieutenant-colonel. He also mentions additional payments that an officer might receive.

6. Sutherland, *His Majesty's Gentlemen*, 3–4. Holmes, *Redcoat*, xix–xx, 111–13.

7. Holmes, *Redcoat*, 174–75 gives a variety of reasons for exchange.

8. Turner, *British Generals*, 59–60, Chapter 4. DCB, 8, 793–96.

9. S. Sutherland, *His Majesty's Gentlemen*, 4–5, 13, n. 21. In cavalry regiments a much higher percentage (45 to 80 percent) of commissions were purchased. For full discussion see Bruce, *The Purchase System*, and Glover, "The Purchase of Commissions," 229–35. Holmes, *Redcoat*, 157–66.

10. Tupper, *Life and Correspondence*, 5–6; Fryer, *Bold, Brave*, 43–4.

11. Tupper, *Life and Correspondence*, 87–9, 92–4, letters of January 10 and February 19, 1811.

12. Fryer, *Bold, Brave*, 44–50. Turner, *British Generals*, 60. On the dangers to the health of troops in the West Indies see M. Duffy, *Soldiers, Sugar and Seapower: The British Expeditions to the West Indies and the War Against Revolutionary France* (Oxford: Clarendon Press, 1987).

13. Tupper, *Life and Correspondence*, 6, 18; Turner, *British Generals*, 60–1.

14. Tupper, *Life and Correspondence*, 349.

15. Edgar, *General Brock*, 13–21, and Tupper, *Life and Correspondence*, 6–17.

16. Denmark, Sweden, Prussia, and Russia. O. Warner, *A Portrait of Lord Nelson* (London: 1963), 238–62; Adkins, *The War for All the Oceans*, 73–91.

17. Tupper, *Life and Correspondence*, 18–22. He was quoting the words of a naval officer, Captain Percy Grace, who was present. Edgar, *General Brock*, 27. Adkins, *The War for All the Oceans*, 84, shows the positions of the ships in Nelson's line.

**Chapter Two**

1. LAC, RG8, C922, 8, Brock to Major Green, September 20, 1802. On Plenderleath see Sutherland, *His Majesty's Gentlemen*, 300.

2. Hunter was also lieutenant governor of Upper Canada. *DCB*, 5, 439–43.

3. Firth, *Town of York*, 72, Brock to Green, July 29, 1803. Lord Selkirk's description of York cited in *Ibid.*, 253. The population in 1802 was 320 and in 1804, 432. *Ibid.*, lxxvii. Green was also military secretary to commander of the forces at Quebec and for a time, military secretary to Colonel Isaac Brock. See *DCB*, 6, 298–300.

4. Turner, "Career," 28–9; see discussion in n. 4. Taylor, *Civil War of 1812*, 106–10.

5. *DCB*, 9, 264–67. FitzGibbon, *A Veteran of 1812*, 16–33. He described his experiences as a prisoner of war.

6. *DCB*, 9, 264. He became ensign and adjutant in 1806 and a lieutenant in 1809. FitzGibbon, *A Veteran of 1812*, 50–1, 56–8. Enid Mallory claims that Brock also taught FitzGibbon "the manners and lifestyle of a gentleman." *The Green Tiger*, 13. See also, 37. Tupper, *Life and Correspondence*, 14–16, 256–59.

7. Turner, "Career," 28–9. FitzGibbon, *A Veteran of 1812*, 52–3.

8. Turner, "Career," 29–32.

9. Turner, "Career," Appendix A; *DCB*, 5, 111. Hitsman, *Incredible War*, 14–5, 19. The battalion had ten companies totaling 650 men. Sutherland, *His Majesty's Gentlemen*, 6.

10. Tupper, *Life and Correspondence*, 72–4.

11. On courts martial see Whitfield, *Tommy Atkins*, 76–7, and Sutherland, *His Majesty's Gentlemen*, 9–10.

12. Tupper, *Life and Correspondence*, 348; cited in Turner, "Career," 31–2. Fryer, *Bold, Brave*, 248, asserts that the executions took place in Montreal.

13. Whitfield, *Tommy Atkins*, 59–71.

14. Simcoe to Major General. Clarke, July 27, 1793. AO, MS83, Simcoe Letterbook, 332–33. *DCB*, 6, 152, R.S. Allen writes of William Claus, in command of militia and British troops at Fort George and Queenston in June and July 1812, that "much of his time was devoted to stemming desertion." Lieutenant Colonel Bisshopp wrote about American inducements to British troops along the Niagara frontier. From Fort Erie, March 21, 1813, Allen, "Bisshopp Papers," 25. For further discussions of the problem see Holmes, *Redcoat*, 316–17; Hickey, *Don't Give Up the Ship!*, 255–62.

15. Cited in Turner, *British Generals*, 86–7. The matter is fully discussed in Turner, "Career," 282–84. The letter, dated February 8, 1804, is in Canadian Archives, RG 4, v. 923, 12–6. For a different view see Whitfield, *Battle of Queenston Heights*, 32, 48–9.

16. The problem of desertion from Sheaffe's command did not completely end. See Sheaffe to Green, York, August 9, 1805, in Firth, *Town of York*, 73.

17. Fryer, *Bold, Brave*, 56–7, 87, speculates that Sheaffe, five years older than Brock, may have felt some jealousy about Brock's rank and his easy manner as commander.

18. Tupper, *Life and Correspondence*, 32, Tupper's reporting of evidence is usually carefully done. What exactly this complaint was about is uncertain. My discussions with experts on the period suggest Sheaffe may have wanted to restrict the soldiers' leisure activities (fishing, visiting town) and "white trowsers" may have meant their work overalls, which would have been none too clean. Brock allowed the men to fish wearing fatigues which were undress uniform and as such would be neater and cleaner than overalls.

19. LAC, RG8, C923, 18–20, Brock to Lieutenant-Colonel. Green, Feruary 19, 1804.

20. This paragraph is based on Turner, "Career," 33.

21. Turner, "Career," 34–5. Fryer, *Bold, Brave*, 92, suggests that Brock was uneasy about leaving Sheaffe in command of the regiment.

22. Turner, "Career," 36–40. Hitsman, *Incredible War*, 21–2.

23. *DCB*, 5, 205–13. His civil secretary was Herman W. Ryland, who favoured an assimilationist policy towards the *Canadiens*. Ouellet, *Lower Canada*, 63–4, 92–4, and Edgar, *General Brock*, 91–3.

24. Dunn was administrator from 1805 to 1807. See *DCB*, 5, 287–93.

25. Sutherland, *His Majesty's Gentlemen*, 60. Tupper, *Life and Correspondence*, 69, Thornton to Brock, April 7, 1808, mentions that Lieutenant-General Prevost was made second in command to Craig. There is very little information on Baynes, who is not included in the usual biographical dictionaries. He may have first joined the army in 1783. When he arrived in Canada he was a lieutenant-colonel in the Nova Scotia Fencibles. He had been ADC to Craig and would serve as adjutant general to the

forces until February 1815. He returned to England as a major-general and died in 1829. On Thornton see *DNB*, 9, 789–90, and Sutherland, *His Majesty's Gentlemen*, 355–56. He had served as ADC to Craig from 1803–06 and returned with Craig to England in 1811. Thornton later served in the Peninsula and under Major-General Robert Ross in the capture of Washington, D.C., where he was wounded and captured. He was wounded again in the attack on New Orleans.

**26.** This paragraph is based on Ouellet, *Lower Canada*, Chapters 2 and 3.

**27.** Ouellet, *Lower Canada*, 92–3; see also, Stanley, *War of 1812*, 54–7; Edgar, *General Brock*, Chapter 9. The scholarly literature dealing with this period is vast. The following quotation is from M. Wade, *The French Canadians, 1760–1967*, vol. 1 (London: Macmillan, 1968), 107.

**28.** Tupper, *Life and Correspondence*, 92–4. See also, 82–3, Baynes to Brock, October 4, 1810; 85, Baynes to Brock, October 11; and 98–100, Baynes to Brock, March 4, 1811.

**29.** Dudley, *Naval War*, I, 26–36; Turner, "Career," 39–43; Prucha, *The Sword of the Republic*, 97. Before the increase, the army had three regiments and a corps of engineers. Skelton, "High Army Leadership," 254.

**30.** Horsman, "On To Canada," 9: "In July 1807 ... Jefferson told a visitor, 'If the English do not give us the satisfaction we demand, we will take Canada.'"

**31.** Cited in *Kingston Gazette*, November 19, 1811. On December 10, this newspaper printed the correspondence between the British minister to Washington and James Monroe that settled the *Chesapeake* dispute. *York Gazette*, on November 20, published a special supplement containing President Madison's message of November 5. Hickey, *War of 1812*, 29–32.

**32.** Dudley, *Naval War*, 1, 40–50; Adkins, *War for all the Oceans*, 362–65.

**33.** LAC, RG8, C676, 12–3, Dunn to Brock, July 29, 1807. Tupper, *Life and Correspondence*, 65–6, Brock to Colonel Gordon, September 6, 1807.

**34.** The documents are in LAC, RG8, C1214, no. 11, 332–34, and the gist is given in Tupper, *Life and Correspondence*, 60–1. Turner, "Career," 39–43.

**35.** Tupper, *Life and Correspondence*, 65–6, Brock to Gordon, September 6, 1807; see Edgar, *General Brock*, 94–7.

**36.** Johnston, *The Glengarry Light Infantry*, 6.

**37.** Stanley, *War of 1812*, 61–3; Hitsman, *Incredible War*, 21–2.

**38.** Brock to Windham, Secretary of War in Britain, February 12, 1807, cited in Turner, "Career," 74. Tupper, *Life and Correspondence*, 46–7.

**39.** Tupper, *Life and Correspondence*, 15–19; Turner, "Career," 45–8. On Gore see *DCB*, 8, 336–41.

**40.** *DCB*, 6, 214–15. Turner, "Career," 62–5. For discussion about the office and how it developed see Whitfield, *Tommy Atkins*, 30–6.

**41.** LAC, RG8, C1214, 70–1, Brock to George Harrison, November 28, 1806. Cited in Turner, "Career," 64.

**42.** Turner, "Career," 65–6, discusses and provides documentary references.

**43.** This paragraph is based on Turner, "Career," 66–9, where the origin of the Jesuit Barracks is explained. See also, Holmes, *Recoat*, 266–70.

**44.** For the army's medical services see Whitfield, *Tommy Atkins*, 38–9; Holmes, *Redcoat*, 95–7; Stanley, *War of 1812*, 433–44.

**Chapter Three**

**1.** Tupper, *Life and Correspondence*, 38, 70. Brock wrote to his brothers, July 20, 1808, that his promotion to brigadier was first announced in the March mail. Turner, "Career," 61.

2. Sutherland, *His Majesty's Gentlemen*, 7, refers to brigadier-general as an appointment rather than a rank for the purpose of enabling colonels "to function as general officers as circumstances demanded."

3. *DCB*, 2, 545–48.

4. Tupper, *Life and Correspondence*, 69, Thornton to Brock, April 7, 1808. See also, Edgar, *General Brock*, 99–101. On the roles and status of the Frobishers see biography of Joseph in *DCB*, 5, 331–34.

5. Tupper, *Life and Correspondence*, 72, Brock to his brothers, September 5, 1808. On Drummond see Turner, *British Generals*, 113–16; *DCB*, 8, 236–39.

6. LAC, RG8, C289, 6–7, Drummond to Lieutenant-Colonel Thornton, May 17, 1810; C549, 52–4, Drummond to Thornton, July 22.

7. Richard Cartwright to Major McKenzie, November 2, 1808, C.E. Cartwright, ed., *Life and Letters of Hon R. Cartwright*, 144–45. The major is not identified but may have been Holt McKenzie of the 41st Foot.

8. H. Strum, "A Most Cruel Murder: The Isaac Underhill Affair, 1809," *Ontario History*, 53 (December 1988), 293–310. Taylor, Civil War of 1812, 109–10.

9. Tupper, *Life and Correspondence*, 76–7, letter dated June 8, 1810.

10. There is little information about him. His father's biography is in *DCB*, 4, 190–91. He is mentioned briefly in Ouellet, *Lower Canada*, 145, 148. On his militia service see L. Lépine, *Les officiers de milice du Bas-Canada, 1812–1815* (Montreal: 1996), 96.

11. Tupper, *Life and Correspondence*, 77–9, letter dated July 9, 1810.

12. Turner, *British Generals*, 103. On de Rottenburg see *DCB*, 6, 660–62.

13. Tupper, *Life and Correspondence*, 79–80, letter dated July 10, 1810.

14. Tupper, *Life and Correspondence*, 82–3, Colonel Edward Baynes to Brock, October 4, 1810.

15. Tupper, *Life and Correspondence*, 85, Baynes to Brock, October 11, 1810.

16. Tupper, *Life and Correspondence*, 92–4, Brock to Irving, February 19, 1811; *Ibid.*, 99–100, Baynes to Brock, March 4.

17. Green to William Claus, July 5, 1810, NHS, *Records of Niagara*, #42, 103–04. Winter picnics were another social activity. See Venning, *Following the Drum*, 193–94.

18. *SBD*, I, 528–29, Duke of York to Prevost, October 7, 1812.

19. Turner, *British Generals*, 80 and n. 102. Sutherland, *His Majesty's Gentlemen*, 163. Prevost wrote that he was willing to take Glegg "into my family." LAC, RG8, C1220, 8, Prevost to Sheaffe, October 21, 1812.

20. Tupper, *Life and Correspondence*, 81, 83–84 for the three letters. Graves, *The War of 1812 Journal of Le Couteur*, 224; DCB, 6, 660.

**Chapter Four**

1. Stanley, *War of 1812*, 49. Preston, *Kingston*, cxii–cxiv. Information on Kingston's population principally from Robert Gourlay. Sheppard, *Plunder*, 35–6 gives the population of 1,000, which may be high, other sources state it was about 600. Sheppard also claims that Upper Canada's population declined during the war. *Ibid.*, 195. For York see Firth, *Town of York*, lxxvi–lxxvii. Robinson, *Life of ... Robinson*, 53, wrote that York had "scarcely 700 inhabitants."

2. Bateau also spelled batteau. These were flat-bottomed boats made of planks. They were about forty feet long and six feet across at their widest part and capable of carrying 9,000 pounds. There was a lot of hard work handling cargo and navigating through rapids for a crew of only five men. See Heriot, *Travels*, 117–18. Stanley, *War of 1812*, 71.

3. Tupper, *Life and Correspondence*, 93, Brock to Irving, February 19, 1811; *Ibid.*, 132, Brock to the Military Secretary, December 11.

4. Tupper, *Life and Correspondence*, 194–96, 198–99.

5. This paragraph is based on Turner, "Career," 81, Appendix D.

6. LAC, RG8, C676, Gore to Craig, February 20, 1809.

7. Tupper, *Life and Correspondence*, 81–2, letter dated September 13, 1810. On Vincent see *DCB*, 7, 888–89. On Glegg see Turner, *British Generals*, 80 and n.102.

8. NHS, *Records*, no. 42, 105–06, William Claus to Lieutenant-Colonel Curry, Niagara, November 17, 1810. Curry was military secretary to General Hunter. On Claus see *DCB*, 6, 151–53, Appendix D; on Heriot, who engaged in horse racing, see *DCB*, 7, 397–98. Vincent had begun his military career in 1781 as an ensign in the 66th Foot and entered the 49th Foot in December 1783 as a lieutenant. He became lieutenant-colonel on June 13, 1811, and major-general June 4, 1813. He was in command of the Niagara frontier in 1813 when the Americans invaded and led the forces in defence of Fort George and at Stoney Creek. Later that year he was sent to command at Kingston and in 1814 at Montreal until he departed for England on sick leave. He eventually became a general and died in London in 1848. See *DCB*, 7, 888–89 and Sutherland, *His Majesty's Gentlemen*, 364.

9. Tupper, *Life and Correspondence*, 87–9, 92–4, letters of January 10 and February 19, 1811.

10. *DCB*, 8, 458–65.

11. Tupper, *Life and Correspondence*, 90, Kempt to Brock, January 17, 1811; see also, page 92, where Baynes refers to this in a letter to Brock of February 14. Kempt had a distinguished military career in North America and Europe. *DCB*, 8, 458–65.

12. *York Gazette*, Friday, February 1, 1811.

13. Tupper, *Life and Correspondence*, 100–02, letters dated April 9 and May 9, 1811. Vesey urged Brock to marry but not to a woman in

Canada. Little is known about John Agmondisham Vesey. The following information was provided by Brian Owen, a curator at the Royal Welsh Fusiliers Museum at Caernarfon. From 1778 Vesey served in the 11th Regiment of Foot as an Ensign and by 1788 he was a lieutenant. The record is blank between 1788 and 1804. He shows up as a lieutenant colonel in the 52nd (Oxfordshire) Foot, then the Nova Scotia Fencibles, the 29th Foot. He was on half-pay in 1811 until June 4, when he (and Isaac Brock) were appointed major generals. He served in the Mediterranean and died in Sicily on December 5, 1811. See Edgar, *General Brock*, 138–39.

14. LAC, RG8, C30, 105–06, Torrens to Prevost, October 18, 1811; Tupper, *Life and Correspondence*, 104–05, Torrens to Brock, October 17.

15. Allen, *His Majesty's* ..., 115–17. On Elliott see *Ibid.*, 112–13.

16. Open letter of Harrison, December 25, 1811, cited in Allen, *His Majesty's* ..., 117. See also, Hitsman, *Incredible War*, 30; Benn, *Iroquois in the War*, 23, 41. "From the American perspective, the reality on the ground was a degree of co-operation between Britain and Natives that was a threat." Black, *America as a Military Power*, 86. For a colourful account of the battle see Berton, *The Invasion of Canada*, 69–77.

17. Tupper, *Life and Correspondence*, 94–6, dated February 27, 1811, and 96–8, dated March 4.

18. Tupper, *Life and Correspondence*, 99–100, Baynes to Brock, March 4, 1811. Baynes wrote about Craig being "extremely weak and debilitated ... with his strength ... visibly sinking under his disease," and that he was apprehensive "of his becoming too ill to be able to undertake the voyage." He died January 12, 1812. The *Quebec Mercury*, August 18, 1812, 260–61, printed an obituary.

19. On Dunn see *DCB*, 5, 287–93. *York Gazette*, July 13, 1811, reported on the elaborate ceremonies accompanying Craig's departure. A week later, on July 20, the *York Gazette* reported Drummond's arrival. He, like Brock, had asked to return to England. His request was approved, but Drummond changed his mind and decided to

remain in Canada. LAC, RG8, C30, 14, 24, Drummond to Craig, February 27, 1811, and Colonel Henry Torrens to Craig, June 8; C550, 84, Torrens to Drummond, August 27.

**20.** *DCB*, 5, 693–98; Turner, *British Generals*, Chapter 2. *SBD*, I, 166–67, General Order, September 14, 1811. This order also directed Brock to take command of Upper Canada. The description comes from the *Quebec Mercury*, September 16, 1811, 293.

**21.** Ontario Archives, State Book E, 404, Brock to Prevost, October 9, 1811. *York Gazette*, October 9, 1811, printed Brock's proclamation, addresses presented to Gore and speeches by a deputation of chiefs of the Six Nations. Edgar, *Ten Years of Upper Canada*, 64–5, George Ridout to his brother, October 19.

**22.** Edgar, *Ten Years of Upper Canada*, 57–60, Thomas Ridout to his brother, September 26, 1811. Thomas described the bad economic conditions in England owing to the enforcement of Napoleon's decrees and the costly burden of maintaining the army in Portugal.

**23.** Tupper, *Life and Correspondence*, 111, October 7, 1811; see also, 112–16, Brock to Irving, October 30 and William Brock to Isaac, October 31. Edgar, *General Brock*, 161–67. For the information on the bankruptcy see Brock, *The Brocks of England*, 84–5, 87–8. William's business had been a source of income for his brothers Daniel, Savery, and Irving. The figure for annual pay comes from "Regulations Relating to General Officers," 212, dated Horse Guards, July 24, 1814. Regulations seem to have remained unchanged from 1811 through 1816 so these figures should be accurate for 1812.

**24.** Edward Ellice, *DCB*, 9, 233–39. The following paragraph is based upon this biography.

**25.** Tupper, *Life and Correspondence*, 281; cited in Edgar, *General Brock*, 296–67.

**26.** Spiers, *Army and Society*, 14. See Holmes, *Redcoat*, 282. See Chapter 2.

27. Preston, *Kingston Before the War of 1812*, 274. Macpherson to Noah Freer (acting aide-de-camp to Prevost), February 2. Even the august Duke of Wellington, although receiving extra allowance as commander-in-chief in the Peninsula, complained that after deduction of income tax he needed additional pay "or I shall be ruined." Wellington to Earl Bathurst, Madrid, August 24, 1812, in *Wellington at War, 1794–1815: A Selection of his Wartime Letters*. Edited and Introduction by A. Brett-James (London: 1961), 240–41.

28. Tupper, *Life and Correspondence*, 151–52, Brock to Military Secretary, February 12, 1812.

29. Turner, "Career," 109–11, n. 56; Tupper, *Life and Correspondence*, 117–21; See 141–42, Brock to the Military Secretary, January 1812, reveals great inefficiency in the provision of supplies for the Indian Department in Upper Canada.

30. *DHC*, 3, 19–20, Report of Lieutenant-Colonel Bruyeres, August 24, 1811. On Bruyeres see *DCB*, 5, 118–19.

31. *DHC*, 3, 20–1, Glasgow's report dated September 18, 1811. Bowering, "Study of the Utilization of Artillery," I, 37. On Glasgow see *DCB*, 5, 346–47.

32. *Kingston Gazette*, November 19, 1811, January 14 and 28, 1812. Hickey, *War of 1812*, 22–4, points out that contrary to Madison's belief Napoleon had not truly removed the French decrees restricting neutral shipping.

33. Tupper, *Life and Correspondence*, 123–30, December 2, 1811; see also, LAC, C673, 171–82. Allen, *Indian Allies*, 118–19.

34. Gore had written in the same vein years before, e.g., LAC, RG8, C676, 64–71, Gore to Sir James Craig, February 20, 1809.

35. Cited in Carter-Edwards, "The War of 1812," 29.

36. *DCB*, 6, 479–80.

37. Tupper, *Life and Correspondence*, 130, Brock to Prevost, December 3, 1811. On Prevost's use of this letter see Turner, "Career," 113.

38. Benn, *Iroquois in the War*, 29–35. See Norton's biography in *DCB*, 6, 550–53; Claus in *Ibid.*, 151–53. See Appendix D.

39. Black, *America as a Military Power*, 85–6.

40. *Journal of Major Norton*, 293.

41. Benn, *Iroquois in the War*, 55, 29–35, 212, n. 88, provides figures for part of 1813. A few of these give an idea of the enormity of supplies needed: 5,000 common guns, 5,000 chiefs guns, 1,000 pistols, 2,000 swords, 16,400 kilograms of gunpowder, and 2,000 coats. *Journal of Major Norton*, cv, cxi, cxx, cxxii.

42. Schmaltz, *Ojibwa of Southern Ontario*, 148.

43. Benn, *Iroquois in the War*, 56. Allen, *His Majesty's Indian Allies*, 113. Schmaltz, *Ojibwa of Southern Ontario*, 167–68. After the war, the role of the Indian Department began to change and, finally, "In 1852 the issue of presents in Upper Canada ceased entirely and was commuted to a money payment beginning with three-fourths the value of the equipment and diminishing one-fourth until final extinction in 1857."

44. Stanley, *War of 1812*, 77–9. See G. Collins, *Guidebook to the Historic Sites of the War of 1812* (Toronto: Dundurn Press, 1998), 182.

45. Fryer, *Bold, Brave*, 18–21, refers to two letters written in August 1812 that mention Brockville before Brock gained fame for the capture of Detroit, but only one could be located. The quotation comes from Thad W.H., Leavitt, *History of Leeds and Grenville from 1749 to 1879* (Belleville, ON: Mika, 1972), 197.

46. *Journals of the Legislative Assembly of Upper Canada*, 1812, 27 (February 14), 56 (February 27), 60 (February 28). *Journals and Proceedings of the Legislative Council of Upper Canada*, 1812, 415 (February 17). The same holds true in these Journals for 1811.

47. RG8, C676, 120, Major McPherson to Noah Freer, July 5, 1812; 124, Richard Cartwright to Prevost, July 5. C688, 169, Colonel Lethbridge to Brock, August 10; 174, Lethbridge to Brock, August 30.

**48.** Printed at Montreal 1812. I want to thank Professor Alun Hughes for bringing this item to my attention.

**49.** Correspondence from LAC with the author, May 5, 2010. The sources listed are RG8, C688B, 178–79. However, there is mention of Elizabethtown in February and March 1813 found in Militia Papers, Upper Canada, 1812. Alien Boards were created in November 1812 to examine residents who claimed exemption from militia service on the grounds of being American citizens. The boards could allow claimants to depart for the United States or could forbid their departure from Upper Canada. Turner, *British Generals*, 92.

**50.** Ron Dale provided this information.

**51.** *Journals of the Legislative Assembly of Upper Canada*, 1818, 478, March 2.

**52.** *Journals of the Legislative Assembly of Upper Canada*, 1819, 161–63, 166–67, July 1; 1821, 400 (March 17), 425 (March 30). The Act passed January 28, 1832, is found in *The Statues of Upper Canada, to the Time of the Union* (Toronto: Robert Stanton, n.d.), 806–17.

**Chapter Five**

**1.** Tupper, *Life and Correspondence*, 151, Brock to Prevost, February 12. See also, 140–41, Prevost to Brock, January 22.

**2.** Hickey, *Don't Give Up the Ship*, 37, for an discussion of the War Hawks see 40–1; Hickey, *War of 1812*, 29–32, and Zuehlke, *For Honour's Sake*, Chapter 6. Hitsman, *Incredible War*, 28–9, 44. The War Hawk who had the most influence on campaigns on the Niagara frontier was Peter B. Porter, whose home was at Black Rock. *ANB*, vol. 17, 707–9.

**3.** Perkins, *Prologue to War*, 70–3. However, British seizures from 1803–12 numbered 917 compared to 558 by France and her allies. See also, Zuehlke, *For Honour's Sake*, 53–4; Borneman, *1812: The War*, 48.

4. Ferrell, *American Diplomacy*, 146–53. The repeal of the Orders may also have been influenced by Wellington's military gains in the Peninsula and from Napoleon's preparations to invade Russia see Harvey, *War of Wars*, Chapters 71 and 75. Hickey, *War of 1812*, 42–3, explains why these British measures failed to prevent the war. He also writes that Madison later stated the war "would have been stayed" if he had known about the repeal of the Orders. Borneman, *1812: The War*, 52.

5. Black, *America as a Military Power*, 60.

6. Hitsman, *Incredible War*, 46–7; Prucha, *Sword of the Republic*, 106; On Dearborn see Appendix D.

7. *DHC*, 3, Armstrong to Eustis, January 2, 1812. On Armstrong see *ANB*, 1, 617–18, Peterson, *Military Heroes of the War*, 107–10, and Hickey, *War of 1812*, 106–08, 202.

8. Stanley, *War of 1812*, 47; Borneman, *1812: The War*, 58–9; Hitsman, *Incredible War*, 46.

9. Skelton, "High Army Leadership," 264–67. This article provides an incisive study of many qualities of army leadership throughout the war period. *DHC*, 3, 42, Governor Tompkins to General Porter, February 29, 1812.

10. Hitsman, *Incredible War*, 46; Borneman, *1812: The War*, 76. We need not be concerned with Major General Thomas Pinckney, commander of the Southern Department.

11. *ANB*, vol. 11, 455–57. Hull, *Memoirs of the Campaign*, 16–8. Hickey, *War of 1812*, 80–1, writes, "Hull eagerly sought a military appointment."

12. Hull, *Memoirs of the Campaign*, 8, 19–26.

13. *ANB*, vol. 21, 738–39. Appendix D. Tompkins had no military experience but was an enthusiastic supporter of the war.

14. *DHC*, 3, 80–3, Tompkins to Eustis, June 27, 1812. See Appendix D. *ANB*, vol. 22, 244–45 for Stephen; 243–44 for Solomon. See also, Hitsman, *Incredible War*, 46, 57; Borneman, *1812: The War*, 70, 72.

15. Hickey, *War of 1812*, 33–7. Upper Canadians were kept informed by newspaper articles. See *Kingston Gazette*, November 19, December 31, 1811, and January 14 and 28, February 4, 1812.

16. Stagg, "Enlisted Men," 619–21; Black, *America as a Military Power*, 46; Skelton, "High Army Leadership," 254. The number may have been as low as 7,000 officers and men. Horsman, *War of 1812*, 30; Carland, "The Simplest Thing" 29.

17. Mann, *Medical Sketches of the Campaigns*, 15. He was appointed at the commencement of the war.

18. Dudley, *Naval War*, 1, 53–60, Secretary of the Navy Paul Hamilton's report, dated December 3, 1811. Five other vessels were laid up in Ordinary. For another estimate see Adkins, *War for All the Oceans*, 375.

19. Dudley, *Naval War*, 1, 273–75.

20. Two memoranda by Brock sent to Prevost in early February 1812 demonstrate this professionalism. *SBD*, I, 288–91.

21. Hitsman, *Incredible War*, 36–8. *DHC*, 4, 85–8, Lovett to Alexander, October 14, 1812. For the colonelcy of this regiment, Prevost appointed Baynes, his adjutant general, and for the lieutenant-colonelcy and actual command, Major Francis Battersby, 8th Regiment. Hitsman suggests that Macdonell was "disgruntled" with receiving only a majority. Stanley, *War of 1812*, 63–4.

22. Lépine, *Les officiers de milice*, 28. Stanley, *War of 1812*, 49, 58, argues this was "a measure of conscription beyond anything" attempted by Brock in Upper Canada. Turner, *British Generals*, 28–9. Hitsman, *Incredible War*, 31–9.

23. *DCB*, 6, 341–45, under Irumberry de Salaberry.

24. Lépine, *Les officiers de milice*, 31–4, 221. Hitsman, *Incredible War*, 36–9. Turner, *British Generals*, 28. The corps would give a very good account of itself during the war.

25. Turner, *British Generals*, 31–2. Tupper, *Life and Correspondence*, 159–61, Baynes to Brock, March 19, 1812.

26. Turner, *British Generals*, 31, 88. LAC, RB8, C, 676, 86–9, Brock to Prevost, February 6, 1812. Tupper, *Life and Correspondence*, 199–200, Baynes to Brock, July 8.

27. *SBD*, 1, 190–91, April 27, 1812. On the failure of the scheme see *DHC*, 3, 144–46, Brock to Prevost, July 26.

28. Turner, *British Generals*, 29. The text of the act is given in *SBD*, 1, 210–26. In the *Quebec Mercury* of August 11, 1812, a retail business called John Mure & Co. advertised, "ARMY BILLS PREFERRED TO CASH."

29. LAC, MG13, WO17, 66, 81, show the numbers on June 25 and July 25, the latter being 1,381.

30. *SBD*, I, 288–89, Two memoranda from Brock to Prevost, February 1812.

31. For legislative members and elections see *Legislators and Legislatures of Ontario: A Reference Guide. Vol. 1: 1792–1866*, D. Forman, ed. (Toronto, 1984).

32. Tupper, *Life and Correspondence*, 147, Brock to Baynes, February 12, 1812. Turner, *British Generals*, 63.

33. On Willcocks and the reasons for opposition, see *DCB*, 5, 854–59, where you will find the names of his supporters in the assembly. See also, Graves, "Joseph Willcocks," 16–8, 23–4.

34. Militia Acts had been amended in 1809 and 1810. One of the reasons was to change regulations allowing pacifists (Quakers, Mennonites, Tunkers) to pay "composition money" in place of serving. See Brock, "Accounting for Difference," 19–30; NHS, *Records*, no. 42, 82. Gray, *Soldiers of the King*, 25–9.

35. Brock also provided details of his proposals for raising a volunteer corps in a memorandum undated but certainly early February 1812. *SBD*, I, 290–91.

36. *Journals of the Legislative Assembly of Upper Canada*, 1812, 1–97. Brock's opening address is on 4–5. See also, Turner, *British Generals*, 68.

**37.** Sheppard, *Plunder, Profit*, 42–3, 53. Turner, *British Generals*, 150–51.

**38.** *Journals of the Legislative Assembly of Upper Canada*, 1812, 97. Appendix B. See Turner, *British Generals*, 68. See also, LAC, MG11, CO42/352, 7–9, Brock to Liverpool, March 23, 1812.

**39.** The act may be found in *DHC*, 4, 5–11. See also, Gray, *Soldiers of the King*, 27, 29–34.

**40.** NHS, *Records*, no. 43, 23–5, circular letter, York, April 8, 1812. See also, Tupper, *Life and Correspondence*, 163–65, Brock to Lieutenant-Colonel Nichol April 8, for the kind of letter sent to militia commanders.

**41.** NHS, *Records*, no. 43, 59–61, Charles Askin to his father, November 18, 1812; 68–71, Askin to his father, December 11. The men would be charged for the shirts and stockings. The sedentary militia, however, lacked clothing. Hitsman, *Incredible War*, 40. Stanley, *War of 1812*, 69 mentions the appeal in York.

**42.** NHS, *Records*, no. 43, 21–3. Colonel Ralfe Clench to Major General Shaw, April 1, 1812. Lieutenant-Colonel Thomas Clark to Shaw, April 3; Lieutenant-Colonel John Warren to Shaw, 12 April.

**43.** Gray, *Soldiers of the King*, 32–42.

**44.** LAC, Q117-2, 296, Prevost to Liverpool, May 18, 1812. Cited in Hitsman, *Incredible War*, 36. A figure of 11,408 is given in the "Annual Return of the Militia of Upper Canada," June 4, 1811, in LAC, RG 5, Upper Canada Sundries, XIII, 5437–38.

**45.** *SBD*, I, 305–09, Brock to Liverpool, May 2, 1812. He earlier had asked Prevost for rations and clothing for the militia. *Ibid.*, 186–89, Brock to Prevost, April 22.

**46.** NHS, *Records*, 43, 28. *SBD*, I, 302–03, Brock to Prevost, May 16, 1812. Brock gave his view in this letter. The outcome was approval to pay annuities to widows and children of militiamen killed or disabled. Turner, *British Generals*, 93. See LAC, RG8, I, C1220, 118–19, Prevost to Sheaffe, January 21, 1813.

**47.** Gray, *Soldiers of the King*, 32–45.

**48.** NHS, *Records*, no. 43, 28–9, George Hamilton to Thomas McKee, May 1812.

**49.** *DCB*, 7, 697–98. Newfield, "Upper Canada's Black Defenders?," 32.

**50.** LAC, RG8, I, vol. 1218, 139, Brock to Freer, January 23, 1812. Cited in Hitsman, *Incredible War*, 40. Brock ordered swords and pistols from Quebec for this corps.

**51.** Gray, *Soldiers of the King*, 157–78, 183. In 1813, these corps would be raised as provincial corps. *Ibid.*, 179–201. Bowering, "Study of the Utilization of Artillery," 1, 37, 39. Malcomson, *Brilliant Affair*, 12, 48, 113, 126.

**52.** Allen, *His Majesty's Indian Allies*, 120–22, 219. The quotations are from this source.

**53.** Tupper, *Life and Correspondence*, 141–42. He mentioned that he had seen "about 800" there in 1810. Aboriginal families in the vicinity of Amherstburg needed increased provisions from British stores during the winter of 1811–12 because they had not received the usual issue of ammunition which forced them to curtail their hunting. *DRIC*, 32–3, Claus to Brock, June 16, 1812.

**54.** LAC, RG8, C 676, 86–9, Brock to Prevost, February 6, 1812; Tupper, *Life and Correspondence*, 147–50, Brock to Baynes, February 12.

**55.** LAC, RG8, vol. 256, 209, "Confidential Communication transmitted to Mr. Robert Dickson," February 27, 1812; 211, Dickson's answer, dated June 18, was received at Fort George on July 14; 229, both enclosed in Glegg to Baynes November 11. See also, *SBD*, I, 431–32, Dickson to Brock, July 13, 1812. On Dickson see *DCB*, 6, 209–11.

**56.** Benn, *Iroquois in the War*, 36 and see 36–9 for an explanation of the disputes over land sales. See also, Allen, *Indian Allies*, 93–5. *SBD*, 1: 302–03, Brock to Prevost, May 16, 1812.

**57.** *Journal of Major Norton,* 287–89.

**58.** *Journal of Major Norton,* 289–93; Benn, *Iroquois in the War,* 39–44.

**59.** Tupper, *Life and Correspondence,* 159–61, Baynes to Brock, March 19, 1812. See also, *Ibid.,* 133–35, Prevost to Brock, December 24, 1811. In April, Brock approved an increase in Claus's salary of £200. *DHC,* 3, 58, Brock to Freer, April 23, 1812. See also, *DRIC,* 32–3, Claus to Brock, June 16, 1812.

**60.** *Journal of Major Norton,* 293–95, The quotations are from this source. Benn, *Iroquois in the War,* 42–6.

**61.** Dudley, *Naval War,* I, 268–73, Lieutenant-Colonel A.H. Pye report to Prevost, December 7, 1811 (Also printed in SBD, I, 240–44). *DHC,* 3, 35–8, Captain Gray to Prevost, January 29, 1812. Pye was deputy quartermaster general and Gray was assistant deputy quartermaster general. Malcomson, *Lords of the Lake,* 25–31; Turner, *War of 1812,* 31. On Andrew Gray see Sutherland, *His Majesty's Gentlemen,* 170.

**62.** Firth, *Town of York,* 80–1, Freer to Brock, April 27, 1812. *SBD,* 1, 258–62, Gray's Report upon the Expediency of Removing the Marine Establishment from Kingston to York…, March 9.

**63.** *DHC,* 3, 35–8, Gray to Prevost, January 29, 1812. Malcomson, *Lords of the Lake,* 29–31. On Yeo see *DCB,* 5, 874–77.

**64.** Tupper, *Life and Correspondence,* 159–61, Baynes to Brock, March 19, 1812.

**65.** *DHC,* 3, 35–8, Captain Gray to Prevost, January 29, 1812. On Grant see *DCB,* 5, 363–67. On Hall, see *DCB,* 6, 308–10.

**66.** Tupper, *Life and Correspondence,* 260–61; Edgar, *General Brock,* 206–07. *DCB,* 6, 539–46.

**67.** *DCB,* 6, 539–46; Turner, "Career," 132–36. See also, Turner, *British Generals,* 69 and references there.

**68.** Tupper, *Life and Correspondence,* 156–57, Brock to Prevost, March 9, 1812.

**69.** *DHC*, 3, 76–7, District General Order, June 27, 1812. Tupper, *Life and Correspondence*, 260, states that Nichol's appointment caused offence "to some of those high in station in the provincial government" without explaining who they were.

**70.** Tupper, *Life and Correspondence*, 260–61.

**71.** Firth, *Town of York*, lxv, lxxxiii, 277–78. Turner, "Career," 139. On Firth see *DCB*, 7, 285–86; on Baldwin see *DCB*, 7, 35–44.

**72.** Firth, *Town of York*, lxxii, 212; Turner, "Career," 150–52. The quotation comes from OA, Strachan Papers, 1812 folder, the appointment of Strachan, July 28, 1812. On Mountain see *DCB*, 6, 523–29. On Strachan see *DCB*, 9, 751–66. Edgar, *Ten Years of Upper Canada*, 75–77, Ridout to his son Thomas, December 18, 1811.

**73.** The election was held in June. Firth, *Town of York*, 252.

**74.** Tupper, *Life and Correspondence*, 140–41, Baynes to Brock, January 23, 1812. Firth, *Town of York*, lxxxiii.

**75.** Charles Askin to his father, February 24, 1812, NHS, *Records ... 1812*, no. 43, 16–7.

**76.** Tupper, *Life and Correspondence*, 161, Baynes to Brock, March 19, 1812.

**77.** Dudley, *Naval War*, I, 73–81; Turner, *War of 1812*, 32, 24–5; Hitsman, *Incredible War*, 47.

**78.** Borneman, *1812: The War*, 47–53; Adkins, *War for All the Oceans*, 372–73. Hickey, *War of 1812*, 43–8, describes the vote on the war bill as "essentially a party vote."

**79.** Hitsman, *Incredible War*, 41, Prince Regent's Instructions, October 22, 1811. Turner, *War of 1812*, 29.

**80.** Prevost to Liverpool, May 18, cited in Hitsman, *Incredible War*, 283–88. Turner, *War of 1812*, 29–30. See also, Hyatt, "Defence of Upper Canada," 20–31.

**81.** LAC, RG8, v. 1218, 308, Prevost to Lord Liverpool (prime minister), July 15, 1812. *Life and Correspondence*, 199–200, Baynes to Brock, July 8. Turner, *War of 1812*, 29–30.

**82.** Tupper, *Life and Correspondence*, 147–50, Brock to Baynes, February 12, 1812. *SBD*, I, 302–03, Brock to Prevost, May 16. Turner, *War of 1812*, 64–5.

**83.** LAC, MG13, W.O.17, 1516, 5–125, provides the figures up to October 1812. Turner, *War of 1812*, 31–2.

### Chapter Six

**1.** Skelton, "High Army Leadership," 255–58.

**2.** *DHC*, 3, 73, H.W. Ryland to Prevost, June 24, 1812, forwarding dispatch from Forsyth, Richardson & Co. and McTavish, McGillivray & Co.

**3.** Hitsman, *Incredible War*, 44, 51, 59–61. Tupper, *Life and Correspondence*, 199–200, Baynes to Brock, July 8, 1812.

**4.** *DHC*, 3, 77, Swift to Governor Tompkins, June 27, 1812; 78–9, Major-General Amos Hall to Governor Tompkins, 28 June; 85, *Federal Republican* of Baltimore, Maryland, July 15.

**5.** *DHC*, 3, Hall to Governor Tompkins, June 28, 1812; 71–3, Colonel Philetus Swift and Benjamin Barton to Governor Tompkins, June 24.

**6.** Cited in Casselman, *Richardson's War of 1812*, 11–12. *DHC*, 3, 85, *Federal Republican* of Baltimore, Maryland, July 15.

**7.** *DHC*, 3, 77–8, Wadsworth to Tompkins, June 28, 1812.

**8.** *DHC*, 3, 101–04, Wadsworth to Tompkins, July 6.

**9.** For troop movements and conditions see *DHC*, 3, 80–3, Tompkins to Eustis, June 27, 1812; 89–91, *Aurora* of Philadelphia, July 11; 96–7, Major General Hall to Tompkins; July 4, 117–19, General Porter to Tompkins, July 9.

**10.** *DHC*, 3, 117–19, General Porter to Tompkins, July 9, 1812; see also, 126–28, *New York Gazette*, July 24. DHC, 3, 117–19, General Porter to Tompkins, July 9, 1812; see also, 126–28, New York Gazette, July 24. Taylor, Civil War of 1812, 140–41.

**11.** Dudley, *Naval War*, I, 282–83, Tompkins to John Bullus, July 13, 1812.

**12.** On Procter see *DCB*, 6, 616–18; Chapter 11 below.

**13.** *DHC*, 3, 76–7, District General Order, June 27, 1812; 91–2, District General Order, July 2.

**14.** Tupper, *Life and Correspondence*, 194–96, Brock to Prevost, July 3, 1812. Brock had not heard that the president had signed a declaration of war.

**15.** *DRIC*, 38–9, enclosure in Hull to Secretary of War, June 26, 1812.

**16.** Hitsman, *Incredible War*, 62. J. Latimer, *1812*, 61, 63, 66. Taylor, *Civil War of 1812*, 157–58, describes Hull as "distracted and erratic," his speech slurred, "and he drank too much." during the difficult march to Detroit.

**17.** Hull, *Memoirs of the Campaign*, 8–9, 35–7. [Hull] *Report of Trial*, 48–9, Colonel McArthur claimed that he warned Hull not to send the baggage by water because the British might know that war had been declared. Armstrong, *Notices of the War*, I, 16–7, 47–8, repeats this account.

**18.** Beall, "Journal," 787.

**19.** On Roberts see *DCB*, 5, 713–14.

**20.** Tupper, *Life and Correspondence*, 194–96, Brock to Prevost, July 3, 1812. Turner, *British Generals*, 69–70.

**21.** For a discussion on the name of this fort and two others see Hickey, *Don't Give Up the Ship*, 252–55. On Roberts see *DCB*, 5, 713–14. On the series of letters see Turner, *British Generals*, 70.

**22.** Beall, "Journal," 791.

**23.** *DCB*, 8, 33–5.

**24.** Borneman, *1812: The War*, 62. Hull, *Memoirs of the Campaign*, 10, 40–50.

**25.** *DHC*, 3, 144–46, Brock to Prevost, July 26, 1812.

**26.** The rest of this paragraph is based on Sugden, *Tecumseh's Last Stand*, 9–10. The description refers to September 1813. Hickey, *Don't Give Up the Ship*, 252–53. Beall, "Journal," 802, in 1812, thought the fort was "very weak," meaning it could be captured easily.

27. *DRIC*, 58–60. Emphasis in original. Hull, *Memoirs of the Campaign*, 10, 45–6.

28. Smith, *A Geographical View*, 84–8. On Smith see *DCB*, 5, 765–66. Taylor, *Civil War of 1812*, 159–61, writes that looting by Hull's troops turned many residents against the invaders.

29. Cited in Hitsman, *Incredible War*, 71–2. Armstrong, *Notices of the War*, I, 19–22. Armstrong claims it took three weeks to complete the carriages and mount two guns and three howitzers.

30. *DCB*, 5, 37–9 provides the biography of John Askin, father of John Jr. and of Charles. There is a little information about these sons.

31. *DRIC*, 63–5. Captain Roberts to Colonel Baynes, July 17, 1812. Included were the terms of capitulation. *SBD*, I, 436–37, John Askin Jr. to Honourable Colonel W. Claus, July 18. Hitsman, *Incredible War*, 72–4.

32. Hitsman, *Incredible War*, 82; Fryer, *Bold, Brave*, 141.

33. Hitsman, *Incredible War*, 74; Benn, *Iroquois in the War*, 49; Allen, *His Majesty's Indian Allies*, 130.

34. *DHC*, 3, 144–46, Brock to Prevost, July 26, 1812. Watson later returned to Sandwich while Allan and Westbrook were arrested. The latter escaped in October and continued to assist the Americans throughout the war. See his biography in *DCB*, 6, 808–10. See also, Stanley, *War of 1812*, 96–8, 275, 279–81. Taylor, *Civil War of 1812*, 142–43, depicts Watson as a disaffected "entrepreneur" and see 159–60, 244.

35. Cited in Hitsman, *Incredible War*, 66.

36. Carter-Edwards, "The War of 1812," 3. Dale, *Invasion of Canada*, 23. Berton, *Invasion of Canada*, 136–37, provides details of the plundering of farms and homes by American patrols.

37. *DHC*, 3, 135–38, dated July 22, 1812. Printed in the *Kingston Gazette*, July 28. Hitsman, *Incredible War*, 68, describes Brock's

proclamation as "a poor effort." Stanley, *War of 1812*, 104–05, believes some people were inspired by the proclamation while many in western Upper Canada were indifferent. S.R. Mealing in his biography of W.D. Powell, asserts, "Powell drafted Brock's celebrated reply of 22 July 1812..." see *DCB*, 6, 609.

**38.** Carter-Edwards, "The War of 1812," 32.

**39.** *DRIC*, 53, 72. AO, Alexander Fraser Papers, MU1063, Series 1, Box 1, Matthew Elliott to Colonel Claus, July 26, 1812. Allen, *His Majesty's Indian Allies*, 132, 136–37; Turner, "Career,"175–76.

**40.** Hitsman, *Incredible War*, 67–8.

**41.** *DHC*, 3, 144–46, Brock to Prevost, July 26, 1812. AO, Alexander Fraser Papers, MU1063, Series 1, Box 1, Matthew Elliott to Colonel Claus, July 26, 1812. Elliott reported many militiamen wanted to go home to reap their crops.

**42.** NHS, no. 9, 44, Norton to Hon. Henry Goulburn, January 29, 1816. *Journal of Major Norton*, 295–97.

**43.** Benn, *Iroquois in the War*, 46–7.

**44.** *Journal of Major Norton*, 297–300.

**45.** Tupper, *Life and Correspondence*, 194–96, Brock to Prevost, July 3, 1812. *DHC*, 3, 144–46, Brock to Prevost, July 26.

**46.** Black, *America as a Military Power*, 76–7.

**47.** Letters of August 4 to Colonel Baynes and August 29 to Lord Liverpool (British prime minister). Cited in Turner, "Career," Appendix G.

**48.** Graves, "Joseph Willcocks," 27–9. On the dinner with Brock see Edgar, *Ten Years of Upper Canada*, 116, Thomas Ridout to his father, May 23, 1812. *DCB*, 5, 858. For the report on his mission see *DRIC*, 209–12, Willcocks to Lieutenant-Colonel John Macdonell, September 1, 1812. AO, Alexander Fraser Papers, MU1063, Series 1, Box 1, Norton to Captain Glegg, August 11.

**49.** *DHC*, 3, 179–80, District General Order, August 14, 1812. Schmaltz, *Ojibwa of Southern Ontario*, 164.

50. *DCB*, 7, 348. Allen, *His Majesty's Indian Allies*, 95, 114–15.Turner, *British Generals*, 80. Gray, *Soldiers of the King*, 48. He died in 1846 in Toronto.

51. LAC, RG8, v. 676, 239–41, Brock to Baynes, July 29, 1812. Turner, "Career," 175.

52. Hitsman, *Incredible War*, 69, refers to Procter as Brock's "most capable subordinate." Carter-Edwards, "The War of 1812," 31.

53. Edgar, *General Brock*, 236–37; Fryer, *Bold, Brave*, 156–57, 179. Dean was released after the capture of Detroit.

54. [Hull] *Report of Trial*, 106–14. He also stated that he did not want to divide his army. Armstrong, *Notices of the War*, I, 18–21.

55. Casselman, *Richardson's War of 1812*, 20–1, where Richardson cites an order of August 6, 1812, reporting on these skirmishes. In July 1812, aged fifteen, he joined the 41st Regiment as a volunteer. He participated in the attack on Detroit and in later military engagements with the 41st. He was captured at the Battle of the Thames, October 5, 1813, and was imprisoned in Kentucky until 1814. He continued to serve in the British Army until 1818. Over the next several years he wrote about his military experiences in novels as well as in newspaper articles, subsequently published as his history of the war. He died in New York City in 1852. See *DCB*, 8, 743–48, and Casselman, *Richardson's War of 1812*, Introduction.

56. Stanley, *War of 1812*, 101–02.

57. *DRIC*, 115–17, Hull to Secretary of War, August 4, 1812. Dale, *Invasion of Canada*, 23–4. On Muir see *DCB*, 6, 529–30.

58. Hitsman, *Incredible War*, 77–8. Casselman, *Richardson's War of 1812*, 33–46. Richardson was present but mistakenly refers to Captain Muir as major. Brock appointed him to that rank temporarily on August 14. *Journal of Major Norton*, 300.

59. *SBD*, I, 389–96, Brock to Prevost, July 28, 1812. Here will be found also the replies of the Assembly and of the Legislative Council. *DHC*, 3, 147–48.

60. LAC, RG8, v. 676, 217–18. *DHC*, 3, 148–49. Cited in Hitsman, *Incredible War*, 74.

61. *DHC*, 3, 151–52, Brock to Prevost, July 29, 1812.

62. *DHC*, 3, 162–63. Turner, *British Generals*, 71–2.

63. Printed in the *Kingston Gazette*, September 5, 1812.

64. *DHC*, 3, 144–46. Brock to Prevost, July 26, 1812. Turner, *British Generals*, 72, 34; Turner, "Career," Appendix E.

65. *DHC*, 3, 167–69, Prevost to Brock, August 12, 1812; 225–26, Prevost to Brock, August 30.

66. Turner, *British Generals*, 110, 118–20. See also, Hickey, *Don't Give Up the Ship*, 271–73.

67. *DHC*, 3, 167–69. Turner, *British Generals*, 33.

68. Latimer, *1812: War with America*, 69–71; Stanley, *War of 1812*, 112–15. Hickey, *War of 1812*, 85–6.

**Chapter Seven**

1. *SBD*, I, 469, Brock to Prevost, August 17, 1812. It is not clear if Brock knew that Sheaffe was on his way from Lower Canada. LAC, RG8, C677, 8–9, Vincent to Colonel Baynes, August 4. RG8, C1219, Prevost to Bathurst, August 17.

2. *SBD*, I, 546–48, Diary of Wm. McCay. Gray, *Soldiers of the King*, lists no McCay but has three McKays, all in flank companies, one in the 2nd York, one in the 4th Lincoln, and one in the 5th Lincoln.

3. *DHC*, 3, 170–71; See also, Casselman, *Richardson's War of 1812*, 48–9.

4. OA, F.B. Tupper Papers, MS496. Tupper, *Life and Correspondence*, 259–60. The writer seems to have been James FitzGibbon.

5. Tupper, *Life and Correspondence*, 242; Edgar, *General Brock*, 232–33.

6. Tupper, *Life and Correspondence*, 261. The author gives no source but many historians repeat this story.

7. Cited in Edmunds, *Tecumseh*, 178. For descriptions of Tecumseh in 1813 see Sugden, *Tecumseh's Last Stand*, 54, 63, 98, 122. See also, Appendix D.

8. Tupper, *Life and Correspondence*, 260. Cruikshank, *General Hull's Invasion*, 277.

9. Tupper, *Life and Correspondence*, 253; Edmunds, *Tecumseh*, 179–80.

10. *DHC*, 3, 179, District General Order, August 14, 1812.

11. *DRIC*, 144–45, Brock to Hull, August 15, 1812, and Hull's reply. See also, Casselman, *Richardson's War of 1812*, 50–1; Hitsman, *Incredible War*, 80. Armstrong, *Notices of the War*, I, 32–5, states that Hull rejected several suggestions to interfere with Brock's preparations, such as, sending a detachment to spike the British guns. Hull, *Memoirs*, 95–6.

12. *SBD*, I, 549–50, Diary of Wm. McCay.

13. *DHC*, 3, 179–80, District General Order, August 14, 1812; *SBD*, I, 463, Brock to Prevost, August 16 and 465–70, Brock to Prevost, August 17. Casselman, *Richardson's War of 1812*, 52.

14. *DHC*, 3, 180–81, District General Orders, August 15, 1812.

15. Hull, *Memoirs*, 60, 65–6.

16. Hull, *Memoirs*, 150–2. [Hull] *Report of the Trial*, 39–40, Snelling claimed that Hull had taken no measures to oppose an enemy crossing. Armstrong, *Notices of the War*, I, 35–8, describes the size and locations of Hull's forces to show they were well positioned to defend the fort. He implies that Hull did not intend to put up any resistance.

17. John Richardson's words in Casselman, *Richardson's War of 1812*, 51–2. *SBD*, I, 550, Diary of Wm. McCay. Cruikshank, *General Hull's Invasion*, 279–80, suggests Brock's total force numbered over 850.

18. *DHC*, 3, 186, Brock to Evans, August 17, 1812. On Evans see Chapter 9.

19. *SBD*, I, 465–70, Brock to Prevost, August 17, 1812. The detachment under Cass and McArthur consisted of 350 Ohio militia but Brock rightly considered it a serious threat.

20. [Hull] *Report of the Trial*, 81.

21. Casselman, *Richardson's War of 1812*, 52; see also 53–55. *Journal of Major Norton*, 300. Stanley, *War of 1812*, 107–09 gives a clear account.

22. Tupper, *Life and Correspondence*, 260–61. Nichol claimed that he had selected the point of landing on the American shore and after crossing in the first boat, he superintended the troops' disembarkation. *DHC*, 8, 247–53, Nichol's memorial, September 24, 1817.

23. Stagg, *Mr. Madison's War*, 205. *DHC*, 3, 220–21, John Lovett to Abraham Van Vechten, August 28, 1812, Lovett heard from one of Hull's captains evidence for the general's odd behaviour. Tomes, *Battles of America*, 2, Chapter 4. Hickey, *War of 1812*, 84.

24. Venning, *Following the Drum*, 265–68, present accounts that appeared the *Boston Times* in August 1755, and in New York newspapers in the summer of 1757. Taylor, *Civil War of 1812*, 203–07, 286.

25. [Hull] *Report of the Trial*, 39–40, 93, 130–31, 153.

26. [Hull] *Report of the Trial*, 152, testimony of Brevet-Major John Whistler.

27. Hull, *Memoirs*, 167, 107–27, 211–12.

28. Cruikshank, *General Hull's Invasion*, 284–85.

29. *Journal of Major Norton*, 300–01. What Norton found was a group of French Canadian women and children taking shelter from the battle.

30. Casselman, *Richardson's War of 1812*, 55, 58; *SBD*, I, 550, Diary of Wm. McCay. See also, Stanley, *War of 1812*, 107–09. Brock reported that his ADCs returned "within an hour" from their talks with Hull. *SBD*, I, 468, Brock to Prevost, August 17, 1812.

31. *SBD*, I, 497, General Return of Prisoners of War Surrendered by Capitulation at Detroit, August16th, 1812.

32. Casselman, *Richardson's War of 1812*, 70–82, cites Hull's letter from Fort George, August 26, to the American secretary at war explaining his decision and Colonel Lewis Cass's letter of September 10 to the Secretary criticizing Hull's leadership. Hull, *Memoirs*, 124–27, Hull claimed that his total force numbered only 1,060 men and he had at the fort only 745 effectives. [Hull] *Report of the Trial*, Appendix II, 23–4, 13, Articles of Capitulation enclosed in his letter of August 26, which he sent from Montreal, dated September 8.

33. Cruikshank, *General Hull's Invasion*, 286–87. *SBD*, I, 495–96, Return of Ordnance and Ordnance Stores taken at Detroit. August 16, 1812.

34. Turner, "Career," 190–91. *SBD*, I, 560, Adjutant General's Office, General Order, February 25, 1815, directed the first distribution of prize money from the capture of Detroit, each private to receive three pounds. Fryer, *Bold, Brave*, 180. Robinson, *Life of Sir John Beverley Robinson*, 29–30, Lieutenant Robinson eventually received £90.

35. Latimer, *1812: War with America*, 68. On hearing news of Hull's surrender, Madison immediately returned to Washington and called a full cabinet meeting only second time of his presidency. Two decisions were reached: they would try to regain control of the lakes and another army would be sent to recover Detroit. Hickey, *War of 1812*, 85–6.

36. Robinson, *Life of Sir John Beverley Robinson*, 29–30. Lieutenant John Beverley Robinson wrote he was at that breakfast.

37. Cited in Casselman, *Richardson's War of 1812*, 59–6. *SBD*, I, 463–65, includes Brock's brief note to Prevost of August 16. While lives were spared, residents' property was taken by native warriors. Taylor, *Civil War of 1812*, 165.

38. *Journal of Major Norton*, 301.

**39.** Cited in Casselman, *Richardson's War of 1812*, 69; Hitsman, *Incredible War*, 82. The question arose in the United States whether or not General Hull could surrender American territory. Antal claims that Brock conquered Michigan as part of his (and Britain's) plan to create a separate native state in the Old Northwest. This plan does not appear in Brock's correspondence with Prevost or with British military authorities. S. Antal, *A Wampum Denied: Procter's War of 1812* (Ottawa: Carleton University Press, 1997).

**40.** *SBD*, I, 506–09, Brock to Lord Liverpool, August 29, 1812. Hitsman, *Incredible War*, 78. Taylor's pays tribute to Brock but disregards Tecumseh's vital contribution. Taylor, *Civil War of 1812*, 163–5.

**41.** Kosche, "Relics of Brock," 56–68. For the story see Tupper, *Life and Correspondence*, 253–54; Edmunds, *Tecumseh*, 180.

**42.** Latimer, *1812: War with America*, 71, Dearborn to Eustis, July 28. Eustis replied in a letter dated August 15 that Dearborn's command did extend to Upper Canada and urged him to launch a diversion to support Hull's invasion.

**43.** *DHC*, 3, 220–21, Lovett to Abraham Van Vechten, August 28, 1812. Mallory, *The Green Tiger*, 27–9.

**44.** *ANB*, vol. 11, 455–57. Stanley, *War of 1812*, 111. See also, Berton, *The Invasion of Canada*, 187–88, and Taylor, *Civil War of 1812*, 169–70.

**45.** *SBD*, I, 539, Extract from an Original Journal of Charles Askin. Tupper, *Life and Correspondence*, 262; Robinson, *Life of Sir John Beverley Robinson*, 30–40. On Peter Robinson see *DCB*, 7, 752–57. His younger brother, John Beverley, in the 3rd York Militia, was also present in the Detroit campaign but it is not clear if he returned on this vessel. See *DCB*, 9, 668–79.

**46.** *SBD*, I, 506–09, Brock to Lord Liverpool, August 29, 1812. Hitsman, *Incredible War*, 85.

**47.** *DHC*, 3, 225–26, Prevost to Brock, August 30, 1812. Hitsman, *Incredible War*, 83–8; Turner, *British Generals*, 88–9. Not all

American officers on the Niagara were pleased by Van Rensselaer's truce. See *DHC*, 3, 193–94, Nicholas Gray to Governor Tompkins, August 19, 1812.

48. *DHC*, 3, 167–69, Prevost to Brock, August 12, 1812. Hitsman, *Incredible War*, 90–1.

49. Dudley, *Naval War*, I, 305; 294–95 Commodore Isaac Chauncey was soon to take over this command.

50. Malcomson, *Brilliant Affair*, 86. Hickey, *War of 1812*, 42–3. For a defence of this armistice see Hitsman, *Incredible War*, 84–8 and Stanley, *The War of 1812*, 86.

51. Dudley, *Naval War*, I, 296–97.

52. Tupper, *Life and Correspondence*, 284–86. Brock to his brothers, September 3, 1812, See Zuehlke, *For Honour's Sake*, 118–21; Hitsman, *Incredible War*, 85.

53. *Kingston Gazette*, September 12, 1812.

54. LAC, C688B, 1–2, Militia General Order, Fort George, August 26, 1812. See page 13.

55. *Kingston Gazette*, September 12, 1812.

56. Tupper, *Life and Correspondence*, 284–86.

57. Fryer, *Bold, Brave*, 186.

58. Tupper, *Life and Correspondence*, 298, letter from inhabitants of Niagara District to Prevost, December 16, 1812. The complete letter is in OA, F.B. Tupper Papers, MS496, Microfilm reel 1.

59. Tupper, *Life and Correspondence*, 284–86. Brock to his brothers, September 3, 1812.

60. Smith, *A Geographical View*, 88–9. Zaslow, *Defended Border*, 211.

61. *DHC*, 3, 268–69, Extract of a letter from _____ to Major General Van Rensselaer, September 16, 1812. The writer is usually considered to have been a spy or informant for the Americans.

62. LAC, C688B, 1–2, Militia General Order, August 26, 1812. See page 11 above. For an example of the oath sworn by militia

officers see OA, F775, MU2102, Miscellaneous Collection #7, September 4, 1812.

63. Bamford and Carroll, *Four Years on the Great Lakes*, 59–60. Wingfield was a Royal Navy officer who arrived at Quebec on May 5, 1813, and served at Kingston from May 16, 1813, until 1816.

64. *Kingston Gazette*, September 5, 1812. In its issue of September 3, the paper reported on elaborate celebrations at Quebec City.

65. *DHC*, 3, 242–43, Brock to Prevost, September 7, 1812; *Kingston Gazette*, September 5.

**Chapter Eight**

1. Van Rensselaer, *A Narrative*, Appendix, 42; Major Gen Van Rensselaer to Major General Brock, September 4, 1812; Major General Sheaffe to Major General Van Rensselaer, September 5.

2. A. Conger Goodyear Bechs, *War of 1812*, MSS, Box 2, vol. 7, 1–6, Nicholas Gray (acting engineer) to General Van Rensselaer, August 31, 1812. Turner, "Career," 244–45. The figures are based upon modern topographical maps. See also, Smith, *Geographical View*, 46, 72–4; Howison, *Sketches of Upper Canada*, 71–3, 110–15.

3. *DHC*, 3, 193–94. Inspector-General Nicholas Gray to Governor Tompkins, August 19, 1812.

4. Wilson, *Enterprises*, 5. The descriptions of the settlements and roads are taken from *Ibid.*, 4–7; Malcomson, *Brilliant Affair*, 12–4; Siebel, *Niagara Portage Road*, 18, 29–33, 131–40.

5. A. Conger Goodyear Bechs, *War of 1812* MSS, Nicholas Gray (acting engineer) to General Van Rensselaer, August 31, 1812. Malcomson, *Brilliant Affair*, 15–6; Siebel, *Niagara Portage Road*, 137.

6. Van Rensselaer, *Narrative*, Appendix, 50–3, Van Rensselaer to Governor Tompkins, September 15, 1812. *DHC*, 3, 253–55, Colonel Van Rensselaer to Major General Lewis, September 11. *SBD*, I, 588–90, Brock to Prevost, September 13. Malcomson,

*Brilliant Affair*, 93–4 Yet, as late as October 5th, a United States army engineer wrote to Van Rensselaer that the fort could not be defended against a cannonade nor could its guns do much damage to the enemy opposite, an estimate that was certainly discredited by the effectiveness of the American bombardment of Niagara on October 13th. *DHC*, 4, 34, Lieutenant Totten to Major General Van Rensselaer, October 5, 1812.

7. Bowering, "A Study of the Utilization of Artillery," 1, 42–3.

8. On Smyth see *ANB*, 20, 325–26, and Chapter 11.

9. Hickey, *War of 1812*, 86.

10. Malcomson, *Brilliant Affair*, 40–7 describes the development of New York state militia from 1807.

11. *DHC*, 3, 125–26, General Order, Albany, July 13. Van Rensselaer was ordered to take up command of New York "between St. Regis and Pennsylvania." *Ibid.*, 177, General Orders, Headquarters, Niagara, August 13, 1812.

12. *DHC*, 3, 224–25, John Lovett to Abraham Van Vechten, September 8, 1812. Lovett was a poet, lawyer, and "boon companion" of Stephen Van Rensselaer. See Taylor, *Civil War of 1812*, 183 175–76; Malcomson, *Brilliant Affair*, 70–1. Abraham Van Vechten was a prominent lawyer who served at different times in New York's assembly, senate and as attorney general. ANB, v. 22, 254–55.

13. Van Rensselaer, *Narrative*, Appendix, 38–41, Major General Van Rensselaer to Major General Dearborn, September 1, 1812, and September 2. Latimer, *War with America*, 74. Malcomson, *Brilliant Affair*, 93, states there were about 800 regulars at this time along the river.

14. Van Rensselaer, *Narrative*, Appendix, 50–3, Major General Van Rensselaer to Major General Dearborn, September 15, 1812; Van Rensselaer to Lieutenant Colonel Fenwick, September 15.

15. *SBD*, I, 588–90, Brock to Prevost, September 13, 1812. Tupper, *Life and Correspondence*, 316–17, Brock to Savery, September 18.

**16.** Van Rensselaer, *Narrative*, Appendix, 45–7, Major-General Van Rensselaer to Major-General Dearborn, September 8, 1812. See also, *Ibid.*, 38–40, Van Rensselaer to Dearborn, September 1; 48–9, Van Rensselaer to Dearborn, September 10; 50–3, Van Rensselaer to Governor Tompkins, September 15.

**17.** Van Rensselaer, *Narrative*, Appendix, 67–72. The two generals exchanged at least ten letters from September 29 to October 12. See also, Malcomson, *Brilliant Affair*, 107–11.

**18.** *DHC*, 3, 276, Dearborn to Van Rensselaer, September 17, 1812; 295, Dearborn to Van Rensselaer, September 26, 1812. In both letters the emphasis is in the originals. See Malcomson, *Brilliant Affair*, 109–11, 117, for details of the units arriving on the Niagara. He gives the figure of 2,350 regulars and 4,050 New York militia.

**19.** Armstrong, *Notices of the War*, 1, 113. Mann, *Medical Sketches*, 11–12, describes the problems of weather and widespread sickness among the troops at Greenbush.

**20.** *DHC*, 3, 238–39, Van Rensselaer to Dearborn, September 5, 1812; 275, Van Rensselaer to Governor Tompkins, September 17. Van Rensselaer, *Narrative*, Appendix, 45–7, Van Rensselaer to Dearborn, September 8; *Ibid.*, 50–3, Van Rensselaer to Tompkins, September 15. This is the source of the quotation.

**21.** *DHC*, 3, 297–98, Van Rensselaer to Dearborn, September 27, 1812.

**22.** *DHC*, 3, 253–55, Colonel Van Rensselaer to Major-General Morgan Lewis, September 11, 1812. Taylor describes the relations between the two Van Rensselaers and British officers opposite as cosy. He also suggests that "Van Rensselaer and his staff" did not expect to defeat Brock's army but rather in the coming battle "to expose Republican folly." *Civil War of 1812*, 184–87.

**23.** *DHC*, 3, 237–38, Colonel Solomon Van Rensselaer to Abraham Van Vechten, September 5, 1812; 253–55, Colonel Van Rensselaer to Major-General Morgan Lewis, September 11; see also, 231,

Solomon Van Rensselaer to his wife, September 1. Malcomson, *Brilliant Affair*, 108, 114.

24. Pennsylvania State Archives, MG6, Jacob Miller Diary, 25–6 Miller was a volunteer from Pennsylvania who served in the Buffalo-Black Rock area throughout October. His diary makes clear how unprepared the Americans at Buffalo were to act against Upper Canada on October 13.

25. Turner, *British Generals*, 33 and n. 45. For the correspondence see *DHC*, 3, 242–43, Brock to Prevost, September 7, 1812; 260, Prevost to Brock, September 14; 299, Brock to Prevost, September 28.

26. Tupper, *Life and Correspondence*, 316–17, Brock to Savery Brock, September 18, 1812; 314–15, Brock to Prevost, September 18.

27. OA, F775, MU2102, Miscellaneous Collection #6, Letterbook of Deputy Commissary General I.W. Cooke, entries for August 11, 15, and 18, 1812.

28. *DHC*, 3, 101–04, Brigadier-General Wadsworth to Governor Tompkins, July 6, 1812; 126–28, *New York Gazette*, July 24. Van Rensselaer, *Narrative*, Appendix, 38–40, Van Rensselaer to Dearborn, September 1.

29. U.S. National Archives, RG59, M588, 7:115, Ensign J. Smith to Colonel Procter, October 18, 1812; *DHC*, 3, 297–98, Van Rensselaer to Dearborn, September 27. Crooks, "Recollections," 32.

30. Bowering, "A Study of the Utilization of Artillery," 1, 41–2.

31. *DHC*, 3, 237–38, Colonel Solomon Van Rensselaer to Abraham Van Vechten, September 5, 1812; 238–39, Van Rensselaer to Dearborn, September 5; Van Rensselaer, *Narrative*, Appendix, 50–3, Van Rensselaer to Tompkins, September 15.

32. Sources sometimes differ in describing the weight and type of ordnance at some points along the Niagara River. Bowering, "A Study of the Utilization of Artillery," 1, 41–3. He mentions "two more field 4 prs, three field 6 prs, one field 12 pr, two garrison 24 prs and two garrison 12 prs," in and near Fort George.

Malcomson, *Brilliant Affair*, 169, puts two guns at Vrooman's Point, a 12-pounder and 18-pounder carronade.

**33.** *DHC*, 3, 283–84, District General Order, September 20, 1812. Another forty-three were sent on September 30th, most of them to be posted at Miller's Creek which lies about seven miles south of Chippawa. *Ibid.*, 304, DGO of September 30th. For other troop dispositions see DGOs in vol. 3, 285–86, September 22; vol. 4, 28, October 2; 44, October 9.

**34.** *SBD*, I, 266–69 provides a description from 1809 of this telegraph system. BECHS, A Conger Goodyear, War of 1812 MSS, Box 2, vol. 7, Nicholas Gray to General Van Rensselaer, August 31, 1812. In his diary, Jacob Miller mentions a black flag "hoisted at the Telegraph" on the Canadian shore opposite Black Rock. Pennsylvania State Archives, MG6, Jacob Miller Diary, 27, October 16, 1812.

**35.** *DHC*, 3, 292, September 25.

**36.** *DHC*, 4, 38. Fort George, October 6, 1812.

**37.** *Journal of Major Norton*, 302–04 and NHS, no. 9, 43–4, Norton to Hon. Henry Goulburn, January 29, 1816. Benn, *The Iroquois*, 88.

**38.** Newfield, "Upper Canada's Black Defenders?," 32–3, 40, n.17, he mentions that Runchey died in 1819 not in 1812. In other sources, Runchey is given credit for leading the corps at Queenston Heights and continuing in command whereas Newfield states that Runchey resigned by October 24. Gray, *Soldiers of the King*, 185–86; E. Green, "Upper Canada's Black Defenders?," OHS, *Papers and Records*, 27 (1931), 368–70, 390–91; Malcomson, *Brilliant Affair*, gives a figure of 38 members, 179, 269, 273–74, 306, n. 11; Hitsman, *Incredible War*, 98, 301, n. 35. The traditional view may need to be revised.

**39.** *DHC*, 4, 40–2, October 8, 1812, these two paragraphs are based on this letter. See also, Van Rensselaer, *Narrative*, Appendix, especially 20–1, 24–5, 30. Armstrong, *Notices of the War*, 1, 116–17, criticized Van Rensselaer's aims as being too limited and strategically unsound. Dale, *Invasion of Canada*, 30, points out the strategic position of Queenston Heights.

**40.** Dudley, *Naval War*, I, 311–14, 336–41, 361–64. On Black Rock see *Ibid.*, 308–09, 355. Hickey, *War of 1812*, 128.

**41.** *DHC*, 4, 45–7, Lieutenant J.D. Elliott to the secretary of the navy, October 9, 1812. See also, 47–9, particularly the "Inquiry respecting the loss of the Detroit," and 63–4, Brock to Prevost, October 11. Tupper, *Life and Correspondence*, 326–27, Brock to Procter, undated. See also, LAC, RG8, C, v. 12031/2A, 39–40, General Order, October 12.

**42.** Tupper, *Life and Correspondence*, 326–27, Brock to Procter undated. See also, LAC, RG8, C, v. 12031/2A, 39–40, General Order, October 12, 1812.

**43.** *DHC*, 4, 79–80, Van Rensselaer to Honourable William Eustis, October 14, 1812. The information about Brock's movements was conveyed to American officers by a spy. The Americans believed that Queenston was lightly garrisoned and could be dominated by guns located on the heights above Lewiston. See Van Rensselaer, *Narrative*, Appendix, 23–4, 29–30.

**44.** Van Rensselaer, *Narrative*, Appendix, 11–2. *DHC*, 4, 79–82, Van Rensselaer to Eustis, October 14, 1812; see also, 40–2, same to Dearborn, October 8; 59–60, same to Brigadier-General Smyth October 10; 60, Lieutenant-Colonel Fenwick to Van Rensselaer, October 10; 62, Van Rensselaer to Fenwick, October 10; 66, same to Smyth, October 11. Scott, *Memoirs*, 56–8. Malcomson, *Brilliant Affair*, 120, is skeptical about the story of the missing oars but offers no other explanation.

**45.** Van Rensselaer, *Narrative*, Appendix, 61. *DHC*, 4, 85–8, Lovett to Alexander, October 14, 1812; *Ibid.*, 146, Lovett to Van Vechten, October 21.

**46.** *DHC*, 4, 68, 95–103, Chrystie to General T.H. Cushing, 22 February 1813.

47. Malcomson, *Brilliant Affair,* 255–58. The "nominal" grand total was 6,714 made up of 2,484 regulars and 4,230 militia.

48. Malcolmson, *Brilliant Affair,* 272–74, 135, 145–47 provided most of the numbers in this paragraph. See also, Gray, *Soldiers of the King,* 91–3. The quotation comes from Cruikshank, *Queenston Heights,* 20–1.

49. On Holcroft see Sutherland, *His Majesty's Gentlemen,* 194. Malcolmson, *Brilliant Affair,* 53.

50. LAC, RG8, C676, 64–71, Gore to Craig, February 20, 1809.

51. On Evans see *DCB,* 9, 245–46 and Sutherland, *His Majesty's Gentlemen,* 138. Evans was also deputy adjutant-general. In December 1812, he was made brevet lieutenant-colonel back-dated to October 13.

52. *SBD,* I, 617–25, Lieutenant Colonel Thomas Evans, October 15, 1812 to _____. See also, MG30, E109, reel M-827, Harold Isadore Hellmuth fonds, Extract from Personal Diary of General T. Evans while serving as an officer on Staff of General Brock. This document provides the same information with minor differences in wording. *DHC,* 4, 66, Brock to Van Rensselaer, October 11, 1812.

53. LAC, RG8, v. 677, October 11, 1812, with the last paragraph dated October 12. Tupper, *Life and Correspondence,* 328, believes this was the final writing ever done by Brock.

54. LAC, MG24, Series A1, 92–6. Tupper, *Life and Correspondence,* 328, quotes a few lines.

55. LAC, RG8, C676, 64–71, Gore to Craig, February 20, 1809.

56. *Journal of Major Norto,* 303–04. Regarding the path, see *SBD,* I, 617–25, Lieutenant-Colonel Thomas Evans, October 15, 1812.

57. Crooks, "Recollections," 40.

58. Duke University, Campbell Family Papers, Major David Campbell to his brother, November 3, 1812. For a discussion of the secondary literature see Turner, *British Generals,* 201, n. 89. Malcolmson, *Brilliant Affair* is the most recent fully researched account. Other

useful accounts are Stanley, *War of 1812*, 121–32 and Hitsman, *Incredible War*, 94–100.

**59.** Crooks, "Recollections," 15–6; *Journal of Major Norton*, 304.

**60.** Van Rensselaer, *Narrative*, Appendix, 63–7, Van Rensselaer to Dearborn, October 14. *DHC*, 4, 85–8, Lovett to Alexander, October 14, 1812; 97, Chrystie to Cushing, February 22, 1813.

**61.** *SBD*, III, part 2, 558, "Journal of Events Principally on the Detroit & Niagara Frontiers." Sunrise at that latitude on October 13 would have been about 6:10 a.m. but the extent of cloud cover is unknown.

**62.** *DHC*, 3, 97–8, Chrystie to Cushing, February 22, 1813. *DHC*, 5, 10–6, Letter from Brown's Point, October 14, 1812. Beverley Robinson, (a shorter version is printed in vol. 4, 103–07) Henceforth cited as Robinson letter. On Robinson see *DCB*, 9, 668–78. Malcolmson, *Brilliant Affair*, 148–50, gives details on the killed and wounded.

**63.** Van Rensselaer, *Narrative*, 26. A. Conger Goodyear Bechs, War of 1812 MSS, Box 2, vol. 7, Colonel H.B. Armstrong to Henry B. Dawson, March 6, 1860. Although written a long time after the battle, when Armstrong was a captain, he gives very clear details. *DHC*, 3, 96–9, Chrystie to Cushing, February 22, 1813.

**64.** *DHC*, 5, 10–6, Robinson letter. *Ibid.*, 9–10, Lieutenant Patrick McDonogh to his sister, October 16, 1812. *Ibid.*, 3, 96–9, Chrystie to Cushing, February 22, 1813. *Ibid.*, 4, 117–18, Extract of a letter from Fort George, October 14, 1812, appeared in the *Quebec Mercury*, October 27. This was Captain Holcroft's account (Henceforth cited as Holcroft's account).

**65.** U.S. National Archives, RG59, M588, 7:115, Ensign J. Smith to Colonel Procter, October 18, 1812.

**66.** *DHC*, 5, 10–6, Robinson letter, October 14, 1812; *Ibid.*, 4, 114–16, Extract of a letter from Upper Canada, dated Brown's Point, October 15. The author, Lieutenant Archibald McLean, refers to the men being called down by a bugle. Van Rensselaer,

*Narrative*, Appendix, 15–6, Report of Captain Wool, October 23.

67. *DHC*, 4, 155–57 has the relevant correspondence; also 98–9, Chrystie to Cushing, February 22, 1813. Van Rensselaer, *Narrative*, Appendix, 15–6, Report of Captain Wool, October 23. Crooks, "Recollections," 40, Crooks was told by Wool that he proposed to Colonel Van Rensselaer to scale the cliff.

68. Tupper, *Life and Correspondence*, 330; OA, Tupper Papers, Sheaffe to Tupper, December 28, 1846; NHS, no. 9, 10, Personal Narrative of W.H. Merritt; *SBD*, I, 617–25, Lieutenant-Colonel Thomas Evans, October 15, 1812; NHS, no. 9, 23, Claus to _____, Dec 4, 1813. In Casselman, *Richardson's War of 1812*, 104, the author, Richardson, writes that Brock was awakened by "an alarm given by the sentinel stationed at the point above Fort George" who had seen and heard firing from Queenston. Richardson was not present but may have heard that from someone who was there. See also, Malcomson, *Brilliant Affair*, 142–43.

69. Crooks, "Recollections," 32–3.

70. U.S. National Archives, RG59, M588, 7:115, Smith to Procter, October 18, 1812.

71. *DHC*, 4, 108–14, Evans to _____, October 15, 1812. Norton in his *Journal of Major Norton*, 304, says Sheaffe gave him this order. NHS, no. 9, 44, Norton to Hon. Henry Goulburn, January 29, 1816. Norton mentions hearing "firing at Queenston," on the morning of October 13. *DHC*, 4, 117–18, cited in Holcroft's account; *Ibid.*, 77–9, William Woodruff to David Thorburn, July 29, 1840.

72. *DHC*, 5, 11–2, Robinson letter. Malcomson, *Brilliant Affair*, 143–48, describes Brock's ride to Queenston. Fryer, *Bold Brave*, 222–23, suggests that because Brock's uniform would be mud-spattered from his ride from Fort George there would be no flash of bright scarlet or gold epaulettes or shiny gorget.

73. NHS, no. 23, 52, McLean to Sir Allan MacNab, July 22, 1860.

74. See V. Begamudré, *Isaac Brock. Larger than Life* (Montreal: XYZ, 2000), xi, 19–27, 31–2, 143–48.

75. NHS, no. 42, 103–04, James Green to William Claus, July 5, 1810; 105–06, William Claus to Lieutenant-Colonel Curry, November 17, 1810. Tupper, *Life and Correspondence*, 87–9, Brock to Irving, January 10, 1811; 100–01, Colonel Vesey to Brock, April 9, 1811. Malcomson, *Brilliant Affair*, 144, attributes the account to family oral tradition. The biography of Susan's father, Aeneas Shaw, is in *DCB*, 5, 752–54.

76. Crooks, "Recollections," 40.

77. *DHC*, 5, 12, Robinson letter; NHS, no. 23, Charles Askin to J. Askin, October 14, says he heard that Brock was at the redan. Charles was too ill to take part in the battle but was in the vicinity of Queenston and knew several of the participants. C. Askin to J. Askin, December 11, *John Askin Papers*, vol. II, 735–36.

78. Van Rensselaer, *Narrative*, Appendix, 15–6, Report of Captain Wool, October 23, 1812.

79. *SBD*, I, 607, Sheaffe to Prevost, October 13, 1812. *DHC*, 4, 116–17, Narrative of Volunteer G.S. Jarvis, 49th Regiment. He was a gentleman volunteer and served throughout the war. *DCB*, 10, 379–80.

80. *DHC*, 4, 114–16, Extract of a letter from Upper Canada, dated Brown's Point, October 15 (Lieutenant Archibald McLean was the writer).

81. U.S. National Archives, RG59, M588, 7:115, Smith to Procter, October 18, 1812. He writes that officers "on the 13th fought in Round Hats from the General to the Lieutenants."

82. *DHC*, 4, 116–17, Narrative of Jarvis. I want to thank Michael Power for his observations on this and other points. Exactly who fired the shot has been a matter of some controversy. Kosche, "Relics of Brock," Appendix G, 100–03 discusses the account of the best known claimant, Robert Walcot. See G. St.-Denis,

"Robert Walcot: The Man Who Could Not Possibly Have Shot General Brock," *Journal of the Society for Army Historical Research*, 83 (Winter, 2005), 281–90; Hickey, *Don't Give Up*, 59–60. Malcomson, *Brilliant Affair*, 152–53.

83. *DHC*, 4, 114–16, Extract of a letter dated Brown's Point, October 15, 1812, for the Jarvis quote. *Ibid.*, 83, Glegg to William Brock, October 14.

84. Reported in *Kingston Gazette*, October 24, 1812.

85. NHS, no. 9, 10, Personal Narrative of W.H. Merritt.

86. NHS, no. 23, 64–7, Charles to John Askin, October 14, 1812.

87. U.S. National Archives, RG59, M588, 7:115, Smith to Procter, October 18, 1812. See Malcomson, *Brilliant Affair*, 153, and Appendix A for his discussion of the hero's last words.

88. *DHC*, 5, 10–6, Robinson letter. Malcomson, *Brilliant Affair*, 153.

89. *DHC*, 5, 10–6, Robinson letter. *Ibid.*, 114–16, Extract of a letter dated Brown's Point, October 15, 1812. McLean managed to crawl "from the battlefield to a nearby village where his wounds were hurriedly dressed." He was still suffering from this wound in April 1813 when the Americans attacked York where he lived. See *DCB*, 9, 512–13. *DHC*, 4, 116–17, Narrative of Jarvis; *Ibid.*, 4, 98–9, Chrystie to Cushing, February 22, 1813. Van Rensselaer, *Narrative*, Appendix, 15–6, Report of Captain Wool, October 23, 1812. *SBD*, I, 623, Lieutenant-Colonel Thomas Evans, October 15, 1812.

90. *DHC*, 4, 83, Glegg to William Brock, October 14, 1812; 88–9, Glegg to Justice Powell, October 14. *DHC*, 5, 6–9, Memoirs of Colonel John Clark.

91. G. St.-Denis, "The House Where General Brock Died?" *Journal of the Society for Army Historical Research*, 86 (2008), 109–19.

92. *DHC*, 4, 88–9, Glegg to Justice Powell, October 14, 1812. *DCB*, 5, 522. Government House, or a government house in earlier documents, had been built in Niagara by D.W. Smith, the surveyor

general of Upper Canada. When the government was moved to York, Smith was obliged to follow and offered to sell his house for conversion to a grammar school. The school board rejected the offer but the government bought it and it became a government house. Brock, as administrator, stayed there. *Correspondence of Russell.* viii–ix, 3, 8, 28–30, 77–8, 104–05. R. Merrit, N. Butler, and M. Power, eds., *The Capital Years. Niagara-on-the-Lake, 1792–1796* (Toronto: Dundurn, 1991), 31–2, 39. On Smith see *DCB,* 7, 811–14.

93. *DCB,* 5, 520–23 for Macdonell's biography. Turner, *British Generals,* 80. Major James Givins was Brock's other provincial ADC. See *DCB,* 7, 347–48 and Gray, *Soldiers of the King,* 48, 54.

94. OA, F775, MU2143, Miscellaneous Coll., Macdonell's appeal to the electors of Glengarry, March 18, 1812.

95. *York Gazette,* October 9, 1811, and Wood, *SBD,* I, 584–85, Brock to Liverpool, August 30, 1812, for his appointment. Tupper, *Life and Correspondence,* 283, Powell to Brock, August 27. On Powell see *DCB,* 6, 605–13.

### Chapter Nine

1. NHS, no. 9, 23, Claus to ____, December 4, 1813. Crooks, "Recollections," 33–4. *SBD,* I, 607, Sheaffe to Prevost, October 13, 1812. Malcomson, *Brilliant Affair,* 158–63.

2. USNA, RG59, M588, 7:115, Smith to Procter, October 18, 1812. Malcomson, *Brilliant Affair,* 162–63 describes the damage done to the American side. *SBD,* I, 621–25, Lieutenant-Colonel Thomas Evans, October 15. Bowering, "A Study of the Utilization of Artillery," 1, 44.

3. Pennsylvania State Archives, MG6, Miller Diary, 24–5. USNA, RG59, M588, 7:115, Smith to Procter, October 18, 1812.

4. *SBD,* I, 621–25, Lieutenant-Colonel Thomas Evans, October 15. After taking further precautions, Evans prepared to ride to Queenston only to learn that the battle was over.

5. *Journal of Major Norton*, 304–06. See also, NHS, no. 9, 44, Norton to Honourable Henry Goulburn, January 29, 1816. *Ibid.*, 8, Personal Narrative of W.H. Merritt. Benn, *The Iroquois*, 91. Malcomson, *Brilliant Affair*, 171–76, gives details of these skirmishes.

6. Smith, *Geographical View*, 90–2.

7. *DHC*, 4, 85–8, Lovett to Alexander, October 14, 1812.

8. Scott, *Memoirs*, vol. 1, 58–9, It seems they were unsuccessful, for Scott mentions only that they attempted to unspike the gun.

9. *DHC*, 4, 95–103, Chrystie to General Thomas H. Cushing, February 22, 1813. Scott, *Memoirs*, vol. 1, 59–64. Malcomson, *Brilliant Affair*, 149–51, 164–69. He points out that out of 3,000 militia in the vicinity, more than 700 crossed.

10. *DHC*, 4, 85–8, Lovett to Alexander, October 14, 1812. When General Van Rensselaer crossed back to the New York shore, men crowded into his boat to return. *Ibid.*, 95–103, Chrystie to Cushing, February 22, 1813.

11. Crooks, "Recollections," 34. Armstrong, *Notices of the War*, 1, 104–07, condemned the refusal as a "cover for cowardice or treason."

12. *DHC*, 5, 11–2, Robinson letter. Turner, *British Generals*, 90.

13. The numbers are taken from Malcomson, *Brilliant Affair*, 274. For timing see Turner, *British Generals*, 90.

14. *DHC*, 4, 95–103, Chrystie to Cushing, February 22, 1813.

15. Crooks, "Recollections," 35. Malcomson, *Brilliant Affair*, 181, writes that it was about 1:00 p.m. when Sheaffe began his march in which case the militiamen's potatoes would have been cooked.

16. The distance by road from present-day Queenston to the marker of "Sheaffe's path" is 1.4 miles. Sheaffe started about 2.5 miles north of Queenston to swing westward. If this was his route, the total distance his men might have marched after leaving the river road until they reached the top of the escarpment would have

been between four and six miles. See Turner, *British Generals*, 90. This paragraph is based on Crooks, "Recollections," 35–6 and *Journal of Major Norton*, 304–08. See also, Malcomson, *Brilliant Affair*, 181–82.

17. Crooks, "Recollections," 35; *DHC*, 4, 117–18, Holcroft's account; *Journal of Major John Norton*, 306; Malcomson, *Brilliant Affair*, 168–71; Benn, *The Iroquois*, 92. Bowering, "A Study of the Utilization of Artillery," 1, 45.

18. *Journal of Major Norton*, 306–08; *DHC*, 4, 95–103, Chrystie to General Thomas H. Cushing, February 22, 1813; *Ibid.*, 118–20, *The War*, October 31, 1812, Scott, *Memoirs*, 59–60, and Benn, *The Iroquois*, 92–4 are the sources for these two paragraphs. See also, Malcomson, *Brilliant Affair*, 172–74, 177–80.

19. Crooks, "Recollections," 35–6.

20. NHS, no. 9, "Campaigns of 1812–1814," Norton to Honourable Henry Goulburn, January 29, 1816.

21. Benn, *The Iroquois*, 94–5. *Journal of Major Norton*, 306–08.

22. Clench was a prominent resident of Niagara and a colonel in the 1st Lincoln Militia. In 1813 he was taken prisoner by the Americans and spent the remainder of the war in captivity. *DCB*, 6, 153–54. Gray, *Soldiers*, 49. *Journal of Major Norton*, 308.

23. This paragraph is based on Crooks, "Recollections," 36–7; *DHC*, 4, 117–18, Holcroft's account; *Ibid.*, 77–9, Woodruff to Thorburn, July 29, 1840, and *Journal of Major Norton*, 304–06; NHS, no. 9, 8, Personal Narrative of W.H. Merritt. He emphasized the brevity of the fight. See also, Malcomson, *Brilliant Affair*, 186–91.

24. RG59, M588, 7:115, Smith to Procter, October 18, 1812. *SBD*, I, 607, Sheaffe to Prevost, October 13. Sheaffe wrote of his debt to Holcroft for the "well directed fire" of his guns "which contributed materially to the fortunate result of the day." Bowering, "A Study of the Utilization of Artillery," 1, 45–6.

25. Other estimates by American officers ranged from 250 to 500 men. See Malcomson, *Brilliant Affair*, 177–78, 183–86.

26. *DHC*, 4, 95–103, Chrystie to Cushing, February 22, 1813. *Ibid.*, 118–20, *The War*, October 31, 1812. Duke University, Campbell Family Papers, Major David Campbell to his brother, November 3. Campbell, who was present, commented on the confusion among his own forces.

27. Turner, *British Generals*, 90 and n. 35 for a discussion of starting and finishing times. *SBD*, I, 607, Sheaffe to Prevost, October 13, 1812. Malcomson, *Brilliant Affair*, 187, 191.

28. *DHC*, 5, 11–2, Robinson letter, *Ibid.*, 4, 114–16, Extract of a letter dated Brown's Point, October 15; *Journal of Major Norton*, 309. Malcomson, *Brilliant Affair*, 187–91.

29. *DHC*, 4, 117–18, Holcroft's account. Scott, *Memoirs*, vol. 1, 61–2.

30. USNA, RG59, M588, 7:115, Smith to Procter, October 18, 1812. Crooks, "Recollections," 37–8, Smith was at Fort George while Crooks was in the battle. *DHC*, 4, 77–9, Woodruff to Thorburn, July 29, 1840. Woodruff, a participant, also mentioned noise and smoke.

31. Turner, *British Generals*, 60, 85–6, 90, on Sheaffe. Brock had led six companies of the regiment. For criticisms of Sheaffe see Crooks, "Recollections," 39–40, and Malcomson, *Brilliant Affair*, 182–83, 186, 188–89. Dale, *Invasion of Canada*, 35–6, describes the advance of Sheaffe's force as "stately and precise." For criticism of General Van Rensselaer see *DHC*, 5, 9–10, Lieutenant Patrick McDonogh to his sister, October 16, 1812; BECHS, War of 1812 Papers, B00-15, Box 1, folder 1, David Willson to Allan Stewart, November 9, 1812.

32. *Montreal Herald*, March 20, 1813, printed a report from London that His Royal Highness had granted Sheaffe a Baronet of the United Kingdom.

33. Crooks, "Recollections," 37–8. *DHC*, 5, 11–12, Robinson letter. Malcomson, *Brilliant Affair*, 191–92.

34. *DHC*, 4, 73–5, Evans, Major of Brigade, October 15, 1812; *Ibid.*, 77–9, Woodruff to Thorburn, July 29, 1840; *DHC*, 5, 11–12,

Robinson letter. For American losses see *DHC*, 4, 143, Van Rensselaer to Dearborn, October 20.

35. *SBD*, I, 605–08, Sheaffe to Prevost, October 13, 1812; *DHC*, 4, 74–5, Return of ordnance and stores captured, Larratt Smith, commissary and paymaster, Quebec, December 1, 1813; *Ibid.*, 146–47, Ridout to his brother, October 21, 1812. Malcomson, *Brilliant Affair*, 195, describes the colours and writes that they were taken to England and put on display there.

36. *DHC*, 4, 102–03, Chrystie to General Thomas H. Cushing, February 22, 1813; *Ibid.*, 118–20, *The War*, October 31, 1812. Scott, *Memoirs*, vol. 1, 63–4. He does not mention any atrocities by native warriors.

37. *DHC*, 5, 9–10, Lieutenant Patrick McDonogh to his sister, October 16, 1812. *Journal of Major Norton*, 309. USNA, RG59, M588, 7:115, Smith to Procter, October 18. Smith mentioned they had trouble restraining warriors. Benn, *The Iroquois*, 95–6.

38. *DHC*, 4, 73–4, Report by Major Evans, October 15, 1812. Malcomson, *Brilliant Affair*, 263–71, gives lower figures for wounded but admits the documentation is incomplete. NHS, no. 9, "Campaigns of 1812–1814," 23, Claus to _____, December 4, 1813. *Journal of Major Norton*, 307–08. USNA, RG59, M588, 7:115, Smith to Procter, October 18, gives lower totals.

39. *Journal of Major Norton*, 310. Crooks, "Recollections," 39.

40. *SBD*, I, 605–8, Sheaffe to Prevost, October 13, 1812. *DHC*, 4, 175–76, Sheaffe to Prevost, November 3.

41. Van Rensselaer, *Narrative*, Appendix, 77–9, Van Rensselaer to Brock, October 13, 1812 (he did not realize Brock was dead), and Sheaffe to Van Rensselaer, October 13. *DHC*, 4, 88, Lovett to Alexander, evening, October 14. For the agreement on the exchange of prisoners signed by Colonel Winder and Major Evans see *DHC*, 4, 89–90.

42. *DHC*, 4, 126–27.

**43.** Scott, *Memoirs*, 1, 67–8, 71–3, 81–2. Hickey, *War of 1812*, 177–80, explains the controversy that erupted over prisoners of "doubtful nationality" who were captured at Queenston. The issue was settled by a convention of July 16, 1814, but the prisoners remained in captivity until the end of the war.

**44.** *SBD*, I, 625–27, Sheaffe wrote three letters and Van Rensselaer one on the 16th.

**45.** *DHC*, 4, 142–43, Sheaffe to Lord Bathurst, October 20, 1812. Sheaffe was writing from York.

**46.** LAC, RG8, v. 1220, 10–2, Prevost to Sheaffe, October 27, 1812. Examples of other critics: See Windsor Public Library, John Stodgell Collection (MS 24 1/13). Series I, Askin Documents, unit 12, Charles Askin to John Askin, November 12, 1812. USNA, RG59, M588, 7:115, Smith to Procter, October 18. See Crooks, "Recollections," 40. See NHS, no. 9, 10–1, Personal Narrative of W.H. Merritt. Turner, *British Generals*, 91.

**47.** *DHC*, 4, 138–39, Prevost, to Brock, October 19, 1812.

**48.** Turner, *British Generals*, 91. The ceasefire ended on November 20.

**49.** USNA, RG59, M588, 7:115, Smith to Procter, October 18, 1812; OA, 496, F.B. Tupper Papers, Microfilm Reel 1, Glegg to [William Brock] October 25.

**50.** Tupper, *Life and Correspondence*, 33. In a note, he cites part of a District General Orders issued by Major Evans; OA, 496, Tupper Papers, Reel 1, Glegg to [William Brock] October 25, 1812. *York Gazette*, October 24.

**51.** Crooks, "Recollections," 39; Tupper, *Life and Correspondence*, 331. *DHC*, 4, 146–47, Ridout to his brother, October 21, 1812. Malcomson, *Brilliant Affair*, 197. Fryer, *Bold, Brave*, 212, suggests that the horse was Alfred, given to Brock by Governor Craig. Brock, because of his rank, could have had the horse brought to Upper Canada if he wished. See Malcomson, *Brilliant Affair*, 144.

**52.** *DHC*, 4, 129–30, Van Rensselaer to Sheaffe, October 16, 1812; Captain Leonard to Van Rensselaer, October 16, 4:00 p.m.

Tupper, *Life and Correspondence*, 331–32. Winfield Scott claimed the credit for obtaining the tribute of minute guns from Fort Niagara. LAC, RG8, C677, 131A, Memoranda by Scott, New York, November 1863.

53. *Kingston Gazette*, November 17, 1812. Kosche, "Relics of Brock," Appendix B, 80. See Malcomson, *Burying General Brock*, 3.

54. Edgar, *General Brock*, 296. *The Gentleman's Magazine and Historical Chronicle*, 389, October 10, 1812. This British order of chivalry, the Most Honourable Military Order of the Bath, was founded in 1725 by King George I. At the time of Brock's appointment, the Order's membership was limited to the sovereign, the Great Master, and thirty-six knights. Prior to 1815 there was only the one class of knight, KB meaning Knights Companion, and the title was for life only. The term "Military" was removed in 1847 by Queen Victoria. The reader may consult Sir Nicholas H. Nicolas, *History of the Orders of Knighthood of the British Empire* (London: 1842), and James C. Risk, *History of the Order of the Bath and Its Insignia* (London: Spink & Son, 1972).

55. Stanley, *War of 1812*, 421–26. This source lists other officers who received the medal as well as recipients of the General Service Medal. See also, Robinson, *Life of Sir John Beverley Robinson*, 30–40.

56. SBD, I, 636–37, Council of Condolence, November 6, 1812. When the Americans occupied Fort George in 1813 they did not disturb the grave. See Chapter 11.

## Chapter Ten

1. Crooks, "Recollections," 39–40.

2. Wilson, "A Rifleman at Queenston," 373–76. Malcomson, *Brilliant Affair*, 158, 252, 257, identifies his unit as "Captain Nathan Parke's rifles of Canandaigua [New York]." See also, 169, 205.

3. LAC, RG8, C673, 183–84, Evans, October 31, 1812. Major Evans had this report from an American-born resident of Upper Canada who recently returned from the United States.

4. *DHC*, 4, 174, Militia District Order, November 1, 1812; 175–76, Sheaffe to Prevost, November 3.

5. Windsor Public Library, John Stodgell Collection (MS 24 1/13). Series I, Askin Documents, unit 12, Charles Askin to John Askin, November 12, 1812. LAC, RG8, C673, 183–84, Evans, October 31. On Bisshopp see *DCB*, 5, 82–3. He was ordered to move to Upper Canada to serve as inspecting field officer of militia. He would die of wounds in July 1813, and is buried in Drummond Hill cemetery. Sutherland, *His Majesty's Gentlemen*, 65–6.

6. *DHC*, 4, 175–76, Sheaffe to Prevost, November 3, 1812.

7. *DHC*, 4, 177, Winder to Smyth, November 3, 1812.

8. BECHS, M81-1, Diary of Colonel George McFeely, 23–8. *DHC*, 4, 233–35, Feeley to Brigadier-General Smyth, n.d. Here is how Colonel Feeley gave her credit: "An instance of extraordinary bravery in a female (the wife of one Doyle, a private in the United States Artillery, made a prisoner at Queenston) I cannot pass over. During the most tremendous cannonading I have ever seen, she attended the six-pounder on the mess-house with red hot shot, and showed fortitude equal to the Maid of Orleans." Hickey, *Don't Give Up the Ship!*, 192, 194. Bowering, "A Study of the Utilization of Artillery," 1, 48–9, A 6-pounder on the roof fired three rounds without shot. Was this the gun that Mrs. Doyle was serving?

9. *ANB*, 20, 325–26, Quoting J.C. Fredriksen. *DHC*, 5, 9–10, Lieutenant Patrick McDonogh to his sister, October 16, 1812; 16–7, Donogh to _____ November 13. *DHC*, 4, 172, General Smyth to General Dearborn, October 30; 239, General Order, November 27; 267–71, Smyth to A Committee of Patriotic Citizens of the Western Counties of New York, December 3. See Stanley, *War of 1812*, 132–38.

10. Malcomson, *Lords of the Lake.*, 43–56; Dudley, *Naval War*, I, 336–38, 343–51, Chauncey to secretary of the navy, November 17, 1812, refers to Captain Brock; Fryer, *Bold, Brave*, 216–17,

sees this gesture of Chauncey's as demonstrating the high regard the Americans had for Isaac Brock.

11. Turner, *British Generals*, 92. Malcomson, *Lords of the Lake* 36, 119–23, He attributes the inability of the Provincial Marine to meet Chauncey's challenge to Brock's failure during 1812 to improve its discipline and drill.

12. Turner, *British Generals*, 92–3. Gray, *Soldiers of the King*, 43–6, 187–94. However, desertion from the militia remained a serious problem. See Stanley, *War of 1812*, 180–82.

13. Spoken in the second session of the 12th Congress. Cited in Latimer, *1812*, 113.

14. Turner, *British Generals*, 93–7; Firth, *Town of York*, 294–311. Benn, *Iroquois in the War*, 106–07, sees a political motive behind the American attack, namely, to help the Republican Governor Tompkins of New York gain re-election. Taylor, Civil War of 1812, 214.

15. Turner, *British Generals*, 95–7. DCB, 8, 793–96.

16. Turner, *British Generals*, 101–04.

17. DCB, 6, 605–13.

18. LAC, RG8, v. 679, 218, Rottenburg to Procter, July 1, 1813.

19. Cited in Casselman, *Richardson's War of 1812*, 205–06. See also, Allen, *His Majesty's Indian Allies*, 144–45, Benn, *Iroquois in the War*, 145–47, Sugden, *Tecumseh's Last Stand*, 53–6, and Edmunds, *Tecumseh and the Quest for Indian Leadership*, 203–12. On the retreat, the battle and some of its consequences, see Sugden.

20. Sugden, *Tecumseh's Last Stand*, Chapter 7, especially 193–95.

21. Turner, *British Generals*, 107–09. The invasion by Wilkinson and Major General Wade Hampton failed. See Stanley, *War of 1812*, 244–68. Turner, *War of 1812*, 78–81.

22. Turner, *British Generals*, 113–18. His opponents were Brigadier-General George McClure and Major General Amos Hall, both militia officers. Stanley, *War of 1812*, 215–19, 221–24.

23. Turner, *British Generals*, 114–15.

24. Turner, *British Generals*, 122–26, 137. The quotation is from a letter to his wife, dated July 27. See also, D.E. Graves, *The Battle of Lundy's Lane on the Niagara in 1814* (Baltimore: Nautical & Aviation, 1993).

25. Turner, *British Generals*, 126–35. See J. Whitehorne, *While Washington Burned: The Battle for Fort Erie 1814* (Baltimore: Nautical & Aviation, 1992). On Izard see page 84.

26. Quoted from Article 9 of the Treaty of Ghent. See Hickey, *War of 1812*, 289–94.

**Chapter Eleven**

1. Crooks, "Recollections," 39; *DHC*, 4, 146–47, Ridout to his brother, October 21, 1812. Turner, *British Generals*, 81.

2. NHS, no. 9, 8–9, Personal Narrative of W.H. Merritt.

3. Allen, "The Bisshopp Papers," 24. Letter dated Montreal, October 22, 1812. Bisshopp was ordered to move immediately to Upper Canada to serve as inspecting field officer of militia. He would die of wounds in July 1813 and is buried in Drummond Hill cemetery. *DCB*, 5, 82–3.

4. Stanley, "Contribution of the Canadian Militia," 34–5.

5. *DHC*, 4, 176, Sheaffe to Prevost, November 3, 1812. NHS, 43, 59–61, Charles Askin (at Chippawa) to his father, November 18. Each militiaman was to receive a blanket but would have to return it. On the delivery of supplies from Lower Canada see OA, F775, MU2102, Miscellaneous Collection #6, Letterbook of deputy commissary general of Montreal, I.W. Clarke, particularly for August 1812.

6. *John Askin Papers*, vol. II, 735–36, C. Askin to J. Askin, December 11, 1812. *DHC*, 4, 275–76, Colonel W. Claus to Captain Jacob A. Ball, December 4.

7. *DHC*, 5, 134–36, Prevost to Sheaffe, March 27, 1813.

8. *DHC*, 5, 29–30, Evans to Powell, January 6, 1813. Powell and Sheaffe were personal friends. See Turner, "Career," 277, n.119. Turner, *British Generals*, 79–80. Sheppard, *Plunder, Profits*, 69–70, refers to this criticism. See also, Malcomson, *Brilliant Affair*, 197–98.

9. Tupper, *Life and Correspondence*, 82–3, Colonel Edward Baynes to Brock, October 4, 1810. See Chapters 3 and 4 above. Turner, "Career," 275–79. Turner, *British Generals*, 91–2, 96, 98–100.

10. *York Gazette*, October 17, 1812. See also, *Kingston Gazette*, October 24 and *Quebec Mercury*, November 3. Turner, *British Generals*, 81–2.

11. *Quebec Mercury*, November 10, 1812.

12. *Montreal Herald*, October 24, 1812.

13. *Kingston Gazette*, November 17, 1812. Uppercase is in the original. Much the same note appeared in a report in the English magazine, *The Gentleman's Magazine and Historical Chronicle*, 490, November 27.

14. *Quebec Mercury*, November 10, 1812, 352; June 22, 1813, 197. See also, K. Walden, "Isaac Brock, Man and Myth: A Study of the Militia Myth of the War of 1812 in Upper Canada, 1812–1912," MA thesis, Queen's University, 1971, Chapter 3.

15. *Montreal Herald*, June 5, 1813. Uppercase in the original. See also, May 29.

16. NHS, no. 15, 17–8. Quoted by permission. There are two versions in OHS, *Papers and Records*, v. 23 (1926), 237–42. E. Fowke and A. Mills, *Singing our History: Canada's Story in Song* (Toronto: Doubleday, 1984), 49–50, 56–7, 59, discuss these songs and provide music for the texts. Gray, *Soldiers of the King*, 130, lists Cornelius Flummerfelt in the 3rd York Flank Company. Poetry was another medium of remembrance. See K. McCabe, ed., *The Poetry of Old Niagara* (St. Catharines: 1999), which contains at least eleven poems mentioning Brock.

17. *DHC*, 5, 159, April 21, 1813.

**18.** *DHC*, 6, 17–22, June 7, 1813. On Simon McTavish see *DCB*, 7.

**19.** OA, Tupper Papers, MS496, Microfilm reel 1. Isaac Todd to [Brock's brother], November 2, 1812. The context makes clear that he addresses William. See *DCB*, 5, 818–22 on Todd.

**20.** Tupper, *Life and Correspondence*, 449–50. *DHC*, 6, 58–9, Bathurst to Sheaffe, June 8, 1813.

**21.** Brock, *The Brocks of England*, 84, 87–9.

**22.** Seibel, *Niagara Portage Road*, 152, provides an illustration as does Malcomson, *Burying General Brock*, 8.

**23.** *Journals of the Legislative Assembly of Upper Canada*, 1814, 159. Malcomson, *Burying General Brock*, 7.

**24.** AO, Gordon Drummond Letterbook (MU 8190), 201, Robert Loring to William Jarvis, March 16, 1815. Tupper, *Life and Correspondence*, 450–51. *Statutes of the Province of Upper Canada* (Kingston, 1831), 187–88, 430, passed January 30, 1826.

**25.** G.J. Lockwood, *The Rear of Leeds and Lansdowne: The Making of a Community on the Gananoque River Frontier, 1796–1996* (Lyndhurst, ON: 1996), 108. NHS, no. 15, Sir Isaac Brock. This coin was issued in 1816 according to Janet Carnochan. Lossing, *Pictorial Field-Book*, 406, has a drawing of the coin.

**26.** *DHC*, 3, 126–28, New York Gazette, July 24, 1812. Duke University, Campbell Family Papers, Major David Campbell to his brother, November 3.

**27.** Scott, *Memoirs*, vol. 1, 67–8. E.A. Cruikshank, *The Battle of Fort George* (Niagara-on-the-Lake: Niagara Historical Society, 1990).

**28.** LAC, RG8, C677, 131A, Memoranda by Scott, New York, November 1863. He also denounced the "miscreants" who destroyed Brock's monument in 1840 and rejoiced that it had been restored.

**29.** NHS, 11, "Reminiscences of Niagara," 19–20. Malcomson, *Burying General Brock*, 13–4 quotes a different source. Symons,

*Battle of Queenston Heights*, 22–3, recounts that Brock's "body ... had undergone little change, his features being nearly perfect ... while that of ... McDonell was on a complete mass of decomposition."

30. *St. Catharines Journal and Welland Canal (Niagara District), General Advertiser*, April 30, 1840, 2. See also, S.A. Otto, "Brock's Two Monuments," *Cuesta*, (1991/92), 16. Seibel, *Niagara Portage Road*, 156–57, 159, 162, provides different views of this monument.

31. *DCB*, 8, 501–02. Malcomson, *Burying General Brock*, 19–23 recounts part of Lett's life. Berton, *Invasion of Canada*, 253–54.

32. Otto, "Brock's Two Monuments," 17. For a description of the memorial, including its architectural aspects see G. McArthur and A. Szamosi, *William Thomas, Architect, 1799–1860* (Guelph, ON: Archives of Canadian Art, Ampersand, 1996), 93–9.

33. *Niagara Mail*, July 20, 1853. NHS, 32, 64. Thomas's letter in the *Chronicle*, July 29.

34. *Niagara Mail*, October 19, 1853, printed a two-page report on the ceremonies accompanying the reburial. See also, Malcomson, *Burying General Brock*, 33–40.

35. Booth, "Research Note: Confusion," 224–29.

36. NHS, no. 23, 40–1. The second quotation comes from NHS, McDougall Papers, Box 47, X992.5.299. Malcomson, *Burying General Brock*, 45–8.

37. Seibel, *Niagara Portage Road*, 167. The statue, sculpted by Ralph Sketch, was presented to the Niagara Parks Commission by Mr. and Mrs. S.G. Bennet.

38. Illustrations of the Guernsey plaques and the Valiants Memorial may be seen on the website *uppercanadahistory.ca*.

39. Hickey, *Don't Give Up the Ship*, 144. For a discussion of literature on Brock see Turner, *British Generals*, 80–1, and notes 105–09. *DCB*, 5, 114–15. Stanley, *War of 1812*, 404–06.

40. Hitsman, *Incredible War*, 41, and see 78, 95–9. Stanley, *War of 1812*, 403, and see 79, 126–27. Babcock, *War of 1812 on the Niagara Frontier*, 52–3, 247.

41. *DCB*, 5, 114. Hickey, *Don't Give Up the Ship*, 144.

42. Malcomson, *Brilliant Affair*, 77. On 152–53 he outlines three critical errors committed by Brock resulting in his death. The first error was Brock ordering Captain William's light company down from the redan, leaving it unguarded. Who gave the order is not clear, it probably occurred before Brock arrived in the village, and without some substantial evidence of Brock's presence or involvement, that decision should not be attributed to him. See Chapter 9 above.

43. Sheppard, *Plunder, Profit*, Chapter 3. Whitfield, *Battle of Queenston Heights*, 24, 27, 30. Turner, *British Generals*, 79, 92–3, 150–51.

44. Black. *America as a Military Power*, 54, 160; Holmes, *Redcoat*, 394, "Officers were expected to lead with demonstrative courage. John Shipp ... told an officer, politely but firmly: 'The words go on don't become [i.e., befit] an officers, Sir.'" The same tradition appeared in British naval tactics of the period. See Harvey, *War of Wars*, 228–35, 268, 451–52, 610, 695–96. Brock's experience in the autumn of 1799 in Holland was not a sound precedent for what he faced early in the morning of October 13, 1812. Venning, *Following the Drum*, 298–302. Hickey, *Don't Give Up the Ship*, 144.

45. Tupper, *Life and Correspondence*, 315–16, Brock to Savery, September 18, 1812. See also, LAC, RG8, v. 677, 90, Brock to Prevost, September 18. Turner, *British Generals*, 78.

46. Turner, *British Generals*, 77–9 has a full discussion. *DCB*, 5, 113, Stacey, his biographer, suggests Brock may have slept in his clothes.

47. Turner, *British Generals*, 82–3, 99, 114, 140, 154–55. Latimer, *1812: War with America*, 3–5.

48. Kosche, "Relics of Brock," 79–80, Glegg to William Brock, December 30, 1813.

**49.** O. Turner, *Pioneer History of the Holland Purchase of Western New York* (Buffalo: Jewett, Thomas & Co., 1849), 188–90. Joseph West was appointed to Fort Niagara in 1802 and remained until 1815 when he retired because of ill health. During the war his family lived on a farm near the fort, and after his death his widow and a daughter continued to reside there. Prior to the war, Elizabeth, Jane, and Emily West were baptized at St. Mark's Church in Niagara (information from baptismal records). The daughter who recorded this incident is not identified. This story is given in brief form by the daughter in NHS, no. 11, 55–6. In NHS, no. 15, *Sir Isaac Brock*, Janet Carnochan gives a slightly different version of the incident. Tupper, *Who was Isaac Brock?*, 1, writes, "In his own family he [Isaac] was chiefly remarkable for his extreme gentleness."

**50.** Casselman, *Richardson's War of 1812*, 116.

**51.** OA, F775MU2143, Miscellaneous Collection 1812. Inventory of Furniture, etc., belonging to the Estate of the Late Major General Brock purchased by Major General Sheaffe. Inventory of Brock's possessions resulting from the Probate of his estate. An Account of Sale of Effects of the later Major General Brock sold at Auction on the 4th of January 1813. Toronto Public Library, Wm. Allan Papers, S123. Inventory of the Effects of Sir Isaac Brock sold at York, November 1812. NHS, no. 15, *Sir Isaac Brock*. Why Brock would own a cow and pigs is hard to imagine or believe.

**52.** Kosche, "Relics of Brock," 79, Glegg to William Brock, December 30, 1813. The rest of this paragraph is based upon Kosche's article and from discussions with Parks Canada personnel.

**53.** OA, Tupper Papers, MS496, Microfilm reel 1, Glegg to [William], October 25, 1812. One of those "friends" was probably James Brock. See Chapter 11.

**54.** OA, Tupper Papers, MS496, Microfilm reel 1, Todd to [William], November 2, 1812.

**55.** Kosche, "Relics of Brock," 80, Glegg to William Brock, December 30, 1813. NHS, no. 11, "Reminiscences of Niagara," 6. Kosche, "Contemporary Portraits," 22–3.

56. Kosche, "Contemporary Portraits," 60–6. He also considers that a miniature (Figure 3, page 27) shows Brock as a teenager. Bayer, *Ontario Collection*, 150, 153, 163–64, 180–81, 372, n.1 and 2. There is also a bust c. 1896 made by Hamilton Plantagenet. For the portrait here see 179. St.-Denis dates Berczy's portrait to 1809–10. Presentation to Niagara Historical Society, April 15, 2010.

57. *DCB*, 5, 70–2.

58. Kosche, "Relics of Brock," 80, Glegg to William Brock, December 30, 1813. NHS, no. 11, "Reminiscences of Niagara," 6. Kosche, "Contemporary Portraits," 22–3.

59. Casselman, *Richardson's War of 1812*, 116.

60. Kosche, "Contemporary Portraits," 23, citing Tupper, Family Records (1835). Despite Richardson's description, Kosche writes that we do not know about his facial features or the colour of his hair. See Janet Carnochan's description in NHS, no. 15.

# Bibiliography

**Abbreviations Used in Reference Notes:**

BECHS   Buffalo and Erie County Historical Society

DCB   *Dictionary of Canadian Biography*

DHC   *Documentary History of the Campaigns upon the Niagara Frontier in 1812–1814*

DNB   *Dictionary of National Biography*

DRIC   *Documents Relating to the Invasion of Canada and the Surrender of Detroit, 1812*

LAC   Library and Archives Canada, Ottawa

NHS   Niagara Historical Society

OA   Ontario Archives, Toronto

RG   Record Group

SBD   Wood, *Select British Documents of the Canadian War of 1812*

## *Archival Sources*

### Archives of Ontario

F775MU2143 Miscellaneous Collection, 1812.

F775MU2102 Fort Detroit Plans.

Alexander Fraser Papers, MU1063, Series 1, Box 1, at Ontario Archives.

### Library and Archives Canada

MG30, E109, microfilm reel M-827, Harold Isadore Hellmuth fonds. Extract from Personal Diary of General T. Evans while serving as an officer on the Staff of General Brock at Queenston.

Record Group 8. British Military and Naval Records. C Series.

### Toronto Public Library

Wm. Allan Papers, S123. Inventory of the Effects of Sir Isaac Brock sold at York, November 1812.

### United States

Buffalo and Erie County Historical Society. (BECHS ) A Conger Goodyear, War of 1812 MSS, Box 2.

Diary of Colonel George McFeely, M81-1.

Duke University, Durham, North Carolina. Campbell Family Papers.

Pennsylvania State Archives, MG6, Jacob Miller Diary.

United States National Archives, RG59, M588, 7:115, Ensign J. Smith to Colonel Procter, October 18, 1812.

### Newspapers

*Kingston Gazette* (The only newspaper published continuously in Upper Canada throughout the war.)

*Montreal Herald*

*Quebec Mercury*

*York Gazette*

# Published Sources

## Primary Sources

Crooks, James, "Recollections of the War of 1812," *Niagara Historical Society*, no. 28, n.d., 28–41.

Cruikshank, E.A., ed. *Campaigns of 1812–1814: Contemporary Narratives by Captain W.H. Merritt, Colonel William Claus, Lieut.-Colonel Matthew Elliott and Captain John Norton.* Niagara: Niagara Historical Society, no.9, 1902.

_____. *Documentary History of the Campaigns upon the Niagara Frontier in 1812–1814.* Nine volumes. Welland: Tribune Press, 1896–1908.

_____. *Documents Relating to the Invasion of Canada and the Surrender of Detroit, 1812.* Ottawa: Canadian Archives, 1912.

Cruikshank, E.A. and A.F. Hunter, eds. *The Correspondence of the Honourable Peter Russell.* Three volumes. Toronto: Ontario Historical Society, 1932–36.

Dudley, William S., ed. *The Naval War of 1812: A Documentary History. Vol. I: 1812.* Washington, D.C.: Naval Historical Center, Department of the Navy, 1985.

Firth, E.G., ed. *The Town of York 1793–1815: A Collection of Documents of Early Toronto.* Toronto: University of Toronto Press for the Champlain Society, 1962.

Graves, Donald, ed. *The War of 1812 Journal of Lieutenant John Le Couteur, 104th Foot. Merry Hearts Make Light Days.* Ottawa: Carleton University Press, 1993.

Hull, William, *Memoirs of the Campaign of the North Western Army of the United States, A.D. 1812*. Boston: True & Greene, 1824.

[Hull, William] *Report of the Trial of Brigadier-General William Hull*. Boston: Russell, Cutler, 1814.

*Journal and Proceedings of the Legislative Council of the Province of Upper Canada*. Seventh Report of the Bureau of Archives for the Province of Ontario. 1910.

*Journals of the Legislative Assembly of Upper Canada, 1812*. Ninth Report of the Bureau of Archives for the Province of Ontario. 1912.

*Journals of the Legislative Assembly of Upper Canada, 1821*. Tenth Report of the Bureau of Archives for the Province of Ontario. 1913.

Klinck, C.F. and J.J. Talman, eds. *The Journal of Major John Norton, 1816*. Toronto: Champlain Society, 1970. (Cited as *Journal of Major Norton*.)

Mann, James. *Medical Sketches of the Campaigns of 1812, 13, 14*. Dedham, MA: 1816.

Preston, R.A. *Kingston Before the War of 1812: A Collection of Documents*. Toronto: Champlain Society, 1959.

Scott, Winfield. *Memoirs of General Scott, Written by Himself*. 2 vols. New York: Sheldon, 1864.

Smith, Michael. *A Geographical View of the Province of Upper Can and Promiscuous Remarks on Govt; In Two Parts with an Appendix*. 1813.

Tupper, F.B. *The Life and Correspondence of Major-General Sir Isaac Brock, K.B.* 2nd ed. London: 1847.

Quaife, M.M., ed. *The John Askin Papers*. Vol. II: 1796–1820. Detroit: 1931.

Van Rensselaer, Solomon. *A Narrative of the Affair of Queenston in the War of 1812.* New York: Leavittt, Lord, 1836.

Wood, William C. H., ed. *Select British Documents of the Canadian War of 1812.* 3 vols. Toronto: Champlain Society, 1920–28.

**Secondary Sources**

Adkins, Roy and Lesley. *The War for All the Oceans: From Nelson at the Nile to Napoleon at Waterloo.* New York: Penguin, 2007.

Allen, Robert S. *His Majesty's Indian Allies: British Indian Policy in the Defence of Canada, 1774–1815.* Toronto: Dundurn Press, 1992.

Armstrong, John. *Notices of the War of 1812.* 2 vols. New York: Wiley & Putnam, 1836–40.

Babcock, Louis L. *The War of 1812 on the Niagara Frontier.* Cranbury, NJ: The Scholar's Bookshelf, 2005.

Bamford, D. and P. Carroll. *Four Years on the Great Lakes, 1813–1816: The Journal of Lieutenant David Wingfield, Royal Navy.* Toronto: Dundurn Press, 2009.

Barr, Daniel P., ed. *The Boundaries Between Us: Natives and Newcomers Along the Frontiers of The Old Northwest Territory, 1750–1850.* Kent, OH: Kent State University Press, 2006.

Bayer, Fern. *The Ontario Collection.* Toronto: Fitzhenry & Whiteside, 1984.

Benn, Carl. *The Iroquois in the War of 1812.* Toronto: University of Toronto Press, 1998.

Berton, P. *The Death of Isaac Brock.* Toronto: McClelland and Stewart, 1993.

_____. *The Invasion of Canada, 1812–1813.* Toronto: McClelland and Stewart, 1980.

Black, J. *America as a Military Power: From the American Revolution to the Civil War*. London: Praeger, 2002.

Bourneman, Walter R. *1812: The War that Forged a Nation*. New York: HarperCollins, 2004.

Bowler, Arthur, ed. *The War of 1812*. Toronto: Holt, Rinehart Winston, 1973.

Brock, Daniel J. *The Brocks of England and the Isle of Guernsey: Together with Many of Their Descendants in North America and Elsewhere*. London, ON: 2005.

Bruce, A. *The Purchase System in the British Army, 1660–1871*. London: 1980.

Casselman, Alexander C., ed. *Richardson's War of 1812 With Notes and a Life of the Author*. Toronto: 1902.

Cruikshank, E.A. *General Hull's Invasion of Canada in 1812*. Ottawa: 1908.

_____. *Queenston Heights*. Niagara Falls, ON: Lundy's Lane Historical Society, 1891.

Dale, Ron. *The Invasion of Canada*. Toronto: James Lorimer, 2001.

Edgar, Matilda. *General Brock*. Revised by E.A.Cruikshank. The Makers of Canada Series, Vol. 4. Toronto: Oxford University Press, 1926.

_____. *Ten Years of Upper Canada in Peace and War, 1805–1815: Being the Ridout Letters with Annotations*. Toronto: William Briggs, 1890.

Edmunds, R. David. *Tecumseh and the Quest for Indian Leadership*. Boston: Little Brown, 1984.

Ferrell, Robert H. *American Diplomacy: A History*. Revised and expanded edition. New York: W.W. Norton, 1969.

FitzGibbon, Mary A. *A Veteran of 1812: The Life of James FitzGibbon*. Toronto: William Briggs, 1894 (reprint 1979).

Fryer, Mary B. *Bold, Brave and Born to Lead: Major-General Isaac Brock and the Canadas*. Toronto: Dundurn Press, 2004

Garraty, J.A. and M.C. Carnes, eds. *American National Biography*. 24 vols. New York: Oxford University Press, 1999.

Gray, William, *Soldiers of the King: The Upper Canadian Militia 1812–1815*. Erin, ON: Boston Mills, 1995.

Halpenny, F.G., ed. *Dictionary of Canadian Biography*. Toronto: University of Toronto Press, 1977–88.

Harvey, Robert. *The War of Wars: The Epic Struggle Between Britain and France: 1789–1815*. New York: Carroll & Graf, 2008.

Hickey, Donald R. *Don't Give Up the Ship! Myths of the War of 1812*. Toronto: Robin Brass, 2006.

_____. *The War of 1812: A Forgotten Conflict*. Chicago: University of Illinois Press, 1989.

Hitsman, J. Mackay. *The Incredible War of 1812: A Military History*. Updated by Donald E. Graves. Toronto: Robin Brass, 1999.

Holmes, Richard. *Redcoat: The British Soldier in the Age of Horse and Musket*. London: HarperCollins, 2001.

Horsman, R. *The War of 1812*. New York: Knopf, 1969.

Howison, John. *Sketches of Upper Canada, Domestic, Local, and Characteristic*. East Ardsley, Yorkshire: S.R. Publishers, 1965.

Johnston, W. *The Glengarry Light Infantry, 1812–1816*. Charlottetown, PEI: 1998.

Latimer, Jon. *1812: War with America*. Cambridge, NJ: Harvard University Press, 2007.

Lépine, Luc. *Les officiers de milice du Bas-Canada, 1812–1815. Lower Canada's Militia Officers, 1812–1815.* Montreal: Société généalogique Canadienne-Française, 1996.

Lossing, Benson J. *The Pictorial Field-Book of the War of 1812.* New York: Harper, 1869.

Malcomson, Robert. *A Very Brilliant Affair: The Battle of Queenston Heights, 1812.* Toronto: Robin Brass, 2003.

_____. *Burying General Brock: A History of Brock's Monuments.* Niagara-on-the-Lake, ON: The Friends of Fort George, 1996.

_____. *Lords of the Lake: The Naval War on Lake Ontario, 1812–1814.* Toronto: Robin Brass, 1998.

_____. *Warships of the Great Lakes, 1754–1834, Rochester.* Kent: Caxton, 2003.

Mallory, Enid L. *The Green Tiger. James FitzGibbon:A Hero of the War of 1812.* Toronto: McClelland and Stewart, 1976.

Markham, F. *Napoleon.* New York: Mentor, 1963.

Niagara Historical Society. *Campaigns of 1812–14.* No. 9. E.A. Cruikshank, ed. Niagara-on-the-Lake, ON: 1902. (Contains accounts by Colonel Claus, Captain Norton, Lieutenant-Colonel Matthew Elliott, and Captain W.H. Merritt.)

_____. *Letters of 1812 from Dominion Archives.* No. 23. E.A. Cruikshank, ed. Niagara-on-the-Lake, ON: 1925.

_____. *Records of Niagara 1805–1811.* No. 42. E.A. Cruikshank, ed. Niagara-on-the-Lake, ON: 1931.

_____. *Records of Niagara. A Collection of Contemporary Letters and Documents, 1812.* No. 43. E.A. Cruikshank, ed. Niagara-on-the-Lake, ON: 1934.

_____. *Records of Niagara. A Collection of Contemporary Documents January to July 1813.* No. 44. Cruikshank, E.A., ed. Niagara-on-the-Lake, ON: 1939.

_____. *Reminiscences of Niagara.* No. 11. Niagara-on-the-Lake, ON: 1911.

_____. *Sir Isaac Brock: Paper Read before York Pioneers, 1ˢᵗ May 1906.* No. 15. Niagara-on-the-Lake, ON: 1913.

Ouellet, Fernand. *Lower Canada, 1791–1840: Social Change and Nationalism.* Toronto: McClelland and Stewart, 1980.

Peterson, Charles J. *The Military Heroes of the War of 1812: With a Narrative of the War.* Philadelphia: J.B. Smith, 1858.

Preston, R.A, S.F. Wise, and H.O. Werner. *Men in Arms: A History of Warfare and Its Interrelationships with Western Society.* Revised edition. New York: Praeger, 1965.

Prucha, Francis P. *The Sword of the Republic: The United States Army on the Frontier, 1783–1846.* Lincoln, NE: University of Nebraska Press, 1969.

Robinson, C.W. *The Life of Sir John Beverley Robinson.* Toronto: Morang, 1904.

Schmaltz, Peter S. *The Ojibwa of Southern Ontario.* Toronto: University of Toronto Press, 1991.

Seibel, George A. *The Niagara Portage Road: A History of the Portage on the West Bank of the Niagara River.* Niagara Falls, ON: 1990.

Sheppard, George. *Plunder, Profit, and Paroles: A Social History of the War of 1812 in Upper Canada.* Montreal: McGill-Queen's University Press, 1994.

Spiers, E.M. *The Army and Society, 1815–1914.* London: Longman, 1980.

Stagg, J.C.A. *Mr. Madison's War: Politics, Diplomacy, and Warfare in the Early American Republic, 1783–1830.* Princeton, NJ: Princeton University Press, 1983.

Stanley, G.F.G. *The War of 1812: Land Operations.* Ottawa: Macmillan, 1983.

Stephen, Sir L. and Sir S. Lee, eds. *The Dictionary of National Biography.* 22 vols. Oxford: Oxford University Press, 1959–60.

Sugden, John. *Tecumseh's Last Stand.* Norman, OK: University of Oklahoma Press, 1985.

Sutherland, S. (comp.) *His Majesty's Gentlemen: A Directory of British Regular Army Officers of the War of 1812.* Toronto: Iser, 2000.

Taylor, A. *The Civil War of 1812: American Citizens, British Subjects, Irish Rebels & Indian Allies.* New York: Knopf, 2010.

Tomes, Robert. *Battles of America by Sea and Land with Biographies of Naval and Military Commanders.* 3 vols. New York: J.S. Virtue, 1878.

Tupper, F.B. *Family Records: Containing Memoirs of Major-General Sir Isaac Brock, K.B.* Guernsey: Stephen Barbet, 1835.

Tupper, H. (comp.) *Who Was Isaac Brock? Short Summary of the Life of Major-General Sir Isaac Brock, K.B.* Guernsey: Clarke, Printer, c.1919.

Turner, W.B. *British Generals in the War of 1812: High Command in the Canadas.* Montreal: McGill-Queens University Press, 1999.

———. *The War of 1812: The War that Both Sides Won.* Second edition. Toronto: Dundurn Press, 2000.

Venning, Annabel. *Following the Drum: The Lives of Army Wives and Daughters, Past and Present.* London: Headline, 2005.

Whitfield, Carol. *The Battle of Queenston Heights.* Canadian Historic Sites, Occasional Papers, no.11. Ottawa: 1974.

_____. *Tommy Atkins: The British Soldier in Canada, 1759–1870.* History and Archaeology, 56. Ottawa: National Historic Parks & Sites Branch, Parks Canada, 1981.

Zaslow, M., ed. *The Defended Border: Upper Canada and the War of 1812.* Toronto: Macmillan, 1964.

Zuehlke, Mark. *For Honour's Sake: The War of 1812 and the Brokering of an Uneasy Peace.* Toronto: Vintage, 2007.


**Articles**

Allen, Robert S. "The Bisshopp Papers during the War of 1812." *Journal of the Society for Army Historical Research,"* 61 (Spring, 1983), 22–29.

Beall, William K. "Journal of William K. Beall." *American Historical Review,* 17 (July 1912), 783–808. Beall was assistant quartermaster General of Hull's army.

Booth, Alan D. "Research Note: Confusion in the Chronological Record of General Brock's Life." *Ontario History,* 83 (September 1991), 224–29.

Brock, Peter. "Accounting for Difference: The Problem of Pacifism in Early Upper Canada." *Ontario History,* 90 (Spring, 1998), 19–30.

Carter-Edwards, Dennis. "The War of 1812 Along the Detroit Frontier: A Canadian Perspective." *Michigan Historical Review,* 13 (Fall, 1987), 25–50.

Carland, John M. "'The Simplest Thing is Difficult': The United States Army and the War of 1812." *Canadian Military History,* 12, 1, and 2 (2003), 29–40.

Glover, Michael. "The Purchase of Commissions: A Reappraisal." *Journal of the Society for Army Historical Research,* 58 (Winter, 1980), 223–35.

Horsman, R. "On To Canada: Manifest Destiny and the United States Strategy in the War of 1812." *Michigan Historical Review*, 13 (Fall, 1987), 1–24.

Johnston, C.M. "William Claus and John Norton." *Ontario History*, 57 (June, 1965), 101–8.

Kosche, Ludwig. "Contemporary Portraits of Isaac Brock: An Analysis." *Archivaria*, 20 (September 1985), 22–66.

_____. "Relics of Brock: An Investigation." *Archivaria*, 9 (1979–80), 33–103.

McGuffie, T.H. "The Significance of Military Rank in the British Army Between 1790 and 1820." *Bulletin of the Institute of Historical Research*, 30 (1957), 207–24.

Newfield, Gareth. "Upper Canada's Black Defenders? Re-evaluating the War of 1812 Coloured Corps." *Canadian Military History*, 18, no. 3 (Summer, 2009), 31–40.

St-Denis, Guy. "The House Where General Brock Died?" *Journal for the Society for Army Historical Research*, 86 (2008), 109–19.

Skelton, W.B. "High Army Leadership in the Era of the War of 1812: The Making and Remaking of the Officer Corps." *William and Mary Quarterly*, 3rd Ser., 51 (April 1994), 253–74.

Stagg, J.C.A. "Enlisted Men in the United States Army, 1812–1815: A Preliminary Survey." *William and Mary Quarterly*, 3rd Ser., 43 (October 1986), 615–45.

Stanley, G.F.G. "The Contributions of the Canadian Militia During the War." In P. Mason, ed., *After Tippecanoe: Some Aspects of the War of 1812*. Toronto: Ryerson, 1963.

Wilson, Jared. "A Rifleman of Queenston." *Publications of the Buffalo Historical Society*, 9 (1906), 373–6.

## *Unpublished Works*

Bowering, Ian. "A Study of the Utilization of Artillery on the Niagara Frontier." Two volumes. Parks Canada, Manuscript Report Series #446, March 1979.

Graves, Donald E. "Joseph Willcocks and the Canadian Volunteers: An Account of Political Disaffection in Upper Can during the War of 1812." MA thesis, Carleton University, 1982.

Hyatt, A.M.J. "The Defence of Upper Canada in1812." MA thesis, Carleton University, 1961.

Turner, W.B. "The Career of Isaac Brock in Canada, 1802–1812." MA thesis, University of Toronto, 1961.

# Acknowledgements

Many significant and valuable contributions have been made by individuals and institutions to my research and writing over the years it has taken me to produce this volume. I sincerely thank all of them and ask forgiveness of any I may have forgotten to name.

Ron Dale, War of 1812 project manager, Parks Canada, deserves special mention, for his careful reading of the first draft has saved me from many an error. He provided much important information and made suggestions that have greatly improved the writing. Clark Bernat and Amy Klassen of the Niagara-on-the-Lake Historical Museum provided help with information and images. Others who have contributed are David Webb, Dan Laroche, and Gavin Watt all of Parks Canada; Dennis Gannon for his indefatigable research in U.S. archives and his assistance in locating illustrations; Sharon Whittaker and Debbie Smith of the Niagara-on-the-Lake Library; David Sharron and Edie Williams of Special Collections, James A. Gibson Library, Brock University; Brian Owen, a curator at the Royal Welsh Fusiliers Museum at Caernarfon, Wales ; Sheila Mackenzie, senior curator, Manuscripts Division, The National Library of Scotland, Edinburgh. The staff at the Archives of Ontario and at the Library and Archives of Canada demonstrated enormous patience, as well as resourcefulness, in answer to my queries. I have also benefited from talking to re-enactors who have a great fund of knowledge.

My wife's patience with my absence while doing research and my virtual absence while writing this text has been a source of amazement to me and is deeply appreciated.

Last, but not least, I wish to thank Dundurn, a great Canadian publishing house. That may read like a commercial but it is true, as a glance at their publishing record shows. The suggestion and encouragement for this book came from Beth Bruder and my early draft was approved by Kirk Howard, president and publisher. Michael Carroll gave me direction and advice, and Cheryl Hawley's editing has greatly improved the manuscript.

The book's opinions and errors are, as always, my responsibility.

# Index

# By the Same Author

The War of 1812
*The War That Both Sides Won*
Wesley B. Turner
978-1-550023367
$16.99

Tragedy and farce, bravery and cowardice, intelligence and foolishness, sense and nonsense — all these contradictions and more have characterized the War of 1812. The real significance of the series of skirmishes that collectively made up the war between 1812 and 1814 is the enormous impact they have had on Canadian and American views of themselves and of each other.

The publication of *The War of 1812: The War That Both Sides Won,* in 1990, provided a contemporary look at the period, and included such developments as the 1975 discovery of the *Hamilton* and *Scourge* on the bottom of Lake Ontario, and the 1987 discovery of the skeletons of casualties at Snake Hill. Now, a decade later, Wesley B. Turner has updated *The War of 1812* to include the volumes of new research that have come to light in recent years. All this new material has been incorporated into this interesting and informative overview of a crucial period in Canada's history.

# OF RELATED INTEREST

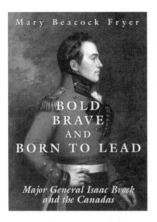

**Bold, Brave, and Born to Lead**
*Major General Isaac Brock and the Canadas*
Mary Beacock Fryer
978-1-770701687
$12.99

Celebrated as the saviour of Upper Canada, Major-General Sir Isaac Brock was a charismatic leader who won the respect not only of his own troops, but also of the Shawnee chief Tecumseh and even men among his enemy. His motto could well have been "speak loud and look big." Although this attitude earned him a reputation for brashness, it also enabled his success and propelled him into the significant role he would play in the War of 1812.

Available at your favourite bookseller.

 **DUNDURN**
www.dundurn.com

What did you think of this book?
Visit *www.dundurn.com* for reviews, videos, updates, and more!